# The Science of Wine

# The Science of Wine

## From Vine to Glass

Jamie Goode

UNIVERSITY OF CALIFORNIA PRESS, BERKELEY – LOS ANGELES

To Fiona

**The Science of Wine**
by Jamie Goode

This edition published by University of California Press
Berkeley and Los Angeles, California

First published in Great Britain in 2005 by Mitchell Beazley
an imprint of Octopus Publishing Group Ltd,
2–4 Heron Quays, London E14 4JP

ISBN 0-520-24800-7

Cataloging-in-Publication Data is on file with the Library
of Congress.

Manufactured in China by Toppan Printing Company

13 12 11 10 09 08 07 06 05
10 9 8 7 6 5 4 3 2 1

Please also visit **www.wine-science.com** for more
information about this book.

Commissioning Editor  Hilary Lumsden
Executive Art Editor  Yasia Williams-Leedham
Production  Gary Hayes

# Contents

# Why wine science?

Wine is remarkable. Consider the following questions and statements. How can this drink of fermented grape juice have assumed such an important place at the centre of many cultures, and maintained this place through millennia? How can it have spread from its origins in Eurasia some 7,000 years ago to become a frequent fixture on dinner tables across the world? People collect it, read books about it, spend large chunks of their disposable incomes on it, and some even give up their well-paid day jobs to go and make it. It has even survived (so far) the technological advances of the twentieth century and the shift from largely rural-based economies to city living. Despite their best efforts, the branders and marketing wizards of modern retailing haven't been able to kill it. In non-wine producing countries it has begun to shed its predominantly elitist image and shows signs of becoming the drink of the masses.

From just one species of vine, *Vitis vinifera*, thousands of different varieties have emerged, each with its own characteristics. The grape vine even has the capacity of transmitting some of the qualities of the site on which it is grown into the wine it produces. As well as making drinks with myriad flavours, textures, and degrees of sweetness and astringency – many of which make perfect foils for different foods – the vine gives us a naturally alcoholic product with pleasant mind-altering and mood-mellowing characteristics. To top it all, it seems that wine also has health benefits when consumed in moderation.

While this book is about wine, its focus is to explore this remarkable substance through a particular lens: that of science. As an ancient drink, wine admittedly has been produced through the ages without the help of a modern scientific world view. And many will argue that what science has brought to wine hasn't really helped it at all; some will go so far to suggest that the so-called "advances" promoted by scientists – such as the use of pesticides, herbicides, and mechanical harvesting to help in the vineyard, and filtration, cultured yeasts, enzymes, and reverse osmosis machines in the winery – have actually been detrimental to wine quality. Certainly, there is little doubt that the potential interventions science has made possible have been abused.

Yet science has a lot to offer wine, at all levels, from industrial production of megabrands to artisanal boutique wines. In this introduction, I'm going to outline why I think science is a fantastically useful tool for wine-growers. Like all tools, however, it can be used correctly or abused. Indeed, one of the goals of this book is to show how it is possible to integrate many of the most interesting and absorbing topics in wine with a scientific understanding of these issues, and that such an integration will assist in the production of more interesting, compelling wines at all levels. Even if the goal is to produce manipulation-free, "natural" wine, a good grounding in wine science will help achieve this target with fewer disasters along the way. For example, people pay a lot of money for wines from a particular patch of ground, or terroir. Wine science can help us understand what is special about that vineyard site, and may thus facilitate identification of similar sites, or help to produce better wines from vineyards less blessed by nature.

## Science is useful

The scientific method can be an incredibly useful tool. It helps us overcome our biases and prejudices, and allows us to answer difficult questions. It helps us to be objective. It presents a coherent model of the world around us that assists our understanding of this environment, and enables us to develop new technologies that actually work. It needs to be emphasized that objectivity is one of the keys to the successful practice of science. By nature we are not objective. We are pulled and pushed in various directions by our inbuilt preconceptions, predilections, and prejudices – often subtly, sometimes not so subtly. Good scientists will step aside and try, as much as possible, to be ruthlessly objective about the phenomena they are studying. The two arms of scientific enquiry are observation and experimentation. Scientists look at what's there, formulate hypotheses, then test those hypotheses by experiment, trying their hardest to disprove them. This is the only way they can be sure their hypotheses are correct.

Let's make this practical. Imagine you had a novel chemical treatment you thought would protect your vines from mildew. How would you test it? Well, you could treat all your vines with it and see how they do. There's a problem with this approach, though. If you get positive results, how do you know they are attributable to your treatment, and not, for example, to the benevolent conditions of this one vintage? The answer is: you don't. This is where the scientific method helps.

A more rigorous and useful approach is to compare the treated population of vines with what scientists term a "control": in this case, a group of vines that

## How science works: part one

The scientific community is a remarkable global enterprise. Researchers across the world are united by a common currency: data published in peer-reviewed scientific journals, and analysis and interpretation of these data. It's a fairly inclusive club, open to all comers – as long as they have good data and are prepared to play by the rules.

How does it work? Scientists are employed by universities, government institutions or private companies. The first group will typically be paid a salary, but will need to fund their research work by means of grants, usually awarded by government-supported funding bodies or industry. To gain credibility and status, researchers need to publish their work in reputable peer-reviewed journals. Their publication record is how they are assessed.

There are many thousands of these journals, and they vary in their scope from the broad to the very narrow. Not all journals are created equal; some have much higher reputations than others. Typically, a scientist (or more commonly, a group of researchers) will write up their results and then choose the most appropriate journal to which to send them. They will want to have them published in the highest-ranking journal possible, but they won't want to send their paper to a journal where it will be rejected, because of the delay in publication that will ensue.

So how do journals decide which papers to accept? This is where "peer review" kicks in, a process vital to the integrity of the scientific literature. Each journal has a board of editors made up of leading researchers in the field covered by the journal, and it also has access to a larger pool of scientists willing to act as referees for papers submitted in their chosen subject areas. A paper will be assessed by one of the editors; if it is clearly unsuitable, it is rejected instantly, but if it is potentially good enough, it will be sent out to two or more scientists for review. They will prepare a report on the paper, checking that it is correct, suitable for the journal in question, and that the science is good. If the referees recommend its acceptance, they might also suggest possible revisions or further experiments. Then the paper and the referees' reports are sent back to the editor, who makes a final decision as to whether to accept it, accept it with revision, or reject it outright.

Journals with good reputations are more fussy than others. Getting your paper into one of the elite band of leading journals can make your career. It should be pointed out that peer review is a slightly controversial process because (1) it involves scientists reviewing the work of their peers, who may well be their competitors, (2) it can take a long time, and (3) because good papers are sometimes rejected while inferior ones get through. It is also worth noting that the scientific publishing process is a highly collaborative venture – neither the scientists publishing work nor those reviewing it get paid, although some publishers make a lot of money from their journals.

Science is highly competitive. The entry ticket into the scientific community is a doctorate (a PhD), which is awarded by a university for the successful completion of an acceptable thesis (a written account of original research undertaken on the subject of choice). This takes from three to five years to achieve. But getting a PhD doesn't guarantee a research job. After you complete your PhD, you need to do what's known as a "post-doc" (post-doctoral research position), a short-term contract (usually three years) to work as a researcher in someone else's lab. After two such positions (preferably with one abroad), if you've been reasonably successful and have published several papers in good journals, then it's time to try to land a proper research job. These are few and far between, and competition for them is fierce. The pay isn't great, either. This is the stage at which many people look for an alternative career or leave academia, opting to work in industry instead. For those who succeed, however, running a successful research group is a highly rewarding career, albeit one that requires gruelling hours and absolute commitment. Despite the competition and the race to be first with each new discovery, it's refreshing to find that scientists are generally quite an open bunch, sharing their results at conferences and distributing reagents freely to other laboratories.

have not been treated, or more precisely, a group of vines that have been sprayed with an inert substance according to the same schedule as the test group in order to rule out the possibility that it is the mere act of spraying that is having the effect, rather than anything specific to the chemical.

So you split your vineyard into two and treat just one half. Still, there is a problem with this experiment. In any vineyard there will be natural variation, and any significant results might be because one part of the vineyard enjoys better conditions than the other. It might be slightly warmer, say, on one side or have different drainage properties. The answer? Subdivide the vineyard further into dozens of different plots, and randomize the treatment so that plots which are treated are interspersed with those which aren't in a way that evens out the environmental variation.

## How statistical analysis can help

Are we sorted? Not yet. Once we get our results we will need to know whether any beneficial effect is significant – that is, what the likelihood is that such a benefit could have been obtained by chance, through natural variation in the measured populations. This is where statistical analysis steps in. Statistics are intrinsic to any good experimental design. Good experiments should be designed from the start with statistical analysis in mind; how many replications (repeated observations) will be necessary to produce a significant result? This can be worked out in advance. Whenever you see a graph or table presenting experimental results, your first question should be: how significant are the differences between the control and experimental treatments?

The number of experimental replications needed depends on the variation in the populations being studied. The variation in a set of results is defined by a statistical term called standard deviation. It's not necessary to go into details about how this is calculated; all we need to know for our purposes here is that measures such as this allow scientists to work out whether or not their results are meaningful. A slightly different example will throw more light on how scientists work and think.

Let's say that you suspect that wine drinking may be beneficial for health by protecting against heart disease; but how do you study this? For ethical and practical reasons, it is rarely possible to do direct experiments. You can't easily isolate a group of people and vary just one parameter in their environment, such

"Statistics are intrinsic to any good experimental design. Good experiments should be designed from the start with statistical analysis in mind; how many replications (repeated observations) will be necessary to produce a significant result? This can be worked out in advance. Whenever you see a graph or table presenting experimental results, your first question should be: how significant are the differences between the control and experimental treatments?"

as whether or not they drink wine, especially when you are looking at a disease process that takes many years to develop.

You could start with animal experiments, looking at the cardioprotective effects of wine consumption on rats or rabbits kept under controlled conditions. The advantage here is that you can study the physiological effects of your treatment in depth; the disadvantage is that while animal models are sometimes helpful, mice, rats, and rabbits are physiologically different from people, a factor that significantly limits the utility of any knowledge obtained in this way. Another avenue of investigation might be to identify a specific physiological process involved in the development of human heart disease, and then study the effects of wine consumption on this "surrogate" process over a limited period in human volunteers – perhaps over a couple of days. Of course, identifying a reliable surrogate process is the key here, and this is always a challenge.

Instead, you could study large populations over time and try to correlate behaviours such as wine drinking with changes in health status, such as the progression of heart disease. This is the science of epidemiology, and it was precisely such a study conducted in the 1950s by Sir Richard Doll that showed conclusively for the first time what many people had suspected: that smoking is harmful to health. The key issues here are recruiting large enough populations to produce statistically significant results, controlling for confounding (more on this in a moment) and having a relevant, easily measurable endpoint (for example, in the case of heart disease, whether or not a heart attack occurs).

So let's say you have decided to look at the influence of wine drinking on the incidence of heart disease in a population of 1,000 randomly selected adults, using the incidence of heart attack as your endpoint. You'd need to get the population to fill in a drinking questionnaire (and here's a source of potential error; most people will under-report the amount they drink), and then follow up the incidence of heart disease in the different groups (*e.g.* non-drinkers versus light drinkers versus heavy drinkers) over a period of time.

What if you find that wine drinkers have reduced levels of heart attacks? Then you'll need to show that the effect is a significant one by using statistics. But we're not finished there; it gets more complicated. Even if there is a significant association between wine drinking and the risk of heart attack, this doesn't prove that wine drinking protects against heart attacks. It might be that the people who choose to drink wine are associated with another trait that is linked to reduced risk of heart attack. For example, on average, wine drinkers might also eat a more balanced diet, or have higher levels of gym membership, or smoke less. It's also well known that low income correlates with poor health status for a variety of unspecified reasons, and people on low incomes might be underrepresented among the population of wine drinkers. These effects are known as "confounding", and they need to be taken into account (*see also* page 195). One way might be to balance the different study groups by socio-economic status, or do a study solely within one profession to iron out any major discrepancies. It's complicated, but unless you take these sorts of precautions you'll end up with an unreliable conclusion.

If you want to know about the health effects of wine, you might also try a clinical trial testing the effects of wine on a group of volunteers. The key to success is using a placebo treatment and "blinding" the study – not letting the subjects know whether they are receiving the actual treatment or the placebo. Variations on this theme include crossover trials, where groups are switched from the treatment to the placebo halfway through. Studies can also be separated according to whether they are prospective (looking at the effects of interventions over a period following the beginning of the trial) or retrospective (using previously gathered data to look back in time from a known endpoint).

Then there's the issue of mechanism. Epidemiology can tell you that a certain intervention or environmental factor has a particular effect on a population, but then you'll want to know why. In the case of wine, if it is clear that moderate drinking protects against heart disease, then what is the biological mechanism? Is it the effect of alcohol, or the effect of another chemical component of the wine? To answer these sorts of questions, scientists frequently turn to animal experiments, simply because doing the equivalent tests on people wouldn't, for the most part, be considered ethical. The goal is that by understanding the mechanism, drug development or other targeted medical treatments might be possible.

## The rise of anti-science

There is no doubt that the application of science has led to many breathtaking technological advances, which show no sign of losing pace. Moore's law – the idea that computer processing power doubles every couple of years – is still holding very nicely. Mobile phones keep getting smaller and packed with more features. The laptop I am writing on is fast and powerful, but because it's eighteen months old, it is already looking a little out of date. My digital camera is twelve months old and for the same money I can now get double the number of pixels, if that's what I really need.

Yet despite this evident utility of science, we live in a culture that is now marked by a strong anti-science sentiment. Back in the 1960s and 1970s, scientists were largely revered; today they are treated with suspicion. Part of the public disenchantment with science lies in the fact that people feel let down – science promised too much and couldn't deliver. For example, scientific progress hasn't led to the nirvana of a happy, disease- and crime-free society. Medical advances against the chief killers in the west – cancer and heart disease – are slow and have included a large number of false dawns. Malaria is still the world's largest killer and our treatments have advanced little. Bacteria are increasingly resistant in the face of our armoury of antibiotics, to the extent that we are facing a very real crisis where people are dying from infections which, a decade ago, would have been easily treatable. Bringing a new drug to market is hideously expensive, with myriad legislative hurdles, and the pipeline of new drugs in development is looking a little short. Consumers, disenchanted by the medical profession's perceived limitations have turned increasingly to scientifically unproven alternative therapies. Even where science seems to offer solutions for problems of the present and the future, such as genetically modified (GM) crop plants, consumers aren't sure they want them.

Perhaps we have expected too much of science – or maybe scientists are guilty of promising what they can't deliver. Science, after all, is a tool; an incredibly useful one, but no more than that. Science can't address issues that belong in the realm of ethics, morality, religion, politics or law. That some scientists have sought to impose their ideas in these realms is not the fault of the scientific method, nor does it mean that science as a tool or process has failed. Instead, society has been wrong to look to scientists to provide enlightenment where they simply cannot. To use a rather far-fetched analogy, if we are going on a journey, science is the engine that helps get us there, but it certainly shouldn't be driving the car.

"Let's be philosophical for a moment. Metaphorically speaking, many people would say that wine has a 'soul'. It's common to find people involved in the production of wine who have a strong sense that there is a 'spiritual' element to what they are doing – that they need to operate with integrity and produce honest wines that reflect a faithful expression of the sites they are working with. Scientists typically find this sort of attitude hard to understand, because ideas like this can't be framed in scientific language."

Scientists have often been guilty of undervaluing or ignoring things that cannot be measured. Let's be philosophical for a moment. Metaphorically speaking, many people would say that wine has a "soul". It's common to find people involved in the production of wine who have a strong sense that there is a "spiritual" element to what they are doing – that they need to operate with integrity and produce honest wines that reflect a faithful expression of the sites they are working with. Scientists typically find this sort of attitude hard to understand, because ideas like this can't be framed in scientific language. But isn't it best if we can establish some sort of dialogue between scientifically literate wine people and those who choose to describe their activities in other terms, such as the proponents of Biodynamics?

## Science and wine

How does all this relate to wine? In this book I am going to be looking at wine through the particular lens of science. I'll be exploring how science is a useful (vital, even) tool in the fields of viticulture, winemaking, and also in terms of helping us understand the human interaction with wine. But I am not suggesting for one minute that wine – this engrossing, culturally rich, life-enhancing, and enjoyable liquid – should be stripped of everything that makes it interesting and turned into an industrially produced, technically perfect, manufactured beverage. Science is a tool that can help wine, but this doesn't mean that wine should belong to the scientists. For this reason, I'll be leaving the familiar, safe ground that you might expect a book about wine science to cover, and venturing into some of the more absorbing issues that get wine lovers talking – such as terroir, Biodynamics, and the production of "natural", manipulation-free wines.

Science has a lot to offer wine. My goal is that by writing this book, which is designed to be accessible to non-scientists (yet still with enough meat to keep scientists engrossed), I'll have facilitated an enhanced understanding of wine that will assist them in their pursuit of this culturally rich and fascinating beverage.

## Accessing the scientific literature

As I've already mentioned, science is published in peer-reviewed journals, of which there are many thousands. So how can the non-scientist approach this scientific literature and glean something useful from it? The first port of call for most will be an online database. There are many of these, and they contain the abstracts (short summaries of methods, results, and conclusions) of each published paper, along with other indexing data. Perhaps the most useful database is *PubMed*, which can be found at www.ncbi.nlm.nih.gov/entrez/.

The skill in researching the literature comes from searching effectively, and then assigning the appropriate level of confidence to the results. Are they significant? Are they reliable? It is hard for non-specialists to do this at all well, but there are a number of clues, the main one being how often the paper is cited by others, and the importance of the journal in which it is published. Not all journals are equal; some are much harder to publish in than others, and will only take the very best studies that represent real breakthroughs. Other journals may publish papers that come from less thorough or extensive studies, or where the interpretation of the data is flawed or subtly biased.

So while you may end up with a long list of articles on the subject you are researching, don't be surprised to find that there may be differing conclusions to the same questions. In any field, while there is a degree of consensus among scientists on some issues, there are usually just as many points of disagreement and intense debate. It's a bit of a minefield for the unwary, so tread carefully and ask the right questions before accepting something as fact.

Finally, a word of warning about "pseudoscience". It's everywhere, and is especially common on the internet and where treatments for human diseases are being discussed. If "results" have not been published in independent, peer-reviewed scientific journals, you should ask why. A useful resource in this regard is the *Quackwatch* website, www.quackwatch.org.

# Section One
# In the vineyard

# 1 The biology of the grape vine

Agiorgitiko and Albariño, Baga and Bourboulenc, Cabernet Sauvignon and Chardonnay, Dolcetto and Durif – there are many thousands of different grape varieties capable of making a bewildering array of different wines, but they all stem from just one species: *Vitis vinifera*. This single species is the source of almost all the wine consumed today. *Vitis vinifera* is commonly referred to as the Eurasian grape vine because of its origin in the Near East at the meeting point of Europe and Asia. This is where *Vitis vinifera* can still be found growing wild. It is estimated that, across the globe, there are some 14,000 to 24,000 different cultivars (the scientific term for plant variety), but because many of these are in fact synonyms, the real figure is perhaps 5,000 to 8,000 varieties – all the offspring of this one "mother vine".

## Vines in the wild

When most people think about grape vines, they envisage pretty vineyards with neat rows of vines arranged on a trellis system, or grown as bushes. Lovely. But this isn't how grape vines grow in the wild. Their natural growth form is as woodland climbers, using trees for support. Where the vine breaks through the canopy into sunlight, it flowers and produces grapes. These are eaten by birds, which disseminate the seeds. Because of this growth form, vines need extensive root systems to enable them to compete for water and nutrients with the trees and bushes they are hitching a ride on; the ability to make the most of limited resources is a prerequisite to this sort of lifestyle. Vines also need shoots capable of rapid elongation to grow towards the outside of the host canopy to find sunlight. When they are in the light, this is the right time for the shoots to produce flowers and thus fruit – a wasted effort if it were to take place in the shade of the canopy. The vine is designed to be a highly competitive plant with a flexible growth form; vines have to adjust to the shape of whatever host plant they are growing on. It's helpful to bear in mind this native state of the vine in considering viticultural issues. Knowing what the vine is "programmed" to do can help in uncovering the scientific basis of effective viticulture.

## Domesticating wild vines

Ancient humans living in the right places would no doubt have been familiar with the wild grape vine and its attractive-looking fruit. It's a mystery how the grape vine was first domesticated, although there have been plenty of guesses. One proposal, known as the palaeolithic hypothesis, seems plausible, although impossible to prove. Imagine early humans foraging for food. They suddenly see some brightly coloured berries growing on vines suspended from trees, so they pick them and eat them. They taste good, so these foragers collect as many as they can in whatever container they have to hand. On the journey home, the weight of the mass of grapes crushes a few, which then start fermenting. The result is a rough and ready wine that collects at the bottom of the container after a few days. If you found this sort of liquid mass at the bottom of a pot, you'd give it a try, wouldn't you? It's hard to imagine any wine produced in this fashion tasting terribly wonderful, but then these folks probably weren't all that fussy.

When they experienced to a small degree the mind-altering effects of this liquid, you can imagine it catching on fairly quickly. It is likely that deliberate planting of grape vines would have soon followed these rudimentary attempts at wine-making. Someone probably planted a few of the seeds, and, with a bit of trial and error, worked out how to make a vineyard. Although it is hard to be precise, it is estimated that this vine "domestication" first occurred 7,000 years ago.

## A primer on plant physiology

Before we examine the specific biology of the grape vine, it's worth taking a brief look at the principles of plant morphology and physiology, as these will help in putting the biology of the vine in context.

Plants are remarkable. From very basic building blocks – water, carbon dioxide, and mineral ions – they make everything they need by capturing energy from sunlight through the process of photosynthesis. With the exception of a few weird organisms that derive their energy from deep-sea hydrothermal vents, all life on earth depends directly or indirectly on photosynthesis for energy. The key molecule involved in capturing light energy from the sun is chlorophyll, which gives plants their green colour. All that is needed to produce a mighty old oak tree is a seed (an acorn in this case), sunlight, carbon dioxide, and a substrate that provides adequate water and mineral ions. It's the same for vines.

The best way to gain an understanding of the concepts underlying plant physiology is to think from first principles and use a bit of poetic licence. You are faced with the task of designing an organism that is going to live on land and derive its energy from sunlight. How are you going to combat the challenges that will be posed by a sedentary, terrestrial lifestyle? You must find a way to ensure that this organism is supplied with water and mineral ions. It must be able to conserve this water – the supply from rainfall will be irregular and unpredictable – but at the same time it needs to be able to exchange gases. The risk of water loss will be made more acute by the fact that the best structure for intercepting light will be thin, with a large surface area (the leaf) that will heat up far beyond ambient temperature in full sunlight. This organism must also be able to orient these photosynthetic tissues in order to capture as much light as possible, even though the direction and strength of this light source will be changing with daily and seasonal variation. Then it will need sufficient protection from the threats of climatic variation, pests, diseases, and predators, plus a way of outwitting the competition and some sort of reproductive strategy. It's a tall order.

Plants have a number of ways of meeting these design requirements. Starting with the finest details, one structure that makes plant cells unique is the cellulose cell wall, formed around the outside of the cell membrane. This confers a rigidity to the cells that enables plants to form organized, structured tissues with a degree of mechanical strength. They can therefore grow away from the ground, and thus away from some pests and competition, to be best placed to intercept light. Plants also have a tissue organization, with a basic body plan of roots, shoots, and leaves, together with more specialized structures such as petals, sepals, stamens, bracts, and tendrils that subserve specific roles. A conduction system made up of "vascular" tissue is crucial to this, allowing the partitioning of water, nutrients, and inorganic ions around the plant from their sites of production or abstraction. There are two main types of vessel: xylem, made up of dead cells that conduct water and some inorganic ions; and phloem, sharing out the food made in photosynthetic parts of the plant such as the leaves.

Roots are important, serving the dual roles of anchorage and uptake of water and solutes. Not only do they take up water and solutes passively, they can also take up mineral ions selectively across a concentration gradient by an active (energy-consuming) process via specialized transport proteins. Roots interact with microbes in the soil in a complex way. Many form specialized mutualistic symbioses (a relationship in which both partners benefit) with specific fungi known as mycorrhizae, which makes the uptake of certain nutrients more effective. Roots from certain species can form specialized structures that house nitrogen-fixing bacteria – another beneficial symbiotic relationship.

Water is at a premium for land-dwelling plants. Its loss is prevented by the cuticle, containing a wax made by the polymerization of a molecule called cutin. In perennial plants (whose structures last more than a season) such as the vine, the outer layer is further specialized and becomes woody via the deposition of another molecule called lignin. Woody tissues are protected from water loss by a polymer, suberin, which lines the inner walls of cork cells, making them highly impermeable to gases and liquids. This protection from water loss is essential, but it also inhibits gas exchange. So plants need specialized openings in the outer layers of their photosynthetic tissues, called stomata. These open and close in response to environmental and physiological signals. Thus the plant must continually weigh up whether to open the stomata for gas exchange or close them to minimize water loss, a delicate balancing act that underlies many viticultural decisions.

## The problem of mobility

Because plants can't move, the problem of predation and disease is a severe one. They are sitting targets. The solution lies in complex chemistry. Plants synthesize a wide array of secondary metabolites – chemicals that many herbivores find aversive – which render them unpalatable. They may also have protective physical structures such as spines, hairs or even stings. In addition, there are specialized pathways to deal with fungal and bacterial attack. In a loose parallel with the immune system of higher animals, plant cells that are under attack can signal to cells around them and throughout their bodies via molecules such as salicylic acid – an active ingredient in aspirin. This stimulates the formation of antimicrobial compounds. Specific cells that are attacked by pathogens can also kill themselves and neighbouring cells. This drastic-sounding measure is an effective way of dealing with alien invasions, often stopping the attack in its tracks.

Plants are almost always fixed in place by their roots, but their aerial parts can still move, albeit very slowly. "Tropism" is the term that describes plant movements; plants are designed to grow in certain directions in response to environmental cues. This means they need a mechanism to sense these cues, then respond to them appropriately. Perhaps the most significant is phototropism: growing in response to light. Plants detect light via a suite of molecules known as phytochromes, which are tuned to pick out certain significant wavelengths. They then usually grow towards sources of light; after all, light equals food. Roots, however, want to grow towards likely sources of water and nutrients; for them, the most significant tropism is positive gravitropism, or growing downwards under the pull of gravity (in the absence of light, shoots show a negative gravitropism, growing away from the ground). Another significant tropism is thigmotropism, a growth response to touch. This is exhibited by vine tendrils.

Plants must not only respond spatially to environmental cues, but they also need to respond temporally – for example, to changes in seasons. Thus plants are equipped to sense factors such as changes in day length and temperature.

# Plant reproduction

Let's expand on the theme of reproduction. The response of plants to their environment also governs the choice between vegetative or sexual reproduction. The former involves the plant producing genetically identical copies of itself; the latter is the more familiar form of reproduction that animals tend to opt for, which involves the reshuffling of the genetic pack through sex to produce genetically different organisms with a mix of genes from the maternal and paternal lines.

Generally (and simplistically) speaking, if conditions are good and a plant is doing well, then, if it can, it opts for vegetative reproduction or just grows larger – after all, there's clearly a good match between the plant genes and the environment and it wants to keep things that way. On the other hand, if conditions are bad, plants will more often choose to reproduce sexually (the "I'm outta here" option), which requires fruit production.

So viticulturalists want to treat their vines harshly enough so that they will focus on fruit production, while giving them just enough of what they need so that they don't suffer from water or mineral deficit, which would hamper their efforts at producing ripe fruit. Thus many viticultural interventions aim at encouraging the vine to partition nutrients to the grapes so that they ripen properly rather than concentrating on growing more leaves and stems (also known in the trade as vegetative growth or "vigour").

## How plants reproduce

Two reproductive options are open to most plants: vegetative and sexual. Simpler plants such as mosses possess an array of vegetative "propagules" – propagational structures – that enable a mature plant to replicate itself, usually in the same locality: a strategy encouraged by favourable conditions. After all, the plant is doing well in that locale, so there's every chance a genetically identical plant would also thrive there. Sexual reproduction involves a jumbling up of the chromosomes, and in simpler plants takes the form of unicellular spores, which are often dispersed over long distances.

The development of multicellular, specialized sexual propagules – also known as seeds – was a major breakthrough for plants. This allows the temporal and spatial separation of plant sex from the establishment of new plants. For example, plants can have sex in the summer (when pollinating insect populations, if these are used, are at their highest), set seed in autumn, and the seeds can be dispersed elsewhere (often over long distances, where conditions may be more suitable) to germinate the following spring, when conditions are more favourable. Seeds are of very little importance for viticulture because no one propagates grape vines from seed, but the process of seed production – "vine sex" – is crucial. This is what produces the grapes.

## Environmental computers

With all these tissues to coordinate and a steadily varying environment to adjust to, it is helpful to think of plants as sophisticated environmental computers. Just as we sense the world around us, then use this information to guide our actions, so do plants. It's simply that whereas we respond quickly – for example, if it is too hot in one place we move somewhere cooler – plants respond over a much longer time-scale. Literally rooted to the spot, they adapt their growth form to best suit local conditions. Thus two genetically identical plants grown in different environments will adopt different growth forms. This morphological plasticity is intended to give plants the flexibility to make the best of particular local conditions. A plant grown in a windy spot will typically exhibit a shorter, stockier stature than one grown in a more sheltered location, for instance, and most plants are able to orient their leaves to capture the maximum amount of sunlight.

How do plants do this? They are able to coordinate the growth and division of their cells in an organized manner by sensing the environment around them

"It is helpful to think of plants as sophisticated environmental computers. Just as we sense the world around us, then use this information to guide our actions, so do plants. It's simply that whereas we respond quickly – for example, if it is too hot in one place we move somewhere cooler – plants respond over a much longer time-scale."

and then conveying this information throughout their growth forms via a suite of signalling molecules known as plant hormones (or "plant growth regulators" as people in the trade prefer to call them). While the precise details of how these operate at cellular level are still being worked out by researchers, the existence of these hormones has been known about since the pioneering experiments of Dutch physiologist Frits Went in the 1920s. There are five different classes recognized: auxins, gibberellins, cytokinins, abscisic acid, and ethylene.

There is one further topic in plant physiology that is highly relevant to viticulture, and falls under the title of "source-sink relationships". Photosynthesis, which is the transformation of light into plant food, takes place in leaves: organs that are specialized for this function. The leaves are therefore the "source". This food is then distributed via the phloem to where it is needed in the plant: the "sinks". Sinks are, most commonly, actively growing regions such as ripening grapes or elongating stems. Their demand or pull on nutrient resources is known as "sink strength". It is important for viticulture that as the grapes are ripening they represent powerful enough sinks to be allocated the nutrient resources that they need for proper maturation. Vines that are still growing vigorously as the grapes go through their crucial ripening process are likely to allocate too many of their food resources to the actively growing shoots, and the grapes may not ripen properly. Part of the job of the viticulturalist is to bring vine vigour, and thus shoot sink strength, under control.

## Vine structure and development

Six main challenges face plants growing out of water. First, they must find enough water and hang on to it, while at the same time being able to exchange gases with the atmosphere. Second, they need to defend themselves against attacks by herbivores or pathogens. Third, they must find enough light for photosynthesis. Fourth, they must reproduce and disperse. Fifth, they must adapt to seasonal rhythms and variability in the environment. Sixth, they need to deal with competition. The ways that plants have met these challenges have shaped and constrained their growth form and physiology. The vine has further constraints and specializations resulting from its lifestyle as a woodland climber.

Let's take a look at how the grape vine works, beginning with the roots. Roots serve two functions: anchorage and uptake. What exactly do vine roots take up from the soil? Like other plants, vines don't need much; they make almost everything themselves. But they do need an adequate supply of water and dissolved mineral ions, termed as macro- and micronutrients. These are inorganic (containing no carbon). Root growth is determined by interplay between the developmental programme of the plant and the distribution of mineral nutrients in the soil. The roots seek out the water and nutrients in the soil, sensing where they are, then preferentially sending out lateral shoots into these areas. Low nutrient levels in the upper layers of the soil cause the roots to grow deeper. This is likely to improve the regularity of water supply to the vine, and such roots can reach depths of three metres (approximately nine feet) or more, sometimes even further. The root system of one vine is capable of supporting an enormous mass of aerial plant structure.

Above ground, the vine has a growth form well-suited to life as a climber. Its shoot system is simple and adaptable, capable of fast growth. The vine never supports itself, so it doesn't waste resources on developing girth. Thin, long shoots are the order, which can produce lateral shoots and eventually become woody. The formation of woody tissue provides protection, particularly during the dormant

"Vines that are still growing vigorously as the grapes go through their crucial ripening process are likely to allocate too many of their food resources to the actively growing shoots, and the grapes may not ripen properly. Part of the job of the viticulturalist is to bring vine vigour, and thus shoot sink strength, under control."

period. At regular intervals buds are formed. These complicated structures, with the potential for leaves, flowers, and tendrils, develop over two seasons, with a rest over the dormant period.

## Shoot morphology

The stem is separated into sections by structures known as nodes. At each node a leaf is formed on one side, with either a tendril or a flower bud on the other. Thus both vegetative (leaf) and reproductive (flower) meristems (the growth region where cells are actively dividing) are formed simultaneously on the same shoot. Light is key to vine growth. In the absence of light, shoots show negative gravitropism, growing away from the ground. Light is the overriding growth cue; shoots are positively phototropic, growing towards light. It is also the chief cue for flowering induction. Tendrils are important for climbing and are modified stems that coil around supporting structures. Do tendrils signal to the shoot when they are coiled around something, in effect telling the shoot to keep on growing because it has adequate support? It's an interesting idea.

## Bud development and flowering

The flowering process in a grape vine is unusual, because it extends for two consecutive growing seasons. Flowering is first induced in latent (dormant) buds during the summer, but initiation and floral development occur the following spring. On flowering induction, the shoot apical meristem (SAM; the region of active cell division) produces lateral meristems; these will give rise either to flowers or tendrils. In Spain, a research group led by José Miguel Martínez-Zapater has proposed that a specific grape-vine gene, VFL, has a role in maintaining indeterminancy – keeping bud fate options open – in meristems as well as specifying flower meristems, its normal role in annual plants. VFL is orthologous to a gene first identified in other plant species as "floricula/leafy" (orthology refers to genes in different species which derive from a common ancestor). In this work they described grape-vine flower development in detail and correlated this with expression of VFL using a technique known as *in situ* hybridization, which shows under the microscope precisely where genes are being expressed in tissue sections.

In grape vines, buds are formed and are first detectable in early spring in the axils (the inside of the join between the stem and leaf stalk) of the current

RIGHT The grape-vine shoot. (1) Growing tip, also known as the primary shoot apical meristem. (2) Tendril. (3) Leaf. Leaves and tendrils arise from portions of the stem known as nodes. The gap between two nodes is known as an internode. (4) Lateral shoot developing in the axil of the leaf, adjacent to (5) an axial bud. This is a Chenin Blanc vine in Vouvray, France.

"It's all for the benefit of the birds – unripe grapes are camouflaged and unappetizing, while ripe grapes stand out with their attractive red or golden colour and taste lovely. The grapes are telling the birds that dinner is served. Seeds are the first part of the grape to reach physiological maturity, around *veraison*, and this makes sense."

year's leaves. These buds consist of several SAMs protected by bracts (scaly structures). The earliest SAM usually develops as a lateral shoot; the rest remain dormant. In the first months of development the SAM produces small protrusions that are the beginnings of leaves. Then, around May to June in the Northern hemisphere, it produces lateral meristems opposite the leaf primordia; the first two or three of these will produce flowers, the rest tendrils. More meristems are produced, so by the end of the growing season the bud contains a shoot containing inflorescence (flowering) meristems, tendrils, and leaves. These are all protected by bracts, scales, and hairs, and become dormant in the autumn. During the following spring, the bud is reactivated, and more meristems are produced. Crucially, the lateral meristems giving rise to inflorescences or tendrils are indistinguishable at the time they form. This keeps the options for the vine wide open, allowing environmental cues to dictate at this late stage whether these lateral meristems should become flowers or tendrils. The decision affecting this choice between tendrils and inflorescences has been the subject of a separate series of studies by researchers in Australia led by Mark Thomas.

Tendrils and inflorescences are homologous structures that can be interconverted by plant-hormone application. Indeed, intermediate structures are commonly observed on vines. The work of Thomas and his colleagues has demonstrated that plant hormones known as gibberellins are major inhibitors of grape-vine floral induction. In the natural habitat of the grape vine, which is a woodland climber, gibberellin would have two roles. It would promote the elongation of the stem and the production of tendrils, while at the same time suppressing fruit production. This suggests that there may well be a connection between light sensing and gibberellin production (or responsiveness to gibberellin), since this is the sort of strategy vines would use if they were in the shade of the host-plant canopy. A vine in the shade would want to delay fruit production and maximize its energy on growing upwards as fast as possible until it breaks through into the light.

When flowers are formed, their development and pollination occur best during a period of warm, settled weather. Domesticated vines are hermaphrodites, and can self-pollinate. Poor weather during this process can result in poor or uneven fruit set, so flowering is one of the critical phases in the vineyard calendar.

## Ancient wine: the new field of molecular archaeology

The science of archaeology must be a frustrating one at times. Detective work of the highest order is necessary to be able to meld together the few remaining pieces of surviving evidence of a bygone era into some sort of coherent story. Patrick McGovern, an archaeologist at the University of Pennsylvania, is probably the leading expert on the ancient origins of wine. But rather than just rely on old fragments of pottery and a few vine seeds, McGovern has turned to advanced molecular biological techniques to provide new evidence to shed light on the origins of wine in ancient civilizations. This new avenue of research has been dubbed "molecular archaeology".

McGovern has collaborated with grape-vine molecular biologists to study the DNA of ancient grape relics such as seeds. Using similar techniques as those employed at the University of California at Davis by Carole Meredith and her colleagues (*see* page.24) to assess relationships among modern-day varieties, McGovern is using microsatellite (sequential) repeats in the ancient DNA to identify the grape variety and its relationship to modern vines. These are stretches of DNA consisting of repeats of simple sequences that can be used as molecular fingerprints. It's a work in progress, as he and his collaborators continue to fine-tune the complex process of extracting useful DNA from ancient plant tissue, then making sense of the results.

As yet, more concrete results have come from the array of chemical techniques that have been used to study residues present on archaeological samples. Together, these are powerful tools for providing scientifically reliable answers to questions that were previously just a matter of conjecture.

## Grape development

As Clark Smith of Vinovation, a California-based company specializing in winemaking services and technologies, emphasizes, grapes are for the birds. The wild vine "designed" grapes to enlist the help of birds for spreading seeds; with their flying habit, birds are pretty mobile, and the sorts of places birds go are promising locations for dispersing seeds. All those sugars in ripe grapes are a reward for potential seed-carrying birds. But the grape vine doesn't want the birds to carry the grapes off too soon, before the seeds are ready for dispersal, or before the onset of autumn, with its rains and favourable conditions for seed germination. The maturation of grapes is therefore cleverly timed, and separated into three phases.

The first phase involves the development of the grape structure; throughout this process the grapes accumulate acids and experience rapid cell division. This second phase, *veraison*, is when red grapes change colour from green to red and the skins of white grapes change from being hard and green to being soft and translucent. The third phase follows this, when growth begins again (but this time through cell enlargement, not division) and grapes accumulate sugar and phenolic compounds, and acids decrease. It's all for the benefit of the birds – unripe grapes are camouflaged (green colour) and unappetizing (highly acidic, containing high levels of leafy-tasting pyrazines, and with harsh tannins), while ripe grapes stand out with their attractive red or golden colour and taste lovely (the sweetest of all fruits, with lower acidity, riper tannins, and the herbaceous pyrazine flavours degraded). The grapes are telling the birds that dinner is served. Seeds are the first part of the grape to reach physiological maturity, around *veraison*, and this makes sense.

### Grape maturity

What is grape maturity in winemaking terms? It depends on the objective. Two types of maturity are talked about in wine circles: sugar accumulation and phenolic (or physiological) maturity; the latter is also referred to as flavour maturity by some. Match the right grape variety to your vineyard climate, do your viticulture well, and you'll reach the goal of perfect maturation: flavour maturity coinciding with a sugar level that will yield

a wine of twelve to thirteen per cent alcohol. There is, however, a disconnection between the physiological processes (which govern the rate of sugar accumulation and loss of malic acid, which are dependent on climatic factors) and the colour, aroma, and tannin development (phenolic maturity), which is less dependent on climate. The result is that, in warmer climates, grapes only reach physiological maturity at sugar levels that are considerably higher than those in cooler regions.

Typically, in the cooler, classic, Old World regions, grape harvest coincides with a shortening of day length and decrease in temperature, and thus sugar accumulation is more gradual. In these regions, the measurement of sugar levels works well as a guide for when to harvest. It is also a simple measurement to make in the field. In these conditions, it is likely that by the time the grapes have accumulated twelve degrees of potential alcohol or so, they will have achieved satisfactory phenolic maturity. Pick at the same sugar levels in many New World regions and you'll end up with unripe flavours in your wines.

Light is crucial in the ripening process. Grapes that are shaded contain less sugar and are more acidic than those exposed to sunlight. Light also affects bud fertility. One of the key viticultural goals is therefore to encourage the vine to produce an open canopy without dense, vigorous growth that could produce shading. This issue is explored further in chapter 10.

## Different varieties, different clones

In taxonomic terms, *Vitis* is what is known as a genus, the "tier" above species. Way back in evolutionary time, this genus split into three lineages. The Eurasian vine *Vitis vinifera* is a single species and is responsible for almost all wine made today. In contrast, there are many different American species of *Vitis*, whose main importance in modern viticulture is to provide phylloxera-resistant rootstocks for grafting *Vitis vinifera* onto. Finally, there are a few Asian species of *Vitis*, of little importance for wine.

"It is remarkable how few new successful varieties have arisen from plant breeding programmes. Even those that have, such as Pinotage, are of questionable worth. Generally, growers are happy with the varieties they have and just want to improve them in ways that don't affect the expression of varietal character."

*Vitis vinifera* may be just one species, but through evolution and numerous cross-fertilizations it has produced thousands of different varieties that are used in wine-growing today. The effect of domestication has been largely to improve the fruitfulness of these various varieties and to distribute them widely.

Vine propagation occurs vegetatively. Cuttings from vines are used to produce new plants which are genetic clones (here the term "clone" means genetically identical) of the parent variety. Attempts to grow vines from seeds are almost certainly doomed to fail because the genetic re-assortment that takes place usually means the loss of positive features of the variety. It is remarkable how few successful new varieties have arisen from plant breeding programmes. Even those that have, such as Pinotage (a misnamed South African cross between Cinsault, known at the time as "Hermitage", and Pinot Noir back in the 1950s), are of questionable worth. Generally, growers are happy with the varieties they have and just want to improve them in ways that don't affect the expression of varietal character.

Within each of the different varieties exists a range of clones (in this context "clones" are variants of the same variety, a different use of the term). Some of these are the product of spontaneous bud mutations, which then result in genetically altered shoots. Almost always, such mutations are neutral or deleterious. Sometimes, however, they are positive, and can be propagated by cuttings taken from an affected shoot, resulting in a new clone of the variety. At other times, the clonal differences reflect nothing more than differing levels of virus infection, or perhaps epigenetic differences (heritable changes not based on DNA-sequence changes). Another mechanism underlying differences between varieties and clones is a process called "chimerism". This is where separate portions of the plant have different genotypes (that is, are of different genetic origins). Mark Thomas and colleagues have demonstrated that the phenotype of Pinot Meunier results from the interaction of two genetically distinct cell layers. They separated the two by tissue culture and showed that one layer is the same as Pinot Noir, while the other is a mutant which produces a short, stubby vine with a fruit cluster at every node instead of the more usual mix of fruit clusters and tendrils. I asked Thomas how common this sort of

**RIGHT** Do old vines produce better wines? This Shiraz vine, planted on its own roots, is over 100 years old, and is from Wendouree in South Australia's Clare Valley. *See* page 90 for a discussion of vine age and quality.

grape-vine chimerism is. "Since our work, other research groups from various countries have looked at other varieties and found similar results," he said. "So I would guess that most, if not all, old varieties would have accumulated somatic mutations."

Modern molecular biological techniques have provided important new insights into the relationships among different grape varieties. Dr Carole Meredith and her colleagues at the University of California at Davis used microsatellite markers (also known as simple sequence repeats – a molecular fingerprinting device) to sort out relationships between grape varieties that weren't apparent from traditional studies. They have confirmed that Zinfandel is the same grape variety as Primitivo (grown in Italy) and Crljenak (from Croatia, also called Pribidrag), and that the parents of Cabernet Sauvignon were Cabernet Franc and Sauvignon Blanc. They have also shown definitively that Chardonnay is the result of what was likely to have been an accidental cross between Pinot Noir and an undistinguished white variety called Gouais Blanc.

In conclusion, from the examples cited here it is obvious that modern science is illuminating the biology of the grape vine. In the next chapter we turn to the interaction of the grape vine with its environment – the important topic of terroir.

## Retrotransposons and grape colour

Have you ever wondered what makes some grapes white and others red? Viticulturalists have presumed that ancestral wild-grape species were all dark-skinned – this makes sense because red grapes change colour from green to red during the ripening process to make them appealing (and visible) to birds – and that white grapes arose by mutation, but the precise details were a mystery. Recently, however, scientists from Japan have uncovered the molecular basis of grape-skin colour, identifying the genetic mutation responsible for white-skinned grapes. In 2004, a research group led by Shozo Kobayashi discovered the gene mutation that is thought to underlie the emergence of white grape skin colour.

Black- or red-skinned grapes owe their colour to a group of red pigments known as anthocyanins. The synthesis of these pigments is controlled by a specific set of genes. Kobayashi's group has shown that a specific sequence of DNA known as a retrotransposon is responsible for turning off the expression of one of those genes, and thus switching off pigment production in white grapes. Retrotransposons are mobile pieces of genetic information that are able to move genes around the genome. They are especially abundant in plants, and are able to induce mutations by inserting next to, or actually into, other genes. "We hypothesize that Gret1 [the specific retrotransposon] originally inserted upstream of one of the anthocyanin-regulating genes of a black-skinned ancestor, and that subsequently a white-skinned grape was produced by spontaneous crossing," says Kobayashi. They also think that this was an ancient mutation, which took place long before grape vines were first cultivated. They have also shown that red pigmentation can be induced i n the skins of white grapes by the insertion of the anthocyanin-controlling gene, and that white grape varieties have mutated to red by the spontaneous removal of the retrotransposon from this gene.

"It makes sense," says Professor Andrew Walker of UC Davis's Viticulture Department, "and backs up observations by breeders, geneticists, and viticulturists with some varieties, particularly Pinot Noir and its colour morphs (Pinot Blanc and Pinot Gris)." These results also explain how a black grape, Cabernet Sauvignon, can have both a red grape (Cabernet Franc) and a white grape (Sauvignon Blanc) as its ancestors.

Renowned grape-vine geneticist Carole Meredith thinks that the work is significant. "It adds to the growing evidence that retrotransposons have long been active in grapes and may well have contributed to characteristics that are important in wine composition and flavour." She adds that there is ongoing research into the role of retrotransposons in the development of clonal variation within varieties. "I think we'll find that retrotransposons are very important in wine grapes," says Meredith. "It adds to previous evidence that white-fruit colour in many varieties may have a single common basis."

She concludes, "this is fascinating work. But a lot of genetic analysis is needed before it can be concluded that this retrotransposon insertion is solely responsible for white-fruit colour in grapes."

# 2 Terroir: how do soils and climate shape wine?

"Terroir" is a concept that is rapidly emerging as the unifying concept of fine wine. Once almost exclusively the preserve of the Old World, it's now a talking point in the New World, too. The traditional, Old World definition of terroir is quite a tricky one to tie down, but it can probably best be summed-up as the possession by a wine of a sense of place, or "somewhereness"; that is, a wine from a particular patch of ground expresses characteristics related to the physical environment in which the grapes are grown. The goal of this chapter will be to give a broad introduction to this hotly debated topic, examining why it is still a controversial issue. Then I'll focus on the scientific underpinnings of this concept, concentrating on teasing out the relationship between vineyard characteristics and wine flavour. It's unfortunate that just the mention of the word terroir rouses such strong negative feelings in some people, because it really is one of the most absorbing topics in the study of wine – something I'm hoping to demonstrate in the following pages.

## Definitions

One of the problems with many discussions of terroir is that this word means different things to different people. Indeed, defining terroir in precise terms is quite difficult, partly because it is a word used in three rather different ways.

### A sense of place

The primary definition is that terroir is the possession by a wine of a sense of place; that is, the wine expresses flavour characteristics influenced by the properties of the vineyard or region from which it hails. Immediately we see that scale is an issue here: environmental variation affects wine flavour, but this variation operates on a number of scales. Wines made from grapes harvested from different parts of the same vineyard may well taste different. On the other hand, there might be characteristics held in common by wines made from larger geographic regions that are evident when these wines are compared with those of other regions: for example, Burgundian Pinot Noirs compared with California Pinot Noirs. And which factors should be included in the definition of terroir? It's clear that human intervention in terms of viticultural and winemaking practices may also confer a sense of place to a wine, but most people wouldn't count the human element as part of terroir.

This raises the interesting question of the differences between terroir and *typicité*. Most definitions of terroir rule out human intervention as part of the equation. But could winemaking play a role in maintaining *typicité*? Certainly, in the classic Old World regions where terroir is so precisely delineated, the fact that winemakers commonly use similar techniques could help lend a distinctive regional style. Winemakers could also be adapting their techniques to best exhibit regional differences in their wines. This *typicité*, which owes more to human intervention than it does to classical definitions of terroir, is still of merit, as it helps to maintain the sort of stylistic regional diversity that makes wine so interesting. In general, though, terroir is easier to conceptualize and is a more useful concept if winemaking is excluded. "I don't see winemaking as part of terroir," says Jeffrey Grosset of Australia's Clare Valley, "but rather that poor winemaking can interfere with its expression and good winemaking can allow pure expression."

### The vineyard site

The next use of terroir is in describing the vineyard site itself: the combination of soils, sub-soils, and climatic factors that affect the way grapes grow on the vine and thus influence the taste of the wine made from them. This is probably the least controversial use of the term, because it is purely descriptive. But then it is probably the least interesting.

### Goût de terroir

Finally, there is a third use of this word. The term *goût de terroir* is sometimes used to describe flavours presumed to be imparted by the individual vineyard site. Thus someone might say that they taste notes of "terroir" in the wine. This is the most confusing use of this word; in scientific terms it is hard to defend because it makes assumptions about mechanisms which can't be demonstrated, as we will see later.

## Terroir in the New World

One interesting question surrounds why there has recently been a sea change in attitude among New World winemakers, where for so long the job of grape-growing was seen merely as a mundane prelude to the work of the all-powerful winemaker. Even fairly recently, the New World response to terroir was typically that it was a last-ditch marketing ploy by European wine-growers who were panicking about their increasing loss of market share. This turnaround has occurred for two reasons. Firstly, New World wine-growers have realized that two of the keys to wine quality are grapes that show homogeneous (even) levels of ripeness, and the recognition of the role that natural variation within and between their vineyards plays. With the increasing adoption of a technique known as precision viticulture, vineyards are commonly broken up into sub-plots sharing similar characteristics (known as natural or basic terroir units) so that vineyard interventions can be precisely targeted to where they are needed.

The second reason is that New World winemakers have realized that regionality is the way forward with fine wine. Yet you don't have to look too far below the surface to see that there are subtle but important differences between Old World and New World notions of terroir. Speaking generally, in the Old World, "terroirists" aim to make wines that express the *typicité* of the specific vineyard site, whereas in the more pragmatic New World, understanding terroir is seen as a route to improved quality. Of course, there are exceptions to this generalization.

## Terroir in practice

Let's try to explain terroir in practical terms. Take a property with three different vineyard sites: one flat, one on a south-facing hillside, and one on a north-facing slope. We're assuming for the sake of simplicity that the same grape varieties and clones are used in all three, that the vineyards share the same geology, and that they are farmed the same way. Three wines are then made, one from each vineyard, in identical fashion. It's likely that all will taste different. That's terroir in action. Typically, vineyard sites will differ not only in one variable, as in this example, but in several. And factors such as differences in slope gradient, orientation or soil type will also influence decisions about which varieties are planted where, bringing further variables into play.

"One Aussie winemaker, Jeffrey Grosset, suggests that the French weren't the first to come up with the concept. 'Terroir is the French word for what some have known in Australia for thousands as years as *pangkarra*,' he says. He explains that this is an Aboriginal word that encompasses the characteristics of a specific place including the climate, geology, and soil/water relations."

## Winemakers' views on terroir

Although the idea that soils and climate influence wine flavour seems to be rather obvious, terroir is in fact a highly controversial concept. It doesn't help that it has long been regarded as the exclusive preserve of the French. "The French feel they have ownership of terroir," says Barossa wine-grower Charlie Melton, "but in good winemaking the idea is universal." Melton prefers not to use the T-word itself, but instead talks of characterization of distinct vineyard blocks. "In the Barossa, the sub-regions have their own character," he says. "Wines from the southern end have finer, slightly sweeter aromatics, and those from the northern end have a *garrigue*-like earthiness rather than sweetness." He points out that the humidity is on average three per cent higher in the southern end, and that the soils in the Barossa vary quite widely, with adjacent blocks sometimes making quite different wines. "Call it terroir if you like," he adds.

Another Barossa *vigneron* I spoke to also takes terroir seriously. Anita Bowen has recently started making wine here. "In selecting my eighty-acre, hilly vineyard site," she explains, "I commissioned a soil survey that involved the excavating of forty-eight sites on a 75 x 75-metre (246 x 246-foot) grid to the depth of 1.7 metres (5.5 feet) to assess the soil profile. This identified four different soil types and provided me with information to marry the nature of the vine variety to the nature of the soil." Does her wine reflect its origins and express characteristics unique to this part of the Barossa? "Yes!" she says emphatically. "Consistently, Shiraz made in this area of the Barossa is rich, ripe with great palate structure and firm tannins, and is less aromatic and more alcohol-driven than Shiraz made in other areas." Bowen is a firm believer in the notion that the Barossa possesses terroir. "Besides climatic differences, there are variations in soil types from the red-brown earths and clays of western slopes through to the sandy soils of the valley floor and predominantly podzolic soils of the eastern slopes and hills. My winemaker friends who take grapes from these different areas can readily identify the different fruit characters and the wine style that will be produced, dependent upon which vineyard in what area of the valley the grapes were grown."

In fact, one Aussie winemaker, Jeffrey Grosset, suggests that the French weren't the first to come up with the concept. "Terroir is the French word for what some have known in Australia for thousands as years as *pangkarra*," he says. He explains that this is an Aboriginal word that encompasses the characteristics of a specific place including the climate, geology, and soil/water relations. France 0, Australia 1.

### Terroir in Argentina

There's also a word in Spanish that's equivalent to terroir. According to Santiago Achaval, president of premium Argentinian winery Achaval-Ferrer, this term is *terruño*. Achaval is an eloquent proponent of this concept. "Our word has the same nuances as the word terroir, plus an additional one: it's the land a man belongs to, not the land that belongs to a man. It describes a man's bond with the land where he was born," he says. "We think the concept of terroir is of the highest importance. Terroir is for us the only source of originality and personality of a wine. It is also a source of neverending wonder: how small distances and slight differences in soil composition, exposure, and even surrounding plant life result in very noticeable differences in the wines."

Achaval refutes the idea that terroir is confined to classic Old World regions. "Argentina does have terroirs in the same way as France and Italy do.

The difference with those other countries is that the discovery of our terroirs is just now beginning. Both France and Italy have been perfecting their knowledge of their soils and microclimates since the early Middle Ages; Argentina started a century ago, with a hiatus during the turbulent economic times between the seventies and eighties. So there's a lot of exploration to be done until we can really say that we know our terroirs, and that we can design their hierarchy; not every vineyard is capable of expressing a powerful personality through its wine. And, as in the rest of the world, there are differences in quality of the wines that are driven only by location." I asked him whether terroir influences the way he works. "Yes it does," he said, "and strongly so."

Achaval-Ferrer is producing what Achaval calls two "ideas" of wine. "One of these 'ideas' of wine is what we define as 'the research into terroir'," he explains. "These are single-vineyard Malbec varietals, all three of them from very old, low-producing vines in very special places in Mendoza. What we are trying to do with these wines is to showcase the difference between the expressions of terroir in Mendoza. By trial and error, by untiring exploration, and by reducing yields to around twelve hectolitres per hectare, we've selected and purchased vineyards that express their personality so strongly that it overcomes vintage variations and can be recognized by blind tasting year after year. We keep the yields similar in all three vineyards, harvest at the same maturity and ferment in the same way, and use the same barrels. In this way, all the differences between these single-vineyards are entirely attributable to terroir.

"The other 'idea' of wine," he continues, "is what we call the 'pursuit of the ideal wine'. It is a blended wine based on Bordeaux varietals. We've named this wine Quimera. In Spanish, *quimera* means an impossible ideal – which is exactly what the pursuit of an ideal wine is. In this wine the 'sense of place' is lost (if you define place as a specific vineyard), but again, the low yields allow a mineral expression and a very noticeable Mendoza character to be found in the wine: a broader 'sense of place'." This comes back to the idea that terroir can operate on different scales, reflecting the fact that natural variation operates at all levels, from micro to macro.

## Terroir in New Zealand

"Terroir is fundamental to our operation," says Jeff Sinnott, a winemaker with Amisfield, a winery in the newly trendy Central Otago region of New Zealand.

"The notion of terroir is fundamental to the wine industries of Old World countries such as France and Germany. It's a philosophical framework within which wine-growers work."

"Our understanding of terroir is that wine is the embodiment of a vineyard's site, climate, the cultivar, and the culture of those who work within it. By understanding our environment, we can better manage our vineyards to produce fruit that truly represents our sense of place." Sinnott adds, "You could accuse terroir of being a somewhat hackneyed term, conveniently used to add to the mystique of the wine industry. But here in Central Otago, as much as in Burgundy, Oregon, California or anywhere that grows and makes quality wine from single-vineyard sources, we strive to make our wines as representative of our environment as possible."

### Objections to terroir

But one New World *vigneron* who objects to the notion of terroir is Sean Thackrey, a Californian winemaker famous for his single-vineyard Orion wine. "My objection is simply that it's so ruthlessly misused, and with such horrifying hypocrisy," he says. "It's very true that fruit grown in different places tastes different. In fact, it's a banality, so why exactly all this excess insistence?" Thackrey himself allows terroir to influence his work ("I don't know how it would be possible to observe the delicacies of change in a particular vineyard more attentively than I do in making the Orion"), but he feels that the French over-emphasize terroir for largely economic motives. He describes it as "an intensely desirable and bankable proposition because their property can then be sold, transferred, and inherited with the full value of the wine produced from its grapes attributable to the property itself". Thus the work of the winemaker and viticulturalist is played down and the role of the vineyard site talked up. "The immense psychological imperative to have wine be born from the earth without human intervention other than caretaking – which may in itself be why there is no French word for 'winemaker' – would make a long and complex book in itself," Thackrey suggests. "Personally, I believe that the quality of French wine is due to a French genius for viticulture and winemaking, just as I believe that the quality of French cuisine is due to a French genius for gastronomy."

## Mechanisms of terroir: a taste of the soil?

The notion of terroir is fundamental to the wine industries of Old World countries such as France and Germany. It's a philosophical framework within which wine-growers work. Local wine laws are built around the concepts of appellations, which lend official sanction to the idea that a combination of certain vineyard sites and grape varieties creates unique wines that faithfully express their geographical origins. Correspondingly, many Old World growers feel they have a duty to make wines faithful to the vineyard sites with which they work. These growers commonly make associations between properties of the

## A key to successful blending

Portugal's Dirk Niepoort, well-known for his groundbreaking Douro table wines, as well as the highly regarded Niepoort ports, adds a slightly different complexion to the debate about terroir "As a rule," he says, "I believe blended wines to be better than single-vineyard wines." This doesn't mean he's a non-believer in the concept of terroir, though. "I believe that terroir is essential," he adds. "I think that a good blender has to be someone who understands, knows, and respects different terroirs." Niepoort maintains that the search for great terroirs is very important to him. "But it is not only finding the terroirs that is important," he concludes. "It is also important to understand them and then adapt your winemaking to them."

wines and the soil types the grapes are grown on. In some cases, these putative associations are quite specific; people will talk about mineral characters in wines and associate them with the minerals in the vineyard, taken up by the roots of the vines. Do chalk, flint or slate soils impart chalky, flinty or slate-like characters to wine? As a scientist who has a working knowledge of plant physiology, I find this notion, which I call the "literalist" theory of terroir, implausible. Yet I can't get away from the fact that an overwhelming majority of the world's most compelling and complex wines are made by people who hold the notion of terroir as being critical to wine quality. Thus, one of the goals of this chapter is to explore the mechanisms of terroir, focusing specifically on soils. Just how do soils affect wine quality? Is it a direct or indirect relationship? What are the scientific explanations for terroir effects?

### Randall's rocks

A nice illustration of the literalist view of terroir comes from a characteristically wacky experiment conducted by Randall Grahm, of California's Bonny Doon. Even though he's from California, Grahm is actually one of the most eloquent proponents of terroir, and he had the unusual idea of bypassing the vine and adding rocks directly to wine to investigate their influence on flavour. "Our experiments were incredibly simplistic and gross in comparison to the very subtle chemistry that occurs in mineral extraction in real soils," he explains. "We simply took interesting rocks, washed them very well, smashed them up, and immersed them in a barrel of wine for a certain period of time until we felt that the wine had extracted some interesting flavours and we were able to discern significant differences between the various types." Surely, this is taking the literalist notion of terroir – that flavour compounds are translocated from the soil to the developing grapes through the vine roots – to its extreme? Grahm continues, "We initially screened a number of different rocks with bench trials and ultimately decided on a few for larger-scale experimentation: rip rap (granite), Noyo cobblestone, black slate, and Pami pebbles. We certainly took the extraction way too far, as we ended up seeing pH rises of 0.5–0.7 units, i.e. from 3.5–4.1 or 4.2, which is clearly beyond the pale for most wines. Obviously, the big pH shift and the lowering of the acidity caused major changes in the texture and mouth-feel of the wine, but we also observed dramatic differences in aromatics, length, and persistence of flavour." Grahm is convinced of the importance of mineral flavours in wine. "In every case," he says, "low doses of minerals (before we really overdid it), added far more complexity and greater persistence on the palate." His view is that minerality in wines has important implications for wine quality. "It is my personal belief that wines that are richer in minerals just present way differently. I believe that, in general, in mineral-rich wines there is a suppression of obvious fruit. What is most striking to me, though, about wines that have higher levels of minerals is that they seem to have a certain sort of nucleus or density around their centre; they are gathered, focused, cohered the way a laser coheres light. It is a different kind of density relative to tannic density – somehow deeper in the wine than the tannins. In any event, I am utterly convinced that minerality is the one true key to age-ability in wines and that everything else – tannin, acidity, sulphur dioxide – plays a far more secondary role." It is unlikely that adding rocks to wines will ever become a common winemaking manipulation, however. Grahm's rock-infused wines ran into some trouble with the regulatory body in California, which found elevated levels of nickel and antimony, among other things, so it looks like this experiment won't be repeated.

BELOW Randall Grahm, a firm believer in "terroir" – this belief led him to experiment by putting rocks in some of his wines.
*Picture courtesy of Claes Lofgren*

## "Minerality" in wine

"Minerality" is a frequently used descriptor in tasting notes, but it is the source of a lot of confusion. Where do "mineral" flavours come from, if not the soil? One explanation could be the presence of reduced sulphur compounds, described commonly by tasters as "reduction" flavours. Wine contains a wide range of these (*see* chapter 18 for a full discussion of the subject) which, at certain levels, in specific contexts, may be mistaken for terroir character. Dominique Delteil of the Institut Coopératif du Vin in Montpellier consults widely for a number of wineries, and his experience is that sulphur characters are often presented by winemakers as "terroir expression". Delteil's contention is that when sulphur compounds are managed better in the winery, suddenly "that famous terroir appears to be a luscious fruit source". The perception of these sulphur compounds depends a great deal on the context. Delteil recalls a recent visit to a grower in Friuli who had a dominant "flinty" character in his wine caused by a sulphur compound, despite appropriate steps in the winery to manage it. This was finally resolved by increasing the fruit expression in the wine, at which point the flint character became an attribute, not a fault.

On other occasions it's likely that sulphur compounds aren't the explanation for "mineral" flavours, and wines with high acidity levels are described as "mineral" by tasters seeking an apt descriptor.

## Scientific views of terroir

While in some circles it is quite common to hear such literalist explanations of terroir, they are treated with a degree of incredulity by many New World viticulturalists. I asked viticultural guru Dr. Richard Smart what he thought of popular notions of terroir which propose direct translocation of flavour molecules from the soil to the grapes, and hence the wine. "This is an absolute nonsense," he replied. "I have never heard this, yet you say it is popular. Who on earth postulated this?" Dawid Saayman, a South African viticultural expert known for his work on terroir, adds that, "I don't believe that the minerals taken up by the vine can register as minerality in the wines. Minerality appears to me to be more the result of absence of fruitiness." But it's pretty much a given that wines made from grapes differing only in the soil in which they were grown taste different. So just what *is* the scientific explanation for these terroir effects? It is an important question, because providing a sound scientific footing for terroir is a worthy cause. Not only will it lend credibility to the concept in the eyes of sceptics, but it will also help the already converted understand and therefore better utlilize terroir effects.

If we are going to frame terroir in scientific language, then we'll need to start with some plant physiology (*see* chapter 1 for a more in-depth account of this). The miracle of the plant kingdom is that these complex organisms build themselves from virtually nothing; all a plant needs to grow is some water, sunlight, air, and a mix of trace elements and nutrients. All the complex structure and chemistry of an oak tree, a daffodil or a grape vine is fashioned from these very basic starting ingredients. What do vine roots take up from the soil? Primarily water, along with dissolved mineral ions. It seems implausible that such a complex structure as a vine is created from virtually nothing by photosynthesis – the capture of light by specialized organelles called chloroplasts, which turn light energy into chemical energy that the plant can use – but that's the way it is. As Richard Smart emphasizes, "All flavour compounds are synthesized in the vine, made from organic molecules derived from photosynthesis ultimately, and inorganic ions taken up from the soil." Professor Jean-Claude Davidian of the Ecole Nationale Supérieure Agronomique in Montpellier echoes these sentiments. "Nobody has been objectively able to show any links between the soil mineral composition and the flavour or fragrance of the wines," he says. "Those who claim to have shown these links are not scientifically reliable."

"A popular notion is that very old vines with deep roots express terroir better than their younger counterparts. 'The claims often made regarding the importance of deep-rooted vines are based on the assumption that roots are better able to exploit the underlying geology,' says Dawid Saayman. 'In turn, this is considered to contribute certain minerals and impart a certain character to the wine. There is no scientific proof for this.'"

## Treat them mean, keep them keen

It is helpful to think about plants as complex environmental computers. Just as we sense the world around us and use this information to guide our actions, so do plants – but over a longer time-scale. Literally rooted to the spot, they adapt their growth form to suit the local conditions. This extends to their reproductive strategies. Generally (and simplistically) speaking, if conditions are good, then plants opt for vegetative growth; if they are bad, they choose to reproduce sexually, which means fruit production. So viticulturalists want their vines to struggle enough to ensure a focus on fruit production, while giving them just enough to ensure they don't suffer from water or mineral deficit. Thus many viticultural interventions aim at encouraging the vine to partition nutrients to the grapes so that they ripen properly, rather than concentrating on growing more leaves and stems (vegetative growth or "vigour").

An example of this "environmental computing" is seen in the growth of plant roots. Root growth is determined by interplay between the developmental programme of the plant and the distribution of mineral nutrients in the soil. Roots grow to seek out water and nutrients in the soil; to do this it appears that they sense where the various nutrients are, then preferentially send out lateral shoots into these areas. Low levels of nutrients in the upper layers of the soil result in roots growing to a greater depth, which will improve the regularity of water supply to the vine. "Vines have roots which can reach up to three metres (nine feet) in depth," reports Davidian. "These can actively take up water and minerals, even though most mineral ions are more abundant at the root surface."

A popular notion is that very old vines with deep roots express terroir better than their younger counterparts. "The claims often made regarding the importance of deep-rooted vines are based on the assumption that roots are better able to exploit the underlying geology," says Dawid Saayman. "In turn, this is considered to contribute certain minerals and impart a certain character to the wine. There is no scientific proof for this." It's also worth mentioning the existence of mycorrhizae. Many plant roots form an association with specific soil fungi, where the fungi hitch a ride on the roots, gaining energy from the plant, while the plant root gains an enhanced absorptive area and ability to extract mineral nutrients from the soil. This is termed "mutualistic symbiosis" because both partners benefit. Some claim that mycorrhizae are important for terroir expression, but this isn't clear from scientific literature. Saayman points out that grape-vine mycorrhizae assist mainly in phosphorus uptake, an element vines usually don't have problems getting enough of. "It is highly unlikely that mycorrhizal associations are prominent enough to contribute to a terroir effect," he concludes.

## How soils affect wine

Soils differ in their chemical and physical properties. According to Victoria Carey, a lecturer in viticulture at Stellenbosch University who specializes in terroir, the latter are more important for terroir effects. "The most convincing indications in scientific literature are that the effect of soil type is through its physical properties, and more specifically, through the water supply to the grape vine," she suggests. Richard Smart agrees, citing the pioneering work of French scientist Gérard Seguin, who conducted a survey of the properties of soils in the Bordeaux region. Seguin couldn't find any reliable link between the chemical composition of the soil and wine character or quality, and maintained that it was the drainage properties of the soil that mattered. He concluded that it is "impossible to

establish any correlation between the quality of the wine and the soil content of any nutritive element, be it potassium, phosphorus or any other [trace element]". The verdict was that it was the physical properties of the soils, regulating the water supply to the vine, that were all-important in determining wine quality. The best terroirs were the ones where the soils were free-draining, with the water tables high enough to ensure a regular supply of water to the vine roots which then receded on *veraison* (when the berries change colour) so that vegetative growth stopped and the vine concentrated its energies on fruit ripening.

The consensus among the viticulture experts I consulted seems to be that the chemical composition of the soil – that is, nutrient availability – is only important when there is excess nitrogen, leading to excess vigour, or when there is a serious deficiency. "Nutrition can be instrumental to the specific growth pattern of the vine and thus can cause a specific canopy architecture and therefore ripening pattern," says Dawid Saayman. "The plant performance therefore modifies the vineyard climate, creating a specific microclimate in the bunch zone, and in this way it can greatly determine the character of the wine," he adds. "Overall, nutrient effects are minimal," adds Smart.

## Soil chemistry effects

But before we give up on soil chemistry as an important factor in terroir, it's worth taking a look at recent research on the effects of mineral nutrition on plant physiology. I spoke to a number of researchers actively working on plant mineral nutrition, to see whether their work might shed some light on the mechanisms of terroir. "I wouldn't be at all surprised if soil chemistry had an effect on the expression of genes that are involved in the production of the compounds that determine flavour," says Professor Brian Forde of Lancaster University (UK). "There is certainly plenty of evidence that plants are tuned to detect and respond

> "Although it seems clear that there is no direct link between soils and wine flavour, by framing their activities within the context of a soil-focused world view and trying to get a bit of 'somewhereness' and minerality into their wines, wine-growers might be vastly increasing their chances of making interesting wine."

to soil nutrients. The balance between the nutrients (nitrogen, phosphorus, potassium, sulphur, and calcium, and even the micronutrients) is likely to be important, and the plant-stress responses elicited by limiting amounts of one nutrient would probably be subtly different from the stress responses elicited if another nutrient is limited." Forde referred me to some publications showing that the levels of various plant chemicals were significantly altered under different nutrient regimes. At a more detailed level, it is now clear that patterns of gene expression in plants are altered by the presence and absence of various nutrients.

I spoke to Professor Malcolm Bennett and Dr. Martin Broadley of Nottingham University, who have studied the effects of phosphate deficiency on plant-gene expression. Broadley believes we will soon have a better idea about the influence of soils on wine flavour. "A large amount of work is underway to understand the molecular biology of grapes, and scientists are identifying genes that influence wine flavour," he explains. "As more grape molecular biology is known, the easier it will be to understand mechanisms of terroir on wine taste. When genes encoding for proteins that influence wine taste are identified, then the effects of different components of terroir (*e.g.* availability of different minerals, soil pH, soil water content) on specific biochemical pathways can be identified and tested. This research may allow current agronomical practices to be improved to enable better-tasting grapes to be produced, or it might even allow varieties of grapes to be selected or bred more effectively."

Even if science leaves us with what currently looks like rather an emasculated version of terroir, I don't think that this necessarily diminishes the importance of this cherished concept. Wine-growers who use terroir as their guiding philosophical framework and focus on the importance of the soil are responsible for a disproportionately large share of the world's most interesting wines. Perhaps Randall Grahm's rock experiments (*see* page 30) aren't so misguided after all. Although it seems clear that there is no direct link between soils and wine flavour, by framing their activities within the context of a soil-focused world view and trying to get a bit of "somewhereness" and minerality into their wines, wine-growers might be vastly increasing their chances of making interesting wine. And that's something the world needs more of.

As with so many other areas of viticulture and winemaking, it seems that more research is needed. While the current consensus is that it's the physical rather than the chemical properties of the soil that are all-important in separating good terroirs from bad ones, there's still the possibility that new data could emerge demonstrating that soil chemical properties can modulate grape characteristics significantly through altering gene expression. What's the use of this research, besides satisfying our intellectual curiosity? In an ideal world we could all drink fine wines such as First Growth Bordeaux and *grand cru* Burgundy every day. We can't, because there isn't much made, and they are expensive. It's all very well if you own a bit of Montrachet, or have vines on the hill at Hermitage, or preside over a Médoc First Growth. However wine-growers with less auspicious terroirs would understandably like to make better wine, and if scientists uncover precisely what it is that makes a great vineyard, then they might be able to implement better management strategies that would improve wines, or engineer vines that perform superbly on indifferent terroirs. After all, there's nothing magical about great terroirs; they're just patches of ground which naturally possess the conditions that encourage grape vines to produce grapes which, when handled correctly in the winery, can make great wines. Wouldn't it be great if top-class wines were affordable for all? What a wonderful scientific objective!

# 3 Precision viticulture

Welcome to the world of satellite imaging, yield monitors, global positioning systems, multispectral digital video, and state-of-the-art software. This all sounds a bit at odds with the traditional images of elderly *vignerons* carefully tending their vines, but they're some of the technological cornerstones of one of the current hot topics in the wine world: precision viticulture ("PV" for short).

In the previous chapter we looked at the rather ethereal, unmeasurable concept of terroir; now we turn to the high-tech, quantative approach of PV. This is a branch of precision agriculture, a relatively recent development in farming that was first proposed in the early 1990s. Its basis is that nature is uneven. Traditionally, farmers have ignored the natural variation in their fields, and have applied the same treatment across a whole area. To be fair, they didn't have access to tools that would let them manage their land in a more sophisticated manner. But over the last couple of decades, affordable technologies have been developed which allow farmers to make accurate maps of this variation, then manage their fields accordingly. For example, some parts might need more fertilizer, others less. Or the soil properties might vary in such a way that certain sections will need irrigating while others won't. It sounds simple, and, conceptually, it is. The tricky bit lies in the practicalities of making useful maps of this variation, then devising ways of treating the different sections differently.

The need for dealing with natural vineyard variation is highlighted by the fact that in vineyards, yields typically vary by eight- to tenfold from the least to most productive bits. Perhaps more detrimental to wine quality is the variation in grape ripening this implies. If wine-growers can manage their vineyards to encourage homogeneous phenolic and sugar-ripeness levels, then quality soars. It only takes a small block of poor-quality grapes to bring down the overall quality level of a vineyard. Despite these clear opportunities for PV, it is only very recently that precision techniques have been applied to vineyards. The pioneers of PV have been viticulturalists in Australia and California who have adopted similar principles, but in practical terms have taken somewhat different approaches.

## Where the emphasis lies

In California, the emphasis has largely been on what is termed "remote sensing". This is where data collection is conducted through gathering aerial images, either by means of satellites or, more commonly, flying an airplane over the vineyards. The pictures that are taken are "multispectral", consisting of overlapping images taken at different wavelengths, each giving different sorts of information.

In Australia, where many vineyards are mechanized, data collection is typically conducted via the use of yield monitors – devices attached to conventional mechanical harvesters – although multispectral remote sensing has been used quite extensively here, too. When used with a global positioning system (GPS), yield monitors enable yield maps to be generated. Each approach has its own benefits. One of the key developers of PV in Australia is Rob Bramley of the Commonwealth Scientific and Industrial Research Organisation (CSIRO).

Why has he concentrated on using yield monitoring? "First," he explains, "you have to harvest the crop, so if you are doing this mechanically you may as well yield-monitor, simply because it is far better to have some data than not. Secondly, remotely sensed information will only ever give you relative information. It is also a fact that an image without ground truthing [testing of geophysical anomalies] is useless. However, I do think that remote sensing is useful, and we use it for mid-season monitoring and as a data layer to help understand the yield map."

## How to target a harvest

Indeed, Bramley used remote sensing in a case study of PV at a vineyard owned by Vasse Felix in the Margaret River region of Western Australia. Crucially, this study showed that there is an economic benefit to be gained. In a demonstration of how straightforward it can be to use PV, Bramley and his colleagues took remotely sensed images of the vineyard and used these as a basis for targeted sampling of fruit just before harvest. On the basis of the results from this sampling, the grapes were then harvested into two separate bins based on their location. The fruit from one block was good enough for the Vasse Felix Cabernet Sauvignon and the rest went to the cheaper Vasse Felix "Classic Dry Red"; previously all the grapes from this vineyard would have gone to the cheaper wine. Even taking into account the increased cost of the PV work and targeted harvesting, the result was a clear economic benefit.

Bramley has also done studies in vineyards in Coonawarra and Mildura. In these projects, yield maps were constructed using harvesting machines fitted with yield monitors and a GPS device. He demonstrated that, for both sites, the patterns of variation were relatively consistent from year to year – which is good news for growers, as it makes it possible for them to adopt targeted management strategies based on variation maps constructed over just a few vintages, cutting costs significantly. These maps are constructed by means of some fairly complicated software known as geographical information systems (GIS). The maps also have a predictive value; for example, consistently low-yielding areas can be expected to be low-yielding the following year.

## PV in the USA

In the USA, the leader of the PV field is Lee Johnson of the NASA Ames Research Center. Johnson began using remote sensing of vineyards in 1993, well before PV was envisaged, as a means to track the spread of phylloxera (see chapter 6). This first project was a collaboration between NASA and the Robert Mondavi Winery; since this initial work, Johnson has been continuing to work with Mondavi to develop PV technologies. Daniel Bosch, vineyard manager at Mondavi, has been involved with the project for a while , and has used the information gained from remote sensing to modify his approach in the vineyard. "We've changed our drip irrigation system on the basis of this," he reports. "In some vineyards we now have two hoses." This allows separate blocks to be irrigated differently, depending on the vigour of the vines. Bosch also uses PV information to cultivate and harvest vineyard sections at different times. But perhaps the most elegant use of the technology is to mount a GPS device on a tractor, couple it to a computer with GIS software, and then selectively remove cover crops from areas of the vineyard that are low-vigour, leaving them in the high-vigour regions where they can act as competition for water and nutrients. This is done automatically as the tractor is driven through the vineyard, and can be targeted precisely, row by row. Nifty, eh?

Along with other California vineyards, Mondavi mostly uses remote sensing as the basis of its PV. Yield monitoring hasn't been widely adopted in California because here mechanical harvesting is not widespread. The early work was done with airplanes flying over the vineyard, but this is quite expensive at around US$20,000 a flight. To make it cost-effective, growers need to band together to split costs. Now there are also commercial satellite operators offering a similar service, and it is likely that, in the future, growers will be able to pay for and access these sorts of images directly on the internet.

But how do these colourful and rather complicated-looking pictures relate to what's happening on the ground? They are obviously indirect measurements of what is happening with the grapes, concentrating on the visible bit of the grape vine: the leaf area. However, Johnson and his colleagues have spent a lot of effort correlating the imaging data with direct measurements of grape quality and yield. They've developed a complex model that has worked out the relationship between the remotely sensed images and physical factors affecting wine quality, and have identified vineyard canopy density, which they term Leaf Area Index (LAI) as a key variable of interest. There's perhaps one advantage of this remote sensing over yield monitoring. "Remotely sensed data allow growers to be proactive, in terms of altering management practices in conditions observed during the growing season," Johnson explains. "Remote sensing can be used, for instance, to subdivide fields for harvest based on observed vine vigour, make irrigation decisions, support pruning decisions, and look for areas that may be more susceptible to mould." However, it should be kept in mind that the best time for acquiring these images is at *veraison*, relatively late in the vine growth cycle, leaving only a short time for any proactive intervention. Is it expensive? "Commercial costs for remote sensing vary widely, but tend to run to around US$12 per hectare," says Johnson.

The chief beneficiaries of PV are likely to be owners of larger vineyards, such as those in the New World. It's hard to imagine a take-up in an area such as Burgundy, where vineyards are already split into tiny plots and there is considerable experience of the performance of different sites. But one of PV's trump cards is that it allows a wine-grower to gain an almost instant understanding of his or her vineyards that would have previously taken decades of patient observation to achieve. And even then, according to Mondavi's Daniel Bosch, experienced vineyard managers' perceptions of where their vineyards vary are sometimes rather different to those revealed by aerial images or yield maps.

## The view from South Africa

Aside from Australia and California, the main early adopter of PV is South Africa. In collaboration with consultant Dr. Phil Freese, who was involved in the early remote-sensing work in California in his capacity as vineyard manager for Mondavi, PV is being used by Warwick, Thelema, and Rustenberg in the Stellenbosch region. Several other South African estates are also trying out PV, along with others in Chile and New Zealand. Mike Ratcliffe of Warwick Estate explained some of the ways he was using PV to improve quality. "We've done some extreme viticulture in a couple of Cabernet blocks. At *veraison* (when the berries change colour) individual bunches were marked as late-ripening (green berries), early-ripening (fully coloured berries), and mixed bunches. The thinking behind this is that a few weeks after *veraison* is completed, the differing ripening stage indications are lost as all the berries were fully coloured and identical. The different-coloured markings were harvested individually at optimum ripeness. We then did a correlation of this information with our NDVI [normalized difference vegetation index, a remotely sensed measure of vine vigour] and found a statistically significant correlation." Ratcliffe goes on to explain that, although this work is labour-intensive, it reduces variation and improves quality significantly. Another measure used by Warwick is leaf water

**RIGHT** An aerial image of vineyards in Stellenbosch, South Africa. Although this is reproduced here in greyscale, it is actually an infrared image indicating the degree of vegetative growth in the vineyards.
*Picture courtesy of Warwick Estate*

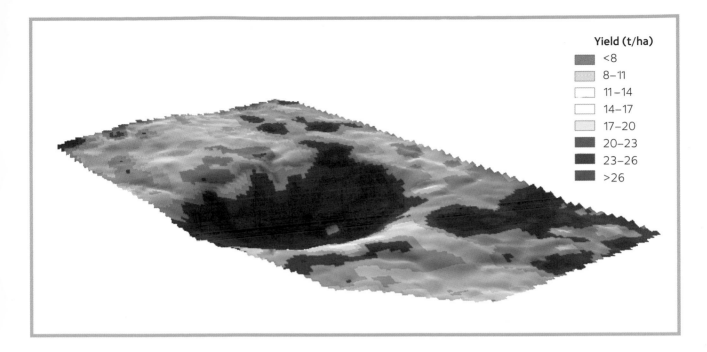

**ABOVE** Variation in yield (vintage 2004) and elevation in a 4.3ha block of Shiraz grapes in Padthaway, Australia. The original is in colour, so the precise details have been lost in this greyscale representation, but the principle of PV is still illustrated. Interestingly, an aerial remotely sensed image of this same block acquired at *veraison* identified the same characteristic zone of a high-yielding, high-vigour area in the centre of the block, seen in this figure as the dark, slightly dipped area. Winemaker assessment of the fruit classified the grapes from the central, high-yielding area to be of "C grade" while the fruit from the rest of the block was "high B grade". This suggests that differential harvest, and perhaps also differential management of the two areas of this vineyard block might be appropriate.

*Figure courtesy of Dr. Rob Bramley*

potential (LWP). This is a direct measure of how much water stress the vine is under. The viticultural goal is to stress the vine just enough, but not too much, at the right time, which enhances fruit quality significantly. "We cross reference the LWP with the NDVI to detect trends and patterns in the vineyards," says Ratcliffe. "This is perhaps our most useful and practically implementable technology used at Warwick."

If this all sounds rather high-tech, there are still lessons to be learned by growers working in a more traditional way in small vineyards. "In principle, PV is for everybody," says the CSIRO's Rob Bramley, "simply because all vineyards are variable." Mondavi's Daniel Bosch suggests a low-tech implementation that would be in the reach of anyone. "Leaf-fall patterns are very similar to the patterns seen by remote sensing." There is therefore a window of about two weeks where a *vigneron* could go through the vineyard during leaf fall and map homogeneous blocks. The following growing season, it would be easy enough to test ripeness levels a couple of weeks before harvest, and if these agreed with the maps, then you could harvest the blocks in the appropriate order. PV in action!

While it's still early days, it's clear that as the technology develops, PV will become more widespread. Potentially, any data relevant to viticulture could be included in PV if the collection is cost-effective enough and the data yields information that will result in targeted management, which in turn results in quality improvements. For example, if they were cheap enough, battery-operated data collectors could be spread around the vineyard in a targeted sampling effort, transmitting relevant information to assist in management decisions. Another area of research concerns the use of ground-penetrating radar, a technique able to reveal sub-surface characteristics of vineyards without the need for digging pits.

It seems the tide has turned. Work in the vineyard used to be seen as a dull, relatively unskilled prelude to the work of celebrity winemakers; now it's the vineyard managers who get the attention. Will flying viticulturalists, brandishing laptops and GPS devices, become as popular as flying winemakers? I wouldn't be surprised. And in a world facing climate change – the subject of the next chapter – PV might become even more critical.

# 4 Global warming: its implications for viticulture

As I write, I'm sitting on an airplane at 39,000 feet. It may be a "small world", but from my current vantage point it looks like an incredibly large one. All I can see is an endless vista of sky and sea. It seems hard to think that human activity, barely visible from this altitude, has had a significant impact on the oceans and atmosphere. But it seems that our interference – most significantly, our use of the sky as a gaseous rubbish tip – has caused profound changes to the environment, with the promise of more to come. The world is getting warmer, and weather is getting less predictable. The oceans are rising. Climate change is here to stay, and it looks like it will have a significant impact on viticulture worldwide.

The data are quite striking. Globally, the average surface air temperature has increased by 0.6°C (approximately 1°F) since the beginning of the twentieth century, with two-thirds of this change occurring since 1970. The warmest year was 1998, and the 1990s the warmest decade since records began in 1860. The growing season for plants in the UK has lengthened by a month since 1900, and our sea level is ten centimetres (four inches) higher now than it was then. But what do the climate scientists say? Are the changes that we've seen merely within the normal parameters of natural climatic variation, or is the human infleunce on the environment finally having a telling impact? The goal of this chapter is to present a brief overview of the science of global warming, and look at the projections for future climate change, examining the implications for wine-growers worldwide. I'll also be reviewing recent work which models the likely effects of climate change over the next fifty years for each of the world's main wine regions.

## What affects climate?

Our climate is the result of a careful balance between energy received by the earth from the sun (which is redistributed by oceanic and atmospheric circulation), and energy reflected from the surface of the earth back into space. Climate varies naturally as the result of interactions between the oceans and the atmosphere, small changes in the orbit of the earth (acting over tens of thousands of years, responsible for the glacial and interglacial cycles), fluctuations in the energy received from the sun (solar output varies with eleven-year cycles), and volcanic eruptions. There's also variation caused by human activity. This occurs mainly through increased emissions of the "greenhouse" gases: primarily carbon dioxide ($CO_2$) and methane. Their presence in the atmosphere traps energy in the lower atmosphere and thus increases the earth's temperature.

The greenhouse effect isn't all bad, however; without any greenhouse gases at all, the average global surface temperature would be around -18°C (-0.4°F). You can have too much of a good thing, though; currently a whopping 6.5 billion tons of carbon enter the atmosphere every year, mainly through the combustion of coal and gas. Yet this picture is complicated by the fact that some pollutants form aerosols: tiny particles or droplets that reflect solar heat into space and act to reduce temperature. Although these aerosols only last for days or weeks, compared with the century or so lifespan of $CO_2$ in the atmosphere, they also alter cloud formation. For a detailed overview of the factors that influence climate change, the reader is referred to the references on page 45, most of which are freely available on the internet. Various climate models suggest that changes in climate prior to 1970 can be explained almost exclusively by natural factors, while those occurring over recent decades are explicable almost entirely by human influences on the environment. So it seems likely that the changes we are seeing really *are* our fault.

## Predicting future climate change

Historical data shows that the climate has changed over the last century, but how can we predict future changes? Today, sophisticated and powerful climate models exist which are able to give some indication These models aren't perfect, but they have improved a lot over recent years, and experts are relatively confident that their predictions are accurate. The most sophisticated of these are known as atmosphere-ocean general circulation models (AOGCMs), which require huge computer resources to run. Probably the best of these is the Hadley Centre Climate Model, developed in the UK, which has been comprehensively validated and is widely used. That global warming is real and caused by human activity is no longer controversial; the current debate centres on the precise effects of increasing atmospheric greenhouse gases. While we can correlate historical climate change with rising $CO_2$ levels, we can't know for sure the nature of this relationship as $CO_2$ levels rise beyond their current atmospheric concentrations.

These climate models have produced various scenarios for future climate change, depending on whether $CO_2$ emissions over the next few decades are reduced, increased or stay the same as they are now (*see* box on page 43). In the UK, the best-case (lowest-emission) scenario is that by the 2080s, the average temperature will be 2°C (3.6°F) warmer, while if emissions increase, parts of the southeast could be as much as 5°C (9°F) hotter. Hot summers will become more frequent and cold winters rarer. Winters will be wetter, summers drier. Sea levels will rise by as much as 86cm (2.8 feet). Most uncertainty surrounds what will happen to the Gulf Stream; this is the sea current that gives the UK and Atlantic-influenced parts of Europe a warmer climate than they really should have. For various reasons, the Gulf Stream is predicted to weaken over the next century by as much as twenty-five per cent, which will have a moderate cooling influence although the precise factors influencing this change are not well-understood. If the Gulf Stream were to disappear altogether, then the consequences for the UK would be disastrous, with the result being a climate somewhat similar to that of St Petersburg in Russia (*see* the box on page 45 about abrupt climate change for more on this).

## Modelling climate change

I asked climate researcher Dr. Phil Jones (University of East Anglia, UK) about the performance of climate models. "The best two are the Hadley Centre model and a German one in Hamburg (ECHAM4). The USA is catching up, but they are behind Canada." How do they work? "They are essentially the same as weather forecast models. You don't give them any climate data, though; you give them your best guess at the initial conditions in the 1960s and a series of factors thought to influence the climate (such as greenhouse gases, the sun, volcanoes and land-usage change). Models are tested against reality; they aren't told anything about reality, though, except what the forcing factors were. They use the basic equations of physics."

How accurate are the models? "There is a lot of uncertainty. Major issues relate to how the models deal with clouds and sea ice," reports Jones. In general, it seems that the scientific community places a reasonable degree of trust in these models: they aren't yet perfect, but they have improved a lot in recent years.

| Predicted temperature rises for selected wine regions by 2050 | |
| --- | --- |
| Wine region | Predicted temperature rise (°C) |
| Southern Oregon, USA | 2.35 |
| Northern California, USA | 2.16 |
| Barossa Valley, Australia | 2.01 |
| South Africa | 0.88 |
| Chile | 1.84 |
| Southern Portugal | 2.85 |
| Rioja, Spain | 2.52 |
| Chianti, Italy | 2.30 |
| Rhine Valley, Germany | 1.51 |
| Mosel Valley, Germany | 1.51 |
| Rhône, France | 2.26 |
| Loire Valley, France | 2.14 |
| Champagne, France | 1.51 |
| Burgundy, France | 2.26 |
| Bordeaux, France | 2.33 |

Source: Dr. Gregory Jones, Southern Oregon University

## The implications for wine

In the light of impending planetary doom, it seems trivial to be thinking of the implications for wine, but that's my job, so I will. A recent study by Dr. Gregory Jones and his colleagues from Southern Oregon University in the USA has done precisely this. His data suggests that global warming has already had an influence on wine quality in many of the world's leading wine regions, and is likely to have further significant effects in the near future.

Jones and his colleagues analyzed fifty years of climate data from twenty-five different wine regions, and compared them with Sothebys' 100-point vintage ratings, looking for any trends. They also ran the Hadley Centre Climate Model to look at the projected temperature changes over the next fifty years. The results are striking. Overall, growing-season temperatures have increased by an average of 2°C (3.6°F) for most of the world's high-quality wine regions over the last fifty years. A couple of degrees doesn't sound much, but it really is – in fact, it's a *huge* increase. In tandem with this rise in temperatures, the quality of vintages has also improved. There is a significant relationship between the vintage ratings and monthly, average, growing-season temperatures in most regions.

A potential confounder is that winemaking and viticulture have improved over the last fifty years, so that what would have been a disastrous vintage some decades ago is now salvageable. Furthermore, because of the rise in prices of fine wines, producers can afford to be more selective, declassifying where necessary; the result is that the overall quality perception of a difficult vintage is improved. Jones accepts that this rise in quality might not just be because of temperature increases, but his data shows that between ten and sixty-two per cent of vintage quality can be explained by growing-season temperature variability, with the greatest effects seen in cool-climate regions such as the Mosel.

Perhaps the most interesting part of the study concerns its predictions for the next fifty years. The Hadley Centre model suggests that the wine regions analyzed can expect an average growing-season temperature increase of 2.04°C (3.67°F) by 2049, on top of the 2°C (3.59°F) rise seen over the last fifty years. This is a very significant change. The largest predicted change is for southern Portugal (2.85°C/5.1°F); the lowest is for South Africa (0.88°C/1.6°F). "From this research," explains Jones, "it appears that the currently cool-climate regions would benefit the most. If the climate warms as the models predict, then these regions will be better able to ripen the fruit and may even be able to consider other varieties that could not ripen there today." He suggests that this might be good news for wineries in England, which experienced a very successful vintage in 2003: "Our research indicates that more of the same is in the future for England." In addition, warmer temperatures could lead to new areas opening up to viticulture.

The news is less encouraging for the warmest wine regions. "For many of the warm-to-hot regions, the negative impacts are already being felt," Jones reports. "In hot regions, grapes ripen to a 'sugar-ripe' condition, but lack flavours that can take time to develop. [It is likely that] other regions, somewhat in between cool-to-hot growing climates, will have to consider other varieties that will produce better crops in a new climate regime. For example, in California's Napa and Sonoma valleys, the climate has become so warm that ripening fruit is not an issue, but retaining acidity and developing flavour have become increasingly difficult. Our analysis shows that this issue could become critical in warm areas like Chianti, Barolo, Rioja, southern France, the Hunter Valley, parts of Chile, and the Central Valley of California."

Other effects of increased temperatures could include harvest periods being brought forward into the warmest parts of the year, reduced water

| Predicted atmospheric and temperature change based on future levels of greenhouse gas emissions | | |
|---|---|---|
| Scenario | Predicted atmospheric $CO_2$ concentration in 2080 | Predicted rise in average global temperature (°C) by 2080 |
| Low emissions | 525 | 2 |
| Medium–low emissions | 562 | 2.3 |
| Medium–high emissions | 715 | 3.3 |
| High emissions | 810 | 3.9 |

# High-alcohol wines: is global warming to blame?

Anyone who's been drinking wine for more than a few years will have noticed that alcohol levels have been creeping up. It used to be common to see red wines on the shelves with eleven or twelve per cent alcohol by volume; now it's rare to find one with less than thirteen per cent, and wines packing fourteen or even fifteen per cent are relatively common. A study from the Australian Wine Research Institute showed a steady increase in alcohol contents of red wines analyzed from vintage 1984 to 2002, such that the mean alcohol concentration was greater than fourteen per cent in 2002; a quarter of the red wines had alcohol concentrations between 14.8 and 16.5 per cent. Is this because global warming is producing riper grapes with higher sugar levels? Partly, but it's also because of advances in viticulture and a tendency to harvest on the basis of phenolic ripeness rather than simple sugar levels. While alcohol can add body and a perception of sweetness to wines, levels are often problematically high in warmer regions, and some winemakers are resorting to sophisticated techniques such as reverse osmosis to remove excess alcohol.

availability, and increased pest and disease burden. So, while it seems that the climate change over the last fifty years has had a mostly positive effect on wine quality, the future could be quite different. And assuming that the projections from the climate models are at all accurate, viticulturalists across the globe will have their work cut out adapting their vineyards to take account of these changes. In some cases, the careful matching of grape variety to vineyard site may have to be reconsidered. Does this mean that we'll have to replant Burgundy with Syrah and Grenache? It's a worrying thought…

One of the common predictions of climate models also has implications for wine. With rising temperatures comes an increased frequency of extreme weather events, and a rising unpredictability of climates. Wine-growers don't want unusual weather; understandably, they like things to be predictable and stable because large fluctuations will almost always be detrimental to vintage quality. Even if growing-season temperatures are very good, a vintage can easily be ruined by extended rain during harvesting, or hailstorms, or a late snap of frost in May.

I asked Greg Jones what sort of reception his work had received from the wine industry. Has anyone disagreed with his conclusions? "No one has disagreed," he answered, "[They've] only been in denial. I was in Napa recently and the numerous growers, winemakers, and industry people I spoke with all agreed that it is becoming too hot to produce balanced wines naturally. Most of the last fifteen to twenty years have been too warm, producing unbalanced wines where some measure of acid or alcohol amelioration has to occur." Jones added that the same is true in other warm-climate wine regions across the world. "My feeling is that people in the industry are willing to admit to the situation, except to the media, because then it might get out to the wine-buying public and produce negative results in the marketplace."

## What can we do about it?
In short, the message of climate change is one that we need to sit up and listen to. Yet it is a contentious subject, not least because, for obvious reasons, it is a highly politicized debate. After all, if laws are brought in to tighten up $CO_2$ emissions, some influential and politically well-connected companies stand to lose a lot of money. On the other hand, there's an incentive for environmental lobby groups to "sex up" the data on the extent of any changes or predictions for the future in order to gain publicity for their cause. This makes a careful and impartial examination of the actual data necessary.

"While it seems that the climate change over the last fifty years has had a mostly positive effect on wine quality, the future could be quite different. And assuming that the projections from the climate models are at all accurate, viticulturalists across the globe will have their work cut out adapting their vineyards to take account of these changes."

The message is that, unless we want to risk environmental catastrophe, we must use less energy, and what we do use needs to be generated without burning fossil fuels. While we don't know for sure – and can't prove – the link between rising greenhouse gases and recent global temperature increases, the data that already exist are strong enough to suggest that we should begin doing something about it now. To do nothing would seem foolishly reckless. I probably sound like a bit of a hippy here, but we need to get away from thinking that just because we can afford the financial cost of energy, we are entitled to use it. Do we really need to air-condition our homes year-round or drive gas-guzzling SUVs? Because of the lifetime of $CO_2$ in the atmosphere, even if greenhouse gas emissions are cut dramatically now, some of the climate change predicted is still inevitable. However, what we do over the next few years will affect the climate of the second half of this century. If we, and our governments, fail to act, the consequences will be serious. And that will be bad news for wine as we know it, too.

## Useful web links

**www.ipcc.ch**
Intergovernmental Panel on Climate Change
**www.met-office.gov.uk/research/hadleycentre/index.html**
Hadley Centre for Climate Prediction and Research
**www.met-office.gov.uk**
UK Met Office
**www.who.int/globalchange/climate/summary/en/**
World Health Organization report on climate change and human health
**www.newscientist.com/hottopics/climate/**
*New Scientist* magazine's special section on climate change

## Abrupt climate changes: should we be concerned?

As well as the gradual changes in climate that are the subject of this chapter, there's another, potentially more worrying scenario involving what's known in the trade as the "Ocean Conveyor" or the "Northern Hemisphere Thermohaline Circulation". This is a global ocean circulation system responsible for shifting heat around the planet. Currently, this massive redistribution system shifts warm waters from equatorial regions northwards between North America and western Europe, and includes the Gulf Stream. This ocean flow releases its heat in cooler northerly regions and is responsible for tempering what would otherwise be a much cooler climate, raising temperatures in North Atlantic regions by as much as 5°C (9°F).

The driving force for this conveyor is the fact that colder water is denser than warm, and saltier water is denser than less salty water. Once this north Atlantic ocean flow, which is very salty, has released its heat, it becomes cooler and sinks, drawing more water from warmer areas and maintaining the flow. What would happen if this water didn't sink? The answer is that the conveyor would cease. Evidence from ice cores suggests that such a conveyor shut-down has occurred several times in the past, leading some commentators to dub it the "Achilles heel" of the world's climate. If the conveyor were to shut down now, the effects would be disastrous for most of Europe's wine-growing regions, with a drop in average temperatures of up to 5°C (9°F). To put it bluntly, Europe's wine regions would be screwed. Finished. Kaput.

It's a paradoxical situation. Global warming could actually prove to be the catalyst for a much colder future for many of us. Signs that global warming has been affecting the vital global conveyor are already emerging.

There are two mechanisms that could result in conveyor shut-off, both involving an influx of fresh water from melting glaciers and sea ice. First, the fresh water would sit at the surface and prevent the transfer of oceanic heat to the atmosphere. Second, this water would dilute the salinity of the north Atlantic, which at some point would be buoyant enough not to sink, removing the driving force behind the conveyor. The evidence currently available is indeed pointing to the fact that the north Atlantic has been getting less saline continuously over the last forty years. Signs of a possible conveyor slow-down have already been recorded. It's not likely that we'll see a complete shut-down over the next couple of decades, but this is a possibility that should concern us now.

# 5 GM vines

Picture the scene: the year is 2025; you wander into your local wine shop. Along with the usual rows of bottles arranged by country of origin, there's a small section hidden over on the right labelled "non-GM wines". By deduction, you realize that everything else here is made from genetically modified (GM) grapes. For some, this represents progress. For others, it's a nightmare.

The subject of genetically modified (GM) crops polarizes opinion. At one extreme we have the scientific perspective. Most scientists are familiar with the use of genetic modification in research as an incredibly useful, everyday technique. For example, the use of "knockout mice", in which a gene is deleted and the consequences of this deletion are then studied, is fundamental to modern developmental biology, and such mice are commonly used as models for human disease. Foreign genes (known as transgenes) are also introduced into experimental mice, and their effects are studied. Because of this familiarity, most scientists can't see why there is such a fuss about GM crops. At the other extreme, many non-scientists regard GM as a disaster in the making, a threat to be resisted at all costs. Their unfamiliarity with the science of genetic modification, together with a growing distrust of the scientific establishment, has helped create a sense of alarm about the way that big agrochemical companies are forcing a new and dangerous-sounding technology on them, without any consultation or public debate.

In this chapter, I'll be attempting to stand back, and present a balanced, factual coverage of this complex and sometimes inflammatory topic. (For those at either pole of the debate, this statement of intent will convince them, no doubt, that I am on the other side. This isn't the case!) I'll look at some of the potential benefits of GM crops in general, together with any disadvantages. Then I'll focus on wine, considering the following questions: to what extent research on GM vines has progressed, what traits are being introduced, how long will it be before we see GM vines, and whether or not it is a good idea.

## Context: the Malthusian precipice

We begin with some necessary non-wine-related context. It is now more than 200 years since Thomas Malthus published his snappily titled Essay on the Principle of Population, as it Affects the Future Improvement of Society with Remarks on the Speculations of Mr Godwin, M. Condorcet and Other Writers. You'll probably recall Malthus's key observation from school geography lessons: while the human population tends to increase geometrically (*i.e.* 2, 4, 8, 16, 32), the means of subsistence – food production – only increases in an arithmetic ratio (2, 4, 6, 8, 10, and so on). The implications are immediately apparent. Once the world's population reaches a certain size, predicted Malthus, it will outstrip the limited food resources, with all sorts of unpleasant consequences.

Fast-forward to the 1950s. The world, and in particular southeast Asia, is teetering on the brink of the Malthusian precipice. A rapid rate of population increase is putting huge pressure on food resources, with the very real threat of widespread famine. That the world was brought back from the brink of this disaster was thanks largely to what is known as the "green revolution". This was a planned international effort aimed at eliminating hunger by improving crop performance, and it was achieved in spectacular fashion, mainly through the development of new crop cultivars together with the use of irrigation, fertilizers, and pesticides. The figures are striking. From 1950 to 1990, agricultural yields increased threefold. And whereas the world's population has doubled since 1950, the proportion of land devoted to farming has hardly increased at all.

Now, however, we are in the aftermath of the green revolution. These increases in crop yields have slowed dramatically, while the global population is still growing. And the gains in yield haven't been made without an environmental cost. There is also a shortage of new arable land, with existing farmland under threat from erosion, salinization, and growing urban sprawl. We currently use about half of the world's available good-quality soil for agriculture; the rest lies under tropical forests. Inevitably, necessary future gains in yield will have to be made by more efficient use of existing land, unless we are to see a dramatic deterioration of natural habitats and biodiversity.

This brings us to the present day. Goodbye green revolution; enter the gene revolution. Over the last couple of decades, plant science has developed increasingly sophisticated tools for the genetic manipulation of crops. Conventional breeding, achieved by crossing plants with the desired traits and leaving nature to do the rest, has produced impressive gains in yield, and some measure of disease and pest resistance. But this is time-consuming and imprecise compared with the genetic techniques now available. Most agricultural research these days involves identifying genes that confer favourable properties, then engineering them into commercially important plants. You might be surprised to learn that figures published in 2002 showed that there are now 5.5 million farmers worldwide growing GM crops, mainly in the USA, China, Canada, and Argentina. These GM crops now cover more than fifty million hectares – an area roughly the size of Spain. The genie is well and truly out of the bottle.

The European Union, for a long time opposed to GM, has recently lifted its moratorium, with the condition that foods containing more than 0.9 per cent of GM ingredients are labelled. In truth, they didn't have much choice. The USA is pro-GM, and saw the EU ban as a restriction of free trade; if the ban had been kept

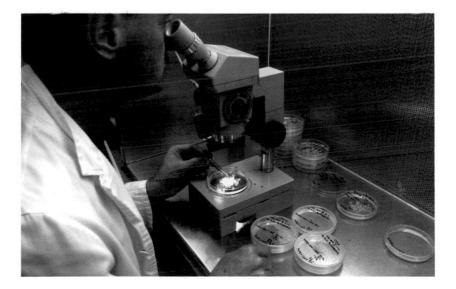

in place, the EU would have been risking a trade war. It's uncertain whether the USA will be happy with the labelling requirement; if it isn't, then the EU may be forced to give in over this as well, with obvious implications for consumer choice.

In the UK, the present Labour government has blown hot and cold. Initially, it was very pro-GM. Then it realized how unpopular GM is with consumers. So, in 2003, the government ran a public debate titled "GM Nation". It was part of a consultation process, including a scientific review and economic analysis, with the goal being to decide whether to say yes or no to GM crops in the UK. At the time of writing, it seems that GM crops will be allowed, but closely regulated, even if consumer resistance means that there is actually no current market for GM food.

## Genetically modified vines

This brings us round to wine. While the technology for genetically engineering most crop plants has been available for a couple of decades, getting it to work with woody plants such as grape vines has proved trickier. It wasn't until 1989 that the first transgenic vine was produced in the laboratory, and it is only in the last few years that scientists have been able to introduce foreign genes into vines with any degree of reproducibility (see "Making GM vines", below). Crucially, there are currently no GM vines being grown on a commercial scale, and we won't be seeing wine made from GM grapes for some years to come.

However, research aimed at producing vines resistant to pests, diseases, and abiotic (non-living) stresses is being undertaken in just about every country with a significant wine industry. The sorts of characteristics being engineered into vines are outlined in "Making GM vines" below. These technological developments have led to alarm among many producers, who feel that GM vines will be a threat. Terre et Vin du Monde, a pressure group of high-profile Burgundian producers, led by Anne-Claude Leflaive, has been particularly vocal in expressing its concerns. A press release circulated in November 2002, called for a ten-year moratorium on the use of GM products in wine, including GM yeasts. The group does not oppose progress, but says that this moratorium would give the industry the necessary time to sift the evidence and make the best decision possible. "After thirty years of irrational chemical treatments," the press release reads, "it is inconceivable to start again making the same mistakes with genetically modified organisms."

## Making GM vines

STEP 1 Take a tissue culture of the grape vine. Take a small piece and induce it to form a callus (new protective layer over a wound) of undifferentiated cells in the laboratory. These cells then have to undergo a process known as somatic embryogenesis; effectively, the development of the vine is initiated from these undifferentiated cells by means of a cocktail of hormones and nutrients. It sounds simple, but this has proved challenging with vines.
STEP 2 Select the transgene (the foreign gene you want to introduce) – for example, one that confers resistance to fungal disease. It is often coupled to another gene which acts as a marker, giving an indication of whether the transgene is successfully incorporated. Research is now under way to decode the grape-vine genome and to identify candidate genes that might confer beneficial properties.

STEP 3 Grape-vine transformation with the desired gene. The two methods commonly used are agrobacterium transformation and biolistic bombardment. Both act to incorporate the transgene into the grape-vine DNA. Because this is an imprecise process, it is necessary to select the successfully transformed plants, which is normally done by using a marker gene.
STEP 4 Voilà – you have your transgenic (or GM) vines. But does the transgene do what you want it to? Now begins the lengthy process of regenerating grape vines from successfully transformed plants, and evaluating their properties, first in greenhouses, then in field tests. And with vines, which typically need three years until the first crop, this is a lengthy process, even if you get it right first time.

I quizzed some experts to see how things are going. Dr. Reinhard Töpfer heads up the Institut für Rebenzüchtung (Institute for Vine Research) at Geilweilerhof in Germany. Since 1999, he has been field-testing GM Riesling and Seyval Blanc vines engineered with a gene from barley that is resistant to fungal diseases. "We expect it will be at least twenty years before we see GM vines in the marketplace," says Töpfer. The reasons for this delay include identifying appropriate genes, getting them to work in the different grape varieties, and the long process of testing, evaluating, and propagating the plants.

"The engineering part is now pretty well-established for the premium varieties like Cabernet Sauvignon, Chardonnay, Riesling, and Shiraz," says Mark Thomas of Australia's CSIRO (*see* page 35). "However, finding the right genes for trait improvement can be difficult." To help with this problem, a public consortium has been formed called the International Grape Genome Program (www.vitaceae.org/) with the goal of discovering all the grape-vine genes. "Research groups from all major wine countries are involved and progress has been rapid, with about half of the expected genes in the grape-vine genome identified," Thomas reports, "but there is still a lot of work to do to use this gene information for the production of improved varieties." CSIRO researcher Simon Robinson is more specific on the time scale. "We calculate that if we had a gene available now and all went well, it would be at least ten years before a GM vine would be ready for any kind of commercial evaluation," he says. As well as Australia, GM vines are being developed and tested in France, Italy, Germany, the USA, South Africa, and Israel, according to Robinson. "There may be others; I'm sure some of the eastern European countries are working in this area and I'd be surprised if China doesn't have GM vines."

The fact that GM vines won't be ready for many years is seen as a positive thing by many, given current consumer opposition to this technology. Everyone is working away in the hope that the current controversy will die down. "Because of the long development and adoption times for any new grape vine, commercial use of GM vines is some way off. I think the debate will be over by the time GM vines are available," says Robinson. Renowned grape-vine geneticist Carole Meredith, of University of California at Davis, agrees. "All the researchers I know are realistic enough to understand that neither consumers nor the wine trade wants transgenic grapes or wine right now," she says – yet research is continuing apace. "Because the work takes many years when you consider the field testing," she explains, "they hope that their work will be better received in the future."

In the meantime, no one wants to be associated too closely with GM research because of its negative image. "I should point out that the Australian wine industry's current position is that no genetically modified organisms are to be used in the production of Australian wine," Robinson states. But even if no GM vines are ever commercialized, he thinks the research is still be worthwhile. "GM organisms are not the only outcome of this research; we are also learning a great deal about how vines function, and this information can enhance conventional breeding and improve viticultural management."

## The benefits

But do we really need GM vines? What's wrong with the ones we already have? The main problem is that viticulture isn't terribly environmentally friendly. Vines are particularly susceptible to fungal diseases such as powdery mildew and bunch rot. This means that vineyards need to be sprayed with fungicide several times each growing season – an expensive and potentially ecologically unsound practice. Even organic and Biodynamic producers still need to spray their vines at times with sulphur and copper fungicides, a cop-out justified along the lines that these are "natural" chemicals. While fungus-resistant grape varieties such as Regent, Rondo, and Phoenix exist, it is highly unlikely that producers will want to switch from superstar varieties such as Cabernet Sauvignon, Chardonnay, Syrah, and Sauvignon Blanc to these relative unknowns. Can you imagine anyone planting Rondo on the fabled slopes of the Côte d'Or? "The great advantage of genetic engineering," explains Meredith, "is the possibility of introducing a specific trait without otherwise disturbing the complex genotype that gives a wine its flavour." Put in simple terms, if you try to breed disease-resistant vines by classical methods, you may succeed, but you'll end up with a new grape variety. And the market doesn't really have any place for new varieties; we're happy with the ones we have.

So a major aim for GM vines lies in engineering fungal resistance into existing varieties. "We have a project in collaboration with French scientists to identify a gene from a wild relative of wine grapes (*Muscadinia rotundifolia*) which provides resistance to powdery mildew," reveals Robinson. "If we could move this gene into wine grapes, the need for fungicide application would be greatly decreased. Another project concerns the genetics of bunch architecture so we can breed looser bunches, which would be less susceptible to rots such as botrytis." Carole Meredith makes an interesting point. "As a consumer, I would much rather drink wine made from a genetically resistant vine than wine containing pesticide residues." Töpfer puts the choice starkly: either we make GM vines that are resistant to fungal diseases, or we keep spraying away.

This is just one of many goals that scientists have in their sights. Provided that researchers can identify the right genes, the sky's the limit. Fancy growing Chardonnay and Cabernet Sauvignon in the UK? All you need to do is to engineer in some genes that will accelerate ripening, along with some fungal-resistant genes to counter our damp climate, and – *bingo!* Likewise, Canadians need not be limited to planting dodgy hybrid vines; they can add some frost-tolerance genes to their favourite *vinifera* varieties – and away they go. Salinity is becoming a problem in irrigated vineyards around the world, so the answer will be salt-tolerant vines. Californian scientists are busy working on producing vines resistant to the deadly Pierce's disease that threatens their industry.

Then there are quality traits that can be manipulated. At the moment, encouraging vines to put all their energy into grape production and focus less on vegetative growth requires labour-intensive, complex, and costly work in the vineyard. If we understood a bit more about the way grape vines partition their nutrient resources, we could engineer vines to automatically produce top-quality fruit. We might even be able to get vines to produce high yields of high-quality grapes: the holy grail of viticulture. This is usually an either/or scenario. It all seems terribly unnatural, but then growing vines at high density on trellises in a vineyard is pretty unnatural; vines are woodland climbers. In such debates, it seems that what is "natural" is what we are familiar and comfortable with.

## The risks

It all sounds a bit too good to be true. What are the potential objections to GM vines? Firstly, there's the safety issue. If we eat GM foods, will we all develop strange and unnatural diseases somewhere down the line? It's highly unlikely. Carole Meredith's position on this issue is clear. "I have no fear whatsoever about the safety of food or wine produced from transgenic vines," she says. "I would consume them in a minute, as I and most Americans do every day with foods already in supermarkets made with transgenic maize and soybean products." Secondly, there's the risk of ecological contamination; the creation of superweed species and genetic pollution (*see* point 3 in the box below). Then we have aesthetic objections (*see* point 4 below). And then there is the "man plays God" argument: we have no right to tamper with the genetic make-up of creation; it's against nature. People in this position will never accept GM grapes or wines.

While I'm generally in favour of the idea of GM vines, I have one serious concern. If scientists manage to develop greatly enhanced GM Syrah, Cabernet or Chardonnay, and consumers change their minds about GM, it is likely that growers will come under severe economic pressure to plant the new, modified varieties. Because of the time, effort, and cost of developing new GM vines, it is likely that just a few varieties will eventually be chosen and just one or two clones from each variety will be used. The implications for diversity are obvious. My fear is that GM vines might represent another significant step in the direction of standardized, taste-alike industrial wine, hastening the progress of soulless big brands, and further severing the connection that wine has with the soil, making it just another manufactured beverage. If this turns out to be the case, it may be wrong to lay the blame at the door of GM, which is just a tool; rather, the problem may be more deep-seated, involving the trajectory of the wine industry as a whole. If the cost of adopting GM vines is increased uniformity and loss of wine diversity, is this a price worth paying?

From a scientific perspective, though, it is encouraging to see how gene technology is enabling rapid advances in our fundamental understanding of the biology of the grape vine. It would be a shame to see such elegant work jeopardized by blinkered opposition from scientifically illiterate but vocal opponents.

## Objecting to GM crops

Objections to GM crops generally fall into five categories:

1 RELIGIOUS/IDEOLOGICAL This is the "man plays God" argument: we have no right to tamper with the genetic make-up of creation as it's against nature. People holding this position will almost certainly never accept GM grapes or wines.

2 DANGER TO HUMAN HEALTH People worry that foodstuffs containing genetically modified ingredients pose a potential health risk. This partly reflects a fear of the unknown. Many of us regularly consume foods containing GM ingredients and there is as yet no evidence of any negative effect.

3 ENVIRONMENTAL THREAT Many are concerned that GM crops could cause the emergence of "superweeds". In this scenario, transgenic crops fertilize closely related wild plants, giving them a competitive advantage. Alternatively, GM crops could spread their transgenes to neighbouring farms, causing genetic pollution and threatening the status of organic producers. Although this is a significant worry for many crops, it isn't such a problem with grape vines, which aren't grown from seed but are vegetatively propagated and grafted onto special rootstocks. Because of this, it would be virtually impossible for GM vines to invade neighbouring vineyards. And

should pollen from a GM vine fertilize a vine in an adjacent vineyard, the transgenes would not find their way into the wine because their expression will be restricted to tissue within the seed of the grape. This is self-evident; if pollen from a Chardonnay vine fertilizes a Pinot Noir vine, the resulting grapes are still very much Pinot Noir.

4 AESTHETIC OBJECTIONS Many people don't like the idea of GM food. For whatever reason, the idea of crops engineered genetically doesn't appeal and they would rather not eat food containing GM ingredients. While this might seem rather subjective, it is a valid, and as wine is a discretionary and often luxury purchase it is highly relevant here. Wine sales are image-led, and GM has a bad image.

5 ANTI-GLOBALIZATION Rightly or wrongly, the current social climate is highly suspicious of large, multinational agrochemical companies. Because GM technologies are covered by a series of patents, some express concern that smaller farmers in developing countries will lose out, and that GM crops will concentrate power in the hands of large companies. In light of this, agrochemical companies must consider how they are seen to behave. Business decisions must be visibly tempered with ethical responsibility and a concern for social justice.

# 6 Phylloxera

Phylloxera is a name firmly written into the history of wine. Back in the late nineteenth century, this tiny aphid caused a vine plague of almost biblical proportions; in the space of a few decades, it brought the world wine industry to its knees. It was overcome by the application of some careful, thorough scientific investigation. After a few false starts, and under intense pressure, scientists worked out the cause of the problem and devised a solution of sorts, one that has proved resilient for more than a century. But the war against phylloxera has never been won. What we are currently experiencing is a prolonged cease-fire. The prospect of this truce between grape vines and their aphid nemesis failing is one that haunts wine-growers worldwide. This chapter traces the history of the epidemic, examines the science behind phylloxera and its control, and considers the risk of new, more virulent forms evolving.

## Outbreak

It's somewhat of an understatement to say that the second half of the nineteenth century was not a particularly good time to be a wine-grower in France. By 1850, an astonishing proportion of the population had livelihoods tied to the vine and its produce. One-sixth of France's state revenues were generated by wine, and one-third of the workforce derived a living from it. But within the space of a few decades, the French wine industry was shaken to its roots by two natural plagues. One of these, the fungal disease oïdium, was remedied fairly quickly, but the other, phylloxera, caused devastation on an enormous scale, and threatened to eradicate viticulture as we know it from the globe. With the benefit of hindsight, of course, we know that it didn't, but at the time it must have seemed a near thing.

The story begins and ends in the USA. This is where the diseases of phylloxera and oïdium – one insect, one fungal – had their origins, and where, rather ironically, phylloxera recently returned to wreak havoc on some of the most expensive wine real estate in the world. How did these natural calamities come about? The grape varieties responsible for almost all the wines that we drink belong to a single Eurasian grape species, *Vitis vinifera.* This species, of the approximately 60 grape-vine species found in the wild, was originally domesticated some 7,000 years ago, in the Neolithic period. Since then, the global wine trade has been built around it. It seems remarkable that the many hundreds of varieties in common use all belong to the same species; the resulting lack of genetic diversity renders them especially vulnerable to attack by pest and disease.

In contrast, the USA has a wide variety of native wild vines, yet there is no historical record of Native Americans ever having cultivated them or wine ever being made from them, despite their abundance. Eventually, European emigrants to North America, anxious to produce wines like those central to the cultures of their homelands, turned to them out of necessity. They had originally tried to grow the Eurasian *Vitis vinifera* varieties, but these had failed spectacularly. It turned out that the reason for this failure was that the *vinifera* vines simply lacked innate protection against the mildew and phylloxera that were endemic to North America, and which the American vine species had learned to exist alongside through co-evolution. While the American varieties grew well and proved robust in the face of disease, their big flaw was that they produced fairly unpalatable wine with a strong "foxy" taste.

Despite these qualitative shortcomings, American vines began to be imported into France in the early decades of the nineteenth century, and, by 1830, two dozen varieties were growing in French nurseries. This was all part of the broader passion at the time for importing novel, exotic plant varieties from around the globe, fuelled by Victorian scientific curiosity, and made possible by the steamship. These imported vines were rapidly disseminated throughout Europe's wine regions by nurserymen and *vignerons* keen to experiment. It turned out that, like so many other introduced non-native species, they were carrying a deadly cargo. While these vines were resistant to both phylloxera and oïdium, they harboured the very organisms that had thwarted the *vinifera* plantings of the European expats.

As you can imagine, the consequences were disastrous. European vineyards, propagated vegetatively and thus vulnerable in their genetic uniformity, were hit first by the devastating fungal disease oïdium. *Oïdium tuckerii* (now known as *Uncinula necator*) was first discovered growing on a greenhouse vine in Kent in 1845. This previously unknown fungus almost certainly arrived from the USA on a botanical sample, and soon spread throughout Europe. Within a few years, wine production in France had collapsed to less than a third of its previous levels.

**BELOW** South Australia is currently free from phylloxera, with most vines still planted on their own roots. This situation is maintained by a careful quarantine; signs like this one in the Barossa are a common feature in South Australian vineyards.

The response of *vignerons* was one of panic. At the time, Louis Pasteur's insightful germ theory of disease was still a few years off, so various explanations for this natural disaster were circulated, some more bizarre than others. In Italy, peasants blamed the railways, so in Tuscany, several miles of track thought to be responsible in some strange metaphysical fashion were torn up and dumped in ditches. This time, though, science provided an answer fairly rapidly and cheaply. French scientists discovered that dusting the vines with elemental sulphur provided protection against the fungus, and by 1858 the problem of oïdium was in retreat.

French wine-growing then entered a short-lived golden age. With the advent of the railways, wine production became separated from consumption, such that northern industrial populations could have their thirst slaked by cheap southern wine. Between 1850 and 1880, the average consumption rose from fifty to eighty litres per head per annum. This prosperity boom for the *vignerons* proved to be a false dawn. Slowly and surely, a catastrophe unfolded in the vineyards of France, which ended up putting global wine production in jeopardy, and ruining the livelihoods of enormous numbers of *vignerons* throughout Europe. The culprit was the tiny root-munching aphid, *Phylloxera vastatrix* (known today by scientists as *Dactylasphaera vitifoliae*). One Monsieur Borty, a small-time wine merchant in the town of Roquemaure in the Gard, had the misfortune of going down in history as inadvertently precipitating this natural disaster. In 1862, he received a case of vines from New York, which he planted in his small vineyard. Two years later, vines in the surrounding area mysteriously began to wither and die. The malady spread. By 1868, the whole of the Southern Rhône was infected, and phylloxera had begun to spread through the Languedoc. Within the space of a decade, it had spread through France and gone global, reaching Portugal's Douro Valley by 1872, Spain and Germany two years later, Australia in 1875, and Italy by 1879. The last French wine region to be affected was Champagne, in 1890.

The response to phylloxera was, again, one of panic. At first, the outward signs – the leaves of affected vines turning yellow and falling prematurely, followed by death of the vine – gave no clue as to the specific nature of the disease. When affected vines were extracted from the ground, their roots were found to be rotten and crumbling, but with no obvious pest present. It was down to Professor Jules-Emile Planchon, a botanist appointed by the government commission established to investigate the outbreak, to identify the culprit. He dug up roots of a healthy vine and observed clumps of minute wingless insects happily gorging themselves. Clever parasites don't kill their hosts, and in their homeland of the USA, phylloxera and grape vines had co-evolved so that they existed alongside each other. However, this cosy relationship hadn't developed with *Vitis vinifera*, and the arrangement was a hopelessly imbalanced one – the parasite load exerted by phylloxera was simply too great, resulting in eventual death of the vine.

## The complex life cycle of phylloxera

Phylloxera has a complicated life cycle, which was only worked out after the plague had begun. The fact that growers were dealing with a largely unknown assailant must have made the crisis doubly terrifying. It's an aphid. Just like the aphids we're more familiar with, which attack the aerial parts of vines, it sucks nutrients from the phloem of host plants. Like many aphids, phylloxera is pathenogenetic, which means it doesn't need actual sex to reproduce. The root-feeding form of phylloxera, the radicicole, is exclusively female. It settles on

# How phylloxera does its damage

There are three potential mechanisms for phylloxera-induced vine damage: removal of photosynthates, physical disruption of the roots, and secondary fungal infections of damaged roots. It is unlikely that the severe, usually fatal vine damage is caused by the first mechanism; on infested vines, there are fewer than 100 individuals per gram of dry root weight, and the loss of photosynthates this causes is not thought to be enough to weaken it significantly. Much more likely is that the vine damage occurs through secondary infections by fungal pathogens. In a controlled greenhouse experiment, University of California entomologist Jeffrey Granett and his colleagues compared control and phylloxera-infected vines grown in sterile soils with soils containing a range of pathogenic fungi. Phylloxera plus fungi caused a much larger loss of biomass (twenty-four to twenty-nine per cent) than phylloxera alone (sixteen per cent). This experiment also showed that phylloxera does cause some damage on its own, which suggests that it may be disrupting the roots in some way independently of secondary infections.

RIGHT Phylloxera galls on the underside of a leaf, which surround the gallicoles, and nodules on roots caused by feeding of the radicicoles.

### The complete life cycle of phylloxera
The winter egg (1) laid in gaps in the vine bark hatches, giving rise to (2) the parthenogenetic female gallicole that attaches to the underside of the leaf and feeds, provoking the formation of a protective gall. These gallicoles lay eggs (3) and can give rise to crawlers which migrate to the roots and feed there, where they are known as radicicoles (4). The radicicoles lay eggs (5) and initiate the sexual stage of the life cycle: a winged female alate (6) lays eggs producing male (7, 8) and female (9, 10) forms. The females lay the winter eggs, taking us back to the start of the cycle.

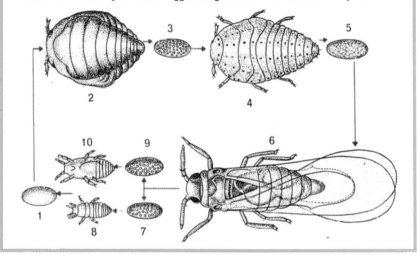

suitable roots and punctures them with its mouthparts and injects saliva; this causes the root cells to grow into a structure known as a gall, which increases the supply of nutrients and provides some protection. Then the aphid lays eggs – loads of them. These hatch and become crawlers, which move along the roots and can also climb the trunk, before being blown into the air and spread by the wind as far as a mile. If they find a suitable feeding site, they'll carry on proliferating, and populations can increase rapidly. Given suitable temperatures, the generation time is around a month, although adult phylloxera are actually laying eggs all the time. In some regions, such as California, phylloxera exists only as the root form. In others, there's also a separate above-ground stage of the life cycle, which is where the complexity begins.

Asexual forms of phylloxera can also develop on the leaves, where they are referred to as gallicoles. They also induce gall formation, and in this case the protective structure that encloses the feeding phylloxera extends below the leaf and opens to the upper leaf surface to allow crawlers out.

The root-dwelling radicicoles are responsible for the sexual phase of the life cycle. They can produce a third growth form, the alate. It is not known how this switch is triggered physiologically. On certain cues, the winged alates crawl up from the roots and can fly, but not very well. Alates deposit eggs of two different sizes on the woody portions of vines, and these hatch to become males and females. These sexual forms are immobile and cannot feed; they just have sex, the female laying an egg that then overwinters.

On hatching the following season, the offspring (known as the fundatrix) then forms leaf galls and carries on with the asexual form of the life cycle. As temperatures drop at the end of the growing season, the root-feeding radicicoles die off while the crawlers hibernate. It is not known how many of these crawlers survive, although the evidence suggests that very few do; the population is reset to almost zero. Nor is it known how many of the eggs laid by the sexual forms survive the winter.

**BELOW** Diseased vines affected by phylloxera.
*Photo courtesy of Claes Lofgren*

# The nightmare scenario

It wouldn't be a huge exaggeration to say that rootstock resistance to phylloxera is the single pillar on which the global wine industry rests. Fortunately, this resistance has proven amazingly durable – to date. This has led to a state of complacency on in the wine industry, which has neglected research on the basic biology of phylloxera and its interaction with the vine.

The spectre of phylloxera is still with us, however, as the Californian wine industry discovered to its cost in the late 1980s. The large expansion of vineyard area which took place in the "Golden State" (its official nickname) during the 1960s and 1970s had largely been on the AXR#1 rootstock, a hybrid cross between American and *vinifera* species. This was considered to be resistant to phylloxera, but even it eventually began to succumb to a new biotype of the pest that had emerged, known simply as biotype B. The consequence was that large areas of California's vineyards had to be replanted onto properly resistant rootstocks. Is this scenario likely to be repeated in other wine regions?

## Defeating phylloxera

Back to the nineteenth century. Faced with the ruin of the entire wine industry, the French government eventually offered a 300,000 franc prize for a remedy. Initial attempts to halt the spread of phylloxera involved uprooting and burning affected vines, but these failed. Remedy after potential remedy was suggested and tried, ranging from the semi-plausible to the outright bizarre. Some of the proposed treatments sounded surprisingly modern, such as biological control (finding a natural enemy of phylloxera) and the interplanting of vines with more attractive hosts for the aphid. They didn't work, though. Perhaps the oddest witchdoctor-style remedy came from the Beaujolais, where schoolboys were released from their classes twice daily to urinate over the vines.

*Vignerons* growing vines on the plains discovered that, where it was possible, seasonal flooding was reasonably effective in killing this subterranean pest. Vineyards in sandy soils were also observed to be immune, but transplanting vine production to the sand dunes was hardly a practical solution. The chemists searched rather randomly for a "magic bullet". At the time, it was known that carbon bisulphide was an effective insecticide, despite the fact that it was highly volatile and explosive when mixed with air. But how could growers get it to where it was needed: deep in the soil? An elaborate array of devices for injecting this rather suspect chemical into the root zones was invented, and before long this was seen as the best bet for heading off the pest. The problem with carbon bisulphide was threefold. It was a relatively expensive treatment, and beyond the reach of many *vignerons*; it would need repeating, year after year; and it wasn't terribly effective, mitigating the worst symptoms of the malaise without being curative.

Another solution was proposed. American vine species, which harboured the invader in the first place, had natural protection against phylloxera. Wherever they had been planted, they thrived, while all around them was a scene of devastation. Yes, the wine they produced tasted fairly bad, but better odd wine than no wine at all, argued the faction that became known as the *Américainistes*. Tastings of wines made using the American vines were set up, but the depressing conclusion was that these foxy wines really weren't good enough.

Then, someone had a brilliant idea. It is not clear who first thought of this, but Henri Bouschet displayed an Aramon (*vinifera*) vine grafted onto American rootstock at a Congrès Viticole in Montpellier in 1874. It soon became clear that, somewhat counter-intuitively, the wine made from *Vitis vinifera* vines grafted onto American rootstocks retained the full character of the *vinifera* variety while benefiting from the phylloxera resistance of the American roots. It completed a rather neat circle: the plague had come from America, but so had the salvation.

"Perhaps the oddest witchdoctor-style remedy came from the Beaujolais, where schoolboys were released from their classes twice daily to urinate over the vines."

The idea spread. The technique of grafting was easy enough to learn, so it could be attempted by just about anyone. The supply of American vines was more of a problem, because many wine regions began to prohibit their importation in order to prevent the remaining phylloxera-free vineyards from succumbing to the pest. Moreover, not everyone was won over by this radical idea of grafting. Many resisted replanting, with the attendant three-year loss of production, and clung tenaciously to their chemical treatments. There was a lengthy battle between the two factions over the ideal solution, but fortunately good sense prevailed and the grafters won the day. The lengthy work of replanting France's vineyards began. It was not a straightforward process, and some of the grander estates, reluctant to pull out their vines, kept them going with insecticide treatments as long as they could. The choice of appropriate grafting material was also complicated by the fact that it took a while to find American vines species that were well-adapted to the chalky soils that dominated some of France's key regions.

There was also an ongoing debate about whether the wines made from grafted vines were quite as good as those made from ungrafted ones; even today, this discussion is hinted at by tasters who refer to the greatness of wines made from pre-phylloxera vines. One thing that replanting did facilitate was a change in the viticultural landscape, with some sites being abandoned and others replanted with new varieties. In addition, the choice of rootstock, with its effect on graft parameters such as vigour, became an additional variable – a new item in the viticultural tool-box. Phylloxera's legacy is that almost all vines grown commercially across the globe are now grafted onto resistant rootstock, with a few notable exceptions, such as vineyards in Chile, which are protected by the Andes on one side and the Pacific Ocean on the other, sealed off at the top and bottom by a desert and Patagonia. Here the vines are planted on their own roots. South Australia also has large areas of non-grafted vines.

## The nature of rootstock resistance

American vine species are resistant to phylloxera. They carry the aphid, but it doesn't kill or damage them: why? Understanding the nature of this resistance would be an important step towards being able to engineer resistance into *vinifera*, a manipulation that might one day be needed if rootstock resistance should fail. What is the difference between the resistant American *Vitis* species and the susceptible *Vitis vinifera*? "We do not know what the physiological and biochemical basis of resistance or susceptibility is," explains entomologist and phylloxera expert Jeffrey Granett, "but we do know that different American *Vitis* species have different mechanisms." This means that if resistance did fail, there's a good chance it would render only certain rootstocks susceptible. Good news.

The current view seems to be that rootstock resistance to phylloxera involves two mechanisms. Firstly, strong rootstocks have some means of severely limiting phylloxera growth on them; perhaps they don't form the protective galls in response to phylloxera feeding. Secondly, they have resistance to pathogenic fungi that invade and damage susceptible vine roots that have been attacked. Yet the big question remains. Should we be expecting the doomsday scenario – the failure of rootstock resistance? Given enough time, is this likely, or even inevitable? "There is evidence on both sides," says Granett.

He and his colleagues have laboratory bio-assay evidence that strains of phylloxera collected from roots and leaves of rootstock plants have higher virulence on the cultivar of origin than on other cultivars or vine species. What does this suggest? Worryingly, it appears that phylloxera strains are gradually being selected for virulence on their hosts – that is, rootstocks are resistant, but they maintain a population of phylloxera at subpathological levels. Over time, those phylloxera that are better equipped to feed on the roots of these vines (those that are more virulent) increase differentially in prevalence.

Could this eventually lead to the selection of phylloxera strains that are able to circumvent the rootstock resistance enough to cause disease? "We don't know whether this appearance is artifact or significant viticulturally," Granett admits. However, there are indications (as yet no firm evidence) that these phylloxera strains which seem to be evolving to overcome rootstock resistance are less "fit" than native strains. On the other side of the coin, as Granett points out, "the rootstocks have lasted more than a century. If they were going to fail, why haven't they?" He also states that quarantines could play an important part in halting the spread of any new virulent phylloxera strain. "The Australians," he concludes, "have had success with their quarantine of South Australia for a long time."

## Avenues for research

With the importance of this issue to the global wine industry, several avenues of research could prove promising for prevention strategies. Firstly, the limiting factor for population growth is gall formation. Phylloxera is thought to manipulate the hormonal signalling of the vine to encourage development of specific morphological structures needed for survival of the aphid on its host. This could be manipulable. Secondly, most vine damage is thought to be due to secondary fungal infection; it might prove possible to manipulate soil ecology to limit pathogen populations. Thirdly, if we understood the genetics of the multiple mechanisms of susceptibility and resistance, we could manipulate them by breeding or genetic engineering. Finally, some soil conditions seem to affect phylloxera incidence; if the mechanisms were understood, these could be targets for intervention.

Science still has an important role to play in the ongoing saga of phylloxera. It saved the day once before, and may be called on again if the doomsday scenario of the emergence of new, more virulent strains should become a reality. Given this, it would seem foolish not to invest in phylloxera research now, while there is no immediate crisis.

# 7  Lutte raisonée and IPM

Science's contribution to viticulture is often cast in a rather negative light. If I ask you to think about science applied in the vineyard, you might well conjure up images of chemicals being sprayed with abandon, obliterating all life but that of the vines. Or your mental picture might be one of space-age trellising and irrigation technologies forcing vines to pump out heroic yields of grapes, which are then turned into mega-litres of soulless, industrial wine. Or geeks in lab coats genetically engineering a new generation of supervines. Yet this is all a misrepresentation. It is science that brings us an understanding of the true complexity of natural systems. The insights from the science of ecology are teaching us how to work with the checks and balances of nature, and encouraging a new, rational, limited-input, environmentally sound means of vineyard management that offers a third way between the ideologically driven approach of Biodynamics and conventional chemical-based agricultural systems.

This new viticultural approach is known in France as *lutte raisonée*, literally the "reasoned struggle". This is based on a scientific concept known as integrated pest management (IPM), and borrows some of the insights from organic farming but without the strait-jacket of strict regulation that typifies organics and Biodynamics. One of the strengths of this new viticulture is that it reconciles the needs of growers with those of the environment in, if you'll excuse the cliché, a win-win scenario.

## Nature's struggle

Imagine a meadow on a midsummer's afternoon. The sun is shining, the air is buzzing with insects, and there's a lovely contrast among the various shades of lush, green vegetation. On the surface things look peaceful enough, but in reality this portrait of natural harmony is actually one of a continual fight for existence. Each organism is in a struggle to grow, survive, and reproduce in the face of hostile, ever-present competition. Plants compete with each other for light, water, and nutrients, at the same time balancing the need to open their stomata (pores in their leaves) to allow gas exchange while restricting the loss of precious water. These plants also represent a useful food source for a number of herbivorous insects and mammals, which in turn have their own predators to worry about. And if that's not enough, there are a host of fungal, bacterial, and viral diseases all waiting to colonize a susceptible plant recipient. Indeed, a lot of plant morphology and chemistry has been shaped by evolution to make plants unpalatable to herbivores and resistant to microbial attack. It's quite a challenge just to survive.

With all these organismal interactions that occur in the environment, a series of checks and balances has evolved, some of them quite sophisticated. Here's an example. When some plants are munched on by certain insect herbivores, they release volatile compounds called semiochemicals. These can be detected at even tiny concentrations by predators of these herbivores. Remarkably, the chemicals released by the plant can give information about the particular organism that's feeding on it, thus specifically alerting the appropriate predator. Effectively, the plant's SOS call has become a "dinner's ready" signal to the predators. This sort of clever balancing act helps ensure the continued survival of the plant, even in the face of attack, through an evolved cooperation with other organisms. It is this sort of complex interaction that IPM attempts to understand and then harness.

## A shift in thinking

The emergence of IPM reflects changing attitudes towards pest control. To illustrate this, let's take a larger perspective on agriculture and, more specifically, viticulture. Since the dawn of agriculture, humans have had problems with pests and diseases. Growing just one crop in a field - monoculture – is asking for trouble. It is shifting the odds firmly in favour of the pest or disease species, because these unwanted guests are kitted out to reproduce fast and explode in numbers once they find a suitable habitat; this may well be your field or vineyard. But, if we are going to farm effectively, then growing crops in a near or absolute monoculture is a prerequisite. However, the larger the extent of monoculture, the higher the risk of losing a substantial portion of the crop to some pest, because natural pest reduction is less likely to occur. And, as agriculture has developed, monoculture has developed to such an extent that ever larger areas are covered with just one crop. In the pursuit of increased yields, weeds have been eradicated by pre-emergence herbicides, and hedgerows and patches of scrub or woodland have been removed.

In the "natural" situation of an ecosystem, checks and balances develop. Biodiversity ensures that there are not only pests, but also predators of those pests present. Any system that is hopelessly imbalanced is unsustainable, so it is selected against. Thus, the ecological systems which have survived are, by definition, sustainable – unless they experience some externally applied change such as climate change or someone planting a large vineyard in the middle of them.

Quite naturally, farmers don't like to lose a portion (or all) of their crop to pests and disease. Traditionally, the response has been to turn to chemists to provide "magic bullets" to eradicate these problems. This approach is flawed, however, because development of resistance on the part of the pest or disease is almost inevitable, given enough time. Apply a strong selective pressure such as a pesticide to a rapid-life-cycle insect, and you are challenging natural selection to come up with a resistance mechanism. Just one mutant with a degree of resistance will be strongly selected for, and will, in a short space of time, be able to restore the population to damaging levels. Natural selection almost always wins.

And bear this in mind: if you have knocked out the pest population, you're likely to have also knocked out the enemies of these pests. Then, when resistance arises to your chemical of choice, the situation will be even worse than before. You'll be without a chemical bullet, and your pest will be without its enemy. You'll sit there looking at your devastated crop, and long for the days when you only lost ten per cent of it. This is the sort of scenario that led to the generation of IPM: a new, smarter paradigm for countering pests, which began to be developed in the 1970s. IPM is a thoroughly scientific, whole-system approach (call it "holistic" if you will) which has largely replaced the rather naïve agrochemical-dependent way of farming – and it is increasing in significance.

The five bedrocks of IPM are knowledge, monitoring, anticipation, timing, and economic thresholds. IPM rests on a thorough scientific knowledge of the biology of pest, weed, and disease organisms in the context of a larger ecosystem.

Practitioners use this knowledge to monitor populations of potential problem organisms and then anticipate when they will reach damaging levels. This is where the concept of economic thresholds steps in. Rather than try to eradicate all pests, farmers need to decide what population levels they can tolerate economically. Finally, timing is a crucial concept that is key to effective implementation of IPM. Chemical inputs may still be needed, but through careful timing these are greatly reduced. Another benefit of IPM is that because it is a multi-pronged strategy and doesn't just rely on the outmoded notion of a chemical bullet, resistance in the pest, weed or disease population is much less likely to arise. In essence, IPM is about reconciling rather disparate aims: farmers wanting to reduce crop losses while at the same time reducing environmental degradation and avoiding pest resistance build-up. Farmers using IPM are making choices based on a broad perspective, which takes into account the whole ecosystem, not just one part of it.

## The IPM tool kit

The strength of IPM is that it offers many potential solutions to agricultural problems. Many of these solutions are still rather experimental; others are tried and tested. They include the topics listed below.

### Biological control

Biological control is one of the foundations of IPM. It's conceptually quite simple: if you have a pest problem, introduce the natural enemies of this pest (be they predators or diseases) and let them control the problem. In practice, it is not quite as simple. In order for the natural enemies to complete their life cycle and establish themselves in a vineyard, there has to be a large enough population of pests for them to prey on, and unless growers want to be re-introducing populations of the natural enemies each time treatment is required, then they must tolerate a degree of pest loss from the continued (but manageable) presence of a sustaining population of pests. They might also have to introduce refuge areas of non-crop plants in and around their fields to sustain diverse populations of insects throughout the year, some of which will be beneficial.

Biological control that isn't properly thought out can go horribly wrong. One of the best examples of failed biological control is the cane toad, *Bufo marinus*. Many years ago, sugar-cane growers in Queensland, Australia, had a problem with cane beetles, and some clever academic identified the cane toad as a natural predator of these beetles. So, in 1935, the cane toad was introduced as a control, and adapted well to life in Australia. However, it quickly became a problem. Not only did it decide not to go after the cane beetles it was intended to control, but it also proved poisonous to local animals; a milky secretion from a gland on the back of its head can prove fatal to any cat, dog or dingo who fancies a cane-toad snack. Even today, cane toads are spreading unchecked through northeastern Australia because they have no natural predators. The recommended humane way of eliminating them is to place them in a plastic bag and put this in a freezer, but locals are known to indulge in the rather more brutal art of cane-toad bashing. In an ironic twist, biological-control agents of the cane toad are now being developed by Australian government researchers. Admittedly, this is a rather extreme example of badly thought-out biological control, but it illustrates the potential dangers that can occur when this control method is attempted without sufficient knowledge of the ecological systems involved.

"It's all very well introducing parasitoids or predators of pests into your vineyard, but they will need somewhere to live, and they might not find your vines an ideal home."

# Headaches for wine-growers: arthropods

Arthropods – the taxonomic group that includes insects and spiders – can be major pests in vineyards. In Europe, the key problems are the grape berry moths *Eupoecilia ambiguella* and *Lobesia botrana*; leafhoppers which act as vectors of viruses and bacteria; and spider mites. In the USA, Pierce's disease, spread by a leafhopper, is a matter of urgent current concern. This isn't forgetting phylloxera, which almost destroyed viticulture worldwide in the latter half of the nineteenth century (*see* page 52). As yet, though, there is no effective biological or even chemical control strategy against this aphid pest. "Insect-eating nematodes will kill phylloxera," says entomologist Jeffrey Granett, "but because the phylloxera are so small, the nematodes cannot complete their life cycle." This means that nematodes would have to be reintroduced at regular periods, which is impractical.

Grape berry moths were already present before vines were widely grown, but they adopted grape vines when vines became a monoculture in certain regions. The larvae feed on grape flowers and cause loss of yield, then later in the season they attack the berries, predisposing them to invasion by botrytis. The likelihood of their attack can be predicted by models based on weather conditions, and the results of population sampling by pheromone traps. Thus spraying can be withheld until the risk is deemed high.

In addition, mating-disruption strategies based on the use of synthetic sex hormones similar to those emitted by females can be employed.

Leafhoppers are a significant problem in European regions, especially for organic growers, where control methods are extremely limited. Perhaps the most serious problem is *Scaphoideus titanus*, which is able to transmit the mycoplasma disease flavescence dorée, with disastrous consequences. Like phylloxera, this is an American introduction to European viticulture, and it came over some time after World War II. The only control is insecticidal sprays, and in some French regions that are affected, spraying is obligatory for all growers. The hunt is on for effective biological control agents.

Pierce's disease is a serious problem in parts of California, and the subject of much current anxiety. It is a bacterial disease (*Xylella fastidosa*): traditionally, it has been spread by a vector with a short flying range. Now, though, it is being spread by a new vector, the glassy-winged sharpshooter, which has a tremendous range, and this the possibility to cause plague-like disease. *Xylella* blocks the vessels of affected vines, thus killing them. There is no effective chemical or biological control, and the disease is so serious that viticulture has to be abandoned in affected areas.

## Natural enemies or "beneficials"

Many IPM strategies rely on the identification of natural enemies of pest arthropods; these are also known as "beneficials". Natural enemies might be predators which eat the problem species, or they might take the form of parasitoids, which are insect parasites. An example of the latter is the parasitic wasp. These creature might lay eggs in a problem caterpillar; the eggs produce larvae that then grow inside the caterpillar, using it as a food source and killing it in the process.

## Biopesticides

These are pesticides that use specific microbes as the active agents. They aren't used as widely as they could be, largely because of a lack of knowledge about them, coupled with an absence of commercial drive. One example is that of *Trichoderma harzianum*, a fungal enemy of another fungus, *Botrytis cinerea*, which causes bunch rot on grapes, and *Ampelomyces quisqualis*, an antagonist of powdery mildew. Some biopesticides are already being used in vineyards.

## "Refuges" or "ecological compensation areas"

It's all very well introducing parasitoids or predators of pests into your vineyard, but they will need somewhere to live, and they might not find your vines an ideal home. Added to this, clean, cultivated vineyards are barren places during the dormant season, with nowhere for overwintering insects to hide. This is where ecological compensation zones come in handy. These are patches of ground given over to specific patterns of vegetation, such as scrubland, woods or hedgerows, which can act as refuge areas for natural enemies of problem species.

This sort of biodiversity can offset some of the negative effects of monoculture. It is likely that the efficacy of these compensation areas will be enhanced by the use of cover crops, or allowing some vegetation to grow between vine rows. Ecological compensation areas are now being trialled in some vineyard regions in France (*see* "Lutte raisonée/IPM in action" opposite). These compensation zones are not a panacea for all vineyard problems, however. While they are intellectually and emotionally appealing, their use needs to be carefully thought through, as there is a risk that growing certain types of vegetation near vineyards could encourage the presence of insect species that actually turn out to be a problem, either directly as pests themselves, or indirectly by acting as transmission agents of viral or bacterial diseases.

## Cover cropping

The ground between vine rows is normally kept clear of weeds by pre-emergence herbicide applications or heavy tillage. Cover cropping is the practice of growing plants between rows instead of leaving them clear, and it offers several potential benefits. These include the promotion of soil life, erosion prevention, and the enhancement of populations of beneficial insects. A range of plants potentially suitable for this purpose already exist. It is now common in some wine regions to grow a cover crop over winter when the threat of erosion is likely to be highest; this crop is then tilled into the soil in spring. But newer strategies involve growing cover crops throughout the growing season, when they can act as

"The danger with many crops is that planting ecological compensation areas increases the habitats for natural enemies, but it may also end up pulling in a larger population of pest species, too."

refuges for beneficials. Studies have shown that these summer cover crops support season-long high populations of predators which can provide biological control for some vineyard pest species. Cover cropping has two potential drawbacks, however; in drier, non-irrigated vineyards, the cover crop can compete with the vine for scarce water resources. It can also enhance the risk of frost damage.

### Semiochemical strategies

Chemical signalling is vital to most insects. They use their acutely sensitive olfactory and pheromone systems to detect food sources and find mates. Where an insect's specific sign-chemical (semiochemical) strategies are known, they can be exploited. For example, mating-disruption strategies involve the use of insect sex pheromones to confuse and thus disrupt the mating behaviour of target species. Experimental work is focusing on ever more sophisticated semiochemical interventions. For example, some insects use their sense of smell to dictate egg-laying behaviour: they will choose not to lay eggs on those plants that have already been laid on, and they can smell the difference. If the semiochemical involved can be identified, then it can be used to mark crop plants and thus discourage egg laying by the pest insect. "Push-pull strategies" can also be employed – plants can be introduced into crop zones that smell repellent to pests, while adjacent target zones of non-crop plants can be planted to pull in pest species, thus diverting pests from the crop.

### Weather monitoring

This can help reduce the number of chemical inputs by predicting when certain pests or diseases are likely to be a problem. Any spray programmes can be scheduled intelligently and applied only when they are really needed. This climatic monitoring is inexpensive to implement, and is actually likely to save money; sprays and the labour required to administer them are costly.

## Lutte raisonée/IPM in action

To get a better idea of how these techniques might look in action, I spoke to a researcher involved in trying to implement ecological compensation areas (known as *zones ecologiques réservoirs* in France) in French vineyards. Marteen Van Helden works for l'Ecole Nationale d'Ingénieurs des Travaux Agricoles (ENITA) in Bordeaux, and his research concerns developing the science behind ecological compensation areas so that they can be used as an IPM tool in vineyards. Currently, he has set up a number of small vineyard plots with experimental hedgerows, and he is monitoring the population dynamics of insect species on the vines and in the hedgerows. "Viticulture is particularly interesting for IPM," explains Van Helden, "because there is very little risk of increasing the pressures of diseases or pests on the vines. This is not the same with other crops."

The danger with many crops is that planting ecological compensation areas increases the habitats for natural enemies, but it may also end up pulling in a larger population of pest species, too. Vineyard insect pests are usually a problem late in the summer; the idea is that, in vineyards in early summer, there will be a build-up of natural enemies on the hedgerows; these eat pest species there and then move to the vines. "Our experiments have been ongoing for five years now," says Van Helden. "We don't have solid results, but a lot of farmers are interested." He explains that this is partly because wine-growing is a matter of image, and

# Headaches for wine-growers: fungi

Fungal diseases are one of the major problems for most wine-growers. *Vitis vinifera* lacks innate resistance to downy and powdery mildew, fungal diseases imported to Europe from the USA in the nineteenth century. The result? Growers have no choice but to spray, either with traditional chemicals such as sulphur and Bordeaux mixture, or with more modern systemic fungicides. *Botrytis cinerea* is another fungal disease that causes grey rot of grape bunches, although when it infects certain already ripe grapes it can become the beneficial "noble" rot that is a crucial component of certain styles of sweet wine. There is currently limited biological control against these fungi in the form of biopesticides, which are not yet widely used.

In the absence of biological control, IPM can still help target chemical treatments more precisely. Knowledge of the biology of these fungal diseases has facilitated the development of risk-assessment indices based on weather conditions. By calculating the index score, a wine-grower can know how much and how often to spray for effective control.

producers like the idea of an attractive countryside for wine tourism. IPM also fits right into the "natural", "wholesome" image that most wineries would like associated with their products. Van Helden is taking advantage of this enthusiasm to see if he can create larger sites to try out IPM, rather than just in his small experimental plots.

In addition to his work in Bordeaux, Van Helden is involved in a project that will see ecological compensation areas being trialled across a whole appellation, Saumur-Champigny in the Loire. "We want to see whether we can recreate functional biodiversity in an existing situation," says Van Helden. "We want to see what we can adapt; we don't want to re-do the landscape entirely." It will be an interesting project because it will help to explore which sorts of landscape elements are most significant for encouraging viable natural enemy populations. It is also important that this experiment is taking place at the scale of a whole appellation. In ecology, scale is quite important, because lots of little isolated plots aren't as useful as a few larger plots, perhaps linked by features such as hedgerows. Small plots suffer from what is termed "island effects". If you have a certain area of a particular habitat, it will support a larger diversity of species if it is all one plot than if it is broken into several different islands, even if the total area is the same in both cases.

Hedgerows are a vital component in this type of project, because they act as refuges and are also linker elements and corridors, but alone, they might not be enough. Some natural enemies prefer larger natural sites such as patches of scrub or woodland. The hedges can act as "roads" directed towards the vineyards. In the vineyard, small landscape elements such as undergrowth provide important refuge areas. In the Saumur-Champigny experiment, Van Helden will be advising growers what types of plants might be useful for ecological compensation areas and vineyard undergrowth. Farmers might find space for these around their plots, or plant hedgerows in or at the boundaries of their vineyards. He estimates that the cost of planting a hedge is around four to five Euros per metre, with some soil preparation, mulching, and a year or two of follow-up also involved. There are possibilities for funding this through the local chamber of agriculture or local government. He hopes that a few keen farmers will start the ball rolling and then others will be encouraged to get involved. On a larger scale, the two organizations planting most hedgerows in France are the railways and motorways. They can be encouraged to collaborate with farmers in this type of project. In some ways, generating successful biodiversity is not just a scientific venture, but a social and cultural one, and it needs to be approached this way.

"The technical services of the CIVC have actually been working on *viticulture raisonée* for a decade; they have found they don't need to enforce it because growers are embracing it readily."

### Champagne – an example to be followed

The Comité Interprofessionnel du Vin de Champagne (CIVC) provides technical support and advice to growers in the region. Champagne claims to be the first wine region in the world to run environmentally friendly programmes on this scale. IPM in Champagne goes under the name of *viticulture raisonée*, and since 2001 the CIVC has issued a *guide practique* for growers. The 2003 version is a 200-page, full-colour guide to viticulture with an emphasis on reducing chemical inputs. The technical services of the CIVC have actually been working on *viticulture raisonée* for a decade; they have found they don't need to enforce it because growers are embracing it readily. They have weather stations throughout the region and provide growers with alerts and advice. This type of project is extremely encouraging, mainly because, with its high take-up and official sanction, it is likely to have a widespread effect on entire vineyard regions, and is relevant to all types of producers, from boutique wineries to industrial giants.

## Headaches for wine-growers: viruses

Viruses are major problems in viticulture. Perhaps the most common is the leafroll virus, which is common throughout vineyards worldwide, and is seen as a downward rolling of the leaf late in the growing season. It doesn't kill the vine, but it substantially delays ripening, reducing wine quality. It is spread mainly by humans employing poor nursery practices, such as taking cuttings from infected vines, although there are reports of transmission by vine mealybugs. The only way to counter leafroll virus is by planting virus-free vines. Other viruses also infect grape vines, and some are transmitted by insects and nematodes, as well as poor cultivation practices.

Virus diseases are frequently overlooked because they rarely kill vines, but instead have an effect on grape quality – for instance by delaying ripening. It is likely that many of the clonal differences seen in different grape varieties are not genetic but instead reflect different levels of viral infection.

# 8 Biodynamics

Many readers will be surprised to see a chapter on Biodynamics in a book on wine science. The language of Biodynamics, with its references to the alignment of the planets, undefined life forces, and the use of bizarrely fashioned preparations, seems totally at odds with a rational, scientific world view. As a consequence, most scientifically literate people have dismissed Biodynamics altogether; alternatively, they have regarded Biodynamic practices as affectations, and explain any benefits merely in terms of increased attention to vineyard management. My goal in this chapter is to try to integrate the insights and practices of Biodynamics with a scientific understanding of viticulture. I'll begin by trying to capture the essence of Biodynamic viticulture, and answer some key questions. How does Biodynamics differ from conventional and organic agriculture? Does it actually work, and if so, how? I'll also address which, if any, aspects of Biodynamics can be explained scientifically.

Back in 1997, the sales team and directors of UK wine merchant Corney & Barrow visited Domaine Leflaive in Burgundy. Anne-Claude Leflaive poured them two wines, blind, and asked them which they liked best. Twelve out of the thirteen preferred the same wine. What was the difference? Well, both were technically the same wine: her 1996 Puligny-Montrachet Premier Cru Clavoillon. But the wines were made from adjacent plots of vines: one organic, the other farmed with Biodynamics, an alternative system of agriculture that represents the focus of this chapter. This latter wine was the one that the Corney & Barrow team had singled out almost unanimously as their favourite. Domaine Leflaive went fully Biodynamic the following vintage.

Anecdotal observations like these don't constitute hard scientific data, but they are common enough – and come from people making serious enough wines – to merit proper attention. Indeed, the roll-call of Biodynamic producers forms a star-studded list (*see* table on page 75), one that is growing steadily.

## What is Biodynamics?

It is helpful to think of Biodynamics not primarily as an agricultural system, but rather as an altered philosophy or world view that impacts on the practice of agriculture in numerous different ways. In other words, in order to farm Biodynamically, you have to think Biodynamically. The system has its roots in a series of lectures delivered in 1924 by Austrian philosopher and scientist Rudolf Steiner. Steiner's mission was to bridge the gap between the material and spiritual worlds through the philosophical method. (Already, I can feel the scientists' hackles rising with the use of these terms.) To this end, Steiner created the "spiritual science" of anthroposophy, which he then used as the basis of the Waldorf School system that persists to this day. It was late in Steiner's life that he turned to agriculture; his eight lectures, entitled *Spiritual Foundations for the Renewal of Agriculture*, were delivered just a year before his death, but they remain the foundation of Biodynamic farming that is practised in vineyards today.

## The farm as a living system

Key to Biodynamics is considering the farm in its entirety as a living system, and seeing it in the context of the wider pattern of lunar and cosmic rhythms. In this holistic view, the soil is seen not simply as a substrate for plant growth, but as an organism in its own right. The idea of using synthetic fertilizers or pesticides is thus anathema to Biodynamic practitioners. Instead, they use a series of special preparations (*see* table on page 76) to enhance the life of the soil, which are applied at appropriate times in keeping with the rhythms of nature. Disease is seen not as a problem to be tackled head-on, but rather as a symptom of a deeper malaise within the farm "organism"; correct the problem in the system and the disease will right itself. Where Biodynamics differs significantly in practice from organic farming is in the use of these preparations and the timing of their application. In other ways the techniques employed are quite similar.

From this outline, we can see why it is difficult to discuss the theoretical basis of Biodynamics scientifically. The undefined "life forces" aren't specified in a concrete way, and we have no means of measuring them. While the concept of lunar rhythms can be framed in scientific forms, the cosmic rhythms that come from the alignment of the planets are undefined. It's hard to see what physical, measurable effect the planets and their movement could have on life on earth.

**RIGHT** A horse being used to plough vines in Vosne Romanée, Burgundy. This is the La Romanée vineyard of Liger Belair.

*Photo courtesy of Bill Nanson, www.burgundy-report.com*

"'The vine is one of the few fruit trees strictly linked to the season,' says Joly. 'The vine is dominated by the earth forces. It goes downwards so it has immense strength in its roots and only goes up a little bit. It couldn't flower in the spring like the cherry or the apple. The more a plant leaves its gravitational forces, the more it can develop its flowers. The vine is waiting for sun to land on earth.'"

## An audience with Nicolas Joly

What better way to try to catch the flavour of the underlying philosophy of Biodynamics than to attend a Nicolas Joly seminar? Joly, who owns Coulée de la Serrant in the Savennières region of France's Loire Valley, is probably the most celebrated and widely quoted proponent of Biodynamic viticulture. "I was trained to be a banker, but I turned out to be a wine-grower," he says. In 1977 he decided that he wanted to make wines that expressed the "spot" of Coulée de Serrant. Early in his tenure, he was visited by an official from the chamber of agriculture. "He said that my mother had been running the estate well," he recalls, "but in an old-fashioned way, and it was now time for some modernity. I was told that if I started using weedkillers, I'd save 14,000 francs." Joly took this advice, but "within two years I realized that the colour of the soil was changing; insects like ladybirds were no longer there; all the partridges had gone." Then fate intervened. Joly read a book on Biodynamics. "I wasn't attracted to the green movement, but this book fascinated me, and I had the crazy idea of trying to practise this concept."

Joly's emphasis is on living forces, and correct timing of viticultural interventions. "The soil has to be alive," he says. "Organic manure is from different animals. Each animal produces very different manure. Some are dominated by heat, like a horse. If you force a cow against its will, it will go down – the earth forces dominate. Wild boar and pigs feed on roots, so their manure will work on the roots." All these different fertilities are essential. "Spring is good for us," he continues. "For a vine, spring is the victory of sun forces over earth forces. In autumn, the law of death comes into force – the law of gravitation comes into force and leaves begin falling. Look how tired we get in the evening. On the first day of spring the days are a bit longer than the nights. The sun attraction is stronger than gravitation.

"The vine is one of the few fruit trees strictly linked to the season. The vine is dominated by the earth forces. It goes downwards so it has immense strength in its roots and only goes up a little bit. It couldn't flower in the spring like the cherry or the apple. The more a plant leaves its gravitational forces, the more it can develop its flowers. The vine is waiting for sun to land on earth. This is what happens at the summer solstice. It withholds its flowering process for the time when the sun lands on earth. The summer solstice is a very important day for a vine. If you taste wines where they flower too early, they have a very good short [first] mouthful but a bad second mouthful. The vines flowering closest to the solstice produce the best wines."

So how is this different to organics? "In Biodynamics we are connecting the vine to the frequencies it needs," Joly explains, "like tuning a radio. We are tuning the plant to the frequencies that bring it life. Organics permits nature to do its job; Biodynamics permits it to do its job more. It is very simple." What does Joly make of inorganic fertilizers? "Fertilizer is a salt," he says. "It takes more water to compensate salt. You are forcing growth through water – the plant has to over-drink, so it grows, and carries on growing after the solstice. The process of growth ends up conflicting with the plant's act of retiring to seed and fruit. The result of this is rot, so you need to counter this with lots of chemicals." And disease? "Disease is a process of constrictive forces and contractive forces. Disease itself doesn't exist. The living agents that bring diseases are just doing their duty. There is no point in fighting hundreds of new diseases."

Joly's Biodynamic philosophy extends to winemaking, too. 'The more you help the vine to do its job by means of a live soil, proper vine selection, and avoiding poisonous treatments, the more harmony there is. If the wine catches this

## Biodynamics lite?

Perhaps the easiest way to illustrate the differences between Biodynamic and conventional viticulture is by asking the following question. If I were a wine-grower, what would I have to do differently to become a certified Biodynamic producer? Is there a minimum set of criteria I would have to meet?

I asked Nicolas Joly what shifting to Biodynamics would entail. "First, you move to organics," he explained, "and if you are confident, then putting in Biodynamics would require as little as six days' extra work in a year for a fifteen-hectare domaine. The problem is moving towards the new understanding of nature. Recreating a model takes a bit of time." Dominique Lafon comes up with a similar figure, estimating that it requires 100 hours' more work a year on fourteen hectares of vineyards to implement Biodynamics.

Anne Mendenhall of Demeter USA (the US arm of Demeter, which is the leading international certification body for Biodynamic agriculture) was more specific about what would be needed to obtain Biodynamic certification. "The full use of Biodynamic methods would be required for two years," she explains. "That is, you'd need to use the two field spray materials, BD 500 and BD 501 [see table on page 76], and compost made with the other six BD preparations." She added that these preparations can be purchased ready to spray, and because of the small quantities involved, they are not expensive. Would I have to keep animals on the farm? "Not absolutely, but it is highly recommended that some livestock be integrated. Chickens running in the vines during the growing season and sheep grazing during the winter have been successful. They are there more to provide the astral component of the farm." And while most Biodynamic practitioners would consider the correct timing of interventions to be crucial to their success, this is not a requirement of the Demeter certification. As Mendenhall points out, "No one has been de-certified for improper timing in the USA."

Interestingly, despite the antipathy of Biodynamics and organics to any chemical treatments, *vignerons* applying these techniques sometimes still have to rely on a chemical solution to the problem of fungal disease. Thus, I would need to use a copper-based treatment, such as Bordeaux mixture, in conjunction with wettable or powdered sulphur in order to ward off mildew and rot. Dominique Lafon mentions that in Europe a limit on the use of copper is being proposed, with a figure of 4kg (8.8lbs) copper per hectare. "This is possible in Burgundy if you're careful," he says.

I asked Biodynamic consultant Jacques Mell, who is based in Reims, why this concession is allowed. "In vineyards, there is no crop rotation," he explains. "Vines stay in the same soil year after year, so they are living on their own excrement. They become feeble because there is no reviving of the soil, and this weakens them. They are in a state of weakness where they are liable to attack."

harmony well, you have nothing to do in the cellar: potentially it is all there." He chooses to use natural yeast, rather than inoculating with yeast cultures: "Re-yeasting is absurd. Natural yeast is marked by all the subtleties of the year. If you have been dumb enough to kill your yeast, you have lost something from that year."

Joly is taking an approach to agriculture that is at odds with my training as a scientist. He is using an altogether different way of describing natural processes: a "picture" language that jars alarmingly with the western rationalistic world view. This is more the language of religion than that of scientifically based viticulture. Yet, at the same time, I have immense respect for the vision of viticulture he is expounding. It has a life and vitality of its own, which exposes some of the intellectual and environmental bankruptcy of chemical-dependent conventional viticultural regimes. And above all, he is making profound, interesting wines.

## Meet Jacques Mell

A common way for a *vigneron* to make this transition to Biodynamics is by hiring a consultant, and Jacques Mell may well be the first flying Biodynamic consultant in Europe. At any one time he consults for around twenty-five growers, and in addition to his contracts in France, he currently has three clients in Italy, although he can't reveal names because of confidentiality clauses.

Trained as a lawyer, Mell discovered organic agriculture in 1967 through his involvement in beekeeping, and Biodynamics ten years later. He formed his own consultancy in 1989. At this time, there were only six wine-growers who practised Biodynamics in France; now he estimates that there are over 100

"'Traditional viticulture artificializes the vineyards, creating an artificial medium,' Espinoza says. 'The result is that the wines are similar to those from other places.'"

(Demeter alone currently has fifty-six certified *vignerons* on its books). Mell deals with general agriculture as well as wine-growing, but is currently seeing a higher take-up among *vignerons*. To hire Mell's services would cost some 1,500 Euros a year, which seems reasonable. "My aim is to make it affordable," Mell explains. "It is not just something for the rich farmers."

One of Mell's clients is Francis Boulard of Champagne Raymond Boulard. Boulard is not yet fully Biodynamic, but was curious enough to experiment with part of his production (in 2003, around one hectare) to see what difference Biodynamics makes. Two years on, he has noted consistent improvements in the Biodynamic plot, and he plans to continue with it. Many growers seem to convert in this fashion; they try Biodynamics a bit, like what they see, and gradually adopt the system more widely. Boulard tells me that he is one of the growers participating in a five-year trial started in spring 2002 by the CIVC. They are systematically comparing three different viticultural regimes: organic, *lutte raisonée*, and Biodynamics. According to Boulard, the CIVC is taking samples of soils and grapes, then comparing finished wines. It will be fascinating to see the results of this experiment, but the CIVC won't comment until all the results are in.

## Biodynamics in the New World

For a Chilean winery, Viñedos Organicos Emiliana (VOE) is unusual. It is dedicated to producing environmentally responsible wines using Biodynamics. The man at the helm of the project, which started in 2000 with the backing of parent company Viña Santa Emiliana, is Alvaro Espinoza, formerly winemaker with Viña Carmen. Espinoza is a true pioneer, and has been single-handedly responsible for introducing Biodynamic viticulture into South America. Santa Emiliana selected three farms in the regions of Maipo, Casablanca, and Colchagua, totalling a substantial 240 hectares, to form the basis of this project, so it is a serious commercial operation and not just a token green-friendly PR gesture. I met with Espinoza to hear about this, listen to his views on Biodynamics, and taste the wines.

It's clear from the outset that Alvaro Espinoza isn't your average Chilean winemaker. "Traditional viticulture artificializes the vineyards, creating an artificial medium," he says. "The result is that the wines are similar to those from other places." His view is very much that organics and Biodynamics facilitate the expression of terroir (*see* page 25), which isn't a word you hear very often in Chile. He also eschews the besetting varietalism that has become an enduring facet of New World winemaking. "I am not aiming to make another Cabernet Sauvignon from Chile," he states. "Blending can add character; that is why we are planting a whole range of varieties." This sounds promising.

So what is the story behind VOE? One of the owners of Santa Emiliana was interested in integrated pest management (IPM), a scientific approach to reducing chemical inputs by targeting interventions just where they are needed (*see* page 60). From here, they progressed to organics in 1998, when plots from three farms were selected as an experiment. Then, in 2000, Espinoza was hired to be responsible for this project. He had previously worked for eight years at Carmen, and first became interested in organic viticulture in the mid-1990s through links with Fetzer, a Californian winery which pioneered organics in the USA. Espinoza decided that conventional viticulture had some severe limitations. "I'd lost my idealism and my connection with the vineyards," he explains. During 1995 he had lots of contact with Fetzer and its offshoot Bonterra team, and started to do some work with Carmen later that year, putting some of its Maipo plots into organics.

In 1998, Alvaro had a sabbatical that proved to be very significant; he went to Mendocino in California and spent six months working on viticulture with the Mexican vineyard workers at Bonterra. While he was there, he had lots of contact with the Fetzers and Alan York, a well-known Californian Biodynamic consultant. Alan York gave him Rudolf Steiner's book, which he says "changed my views about nature". Steiner's views seemed "very logical", and Espinoza's return to Chile, with its environmentally unfriendly industrial-scale viticulture, proved an immense shock.

He left Carmen in 2000 to work for VOE. At VOE, the three Biodynamic farms are being treated as closed units of production. There are three main pillars to the vineyard work, which embrace IPM techniques in addition to Biodynamics. Firstly, they aim to increase the biodiversity of the farms with cover cropping and biological corridors. "Monoculture helps to develop pests," says Espinoza. Secondly, there is composting: adding fertility to the soil and preserving healthy plants with natural nutrients. Finally, there is alternative pest-management work, which involves compost teas and biological products such as *Bacillus subtilis* and *Trichoderma* (a fungus that has anti-botrytis and anti-oïdium action). Espinoza is leaving an increasing amount of flowers in the vineyards to encourage insects.

The move to Biodynamics has proven to be a complicated process. "In 2000, we started to be in contact with Demeter," Espinoza says. In Chile, there is no Biodynamic association, so Espinoza has had to make all the Biodynamic preparations himself – a challenging task. Initially, he had a problem getting yarrow, which isn't native to the wine-growing regions of Chile. More complicated was getting red deer bladders, which are used to ferment some preparations; there aren't any red deer in Chile. "Now we have enough to sell to others," he says. "For me, the main view is the sustainable view of the farm – seeing it as an organism." With this goal in mind, Espinoza is bringing animals to the farms to close the cycle

**RIGHT** Viñedos Organicos Emiliana's Biodynamic Los Robles vineyard in Chile.
*Photo courtesy of VOE Vintage Roots Ltd*

of nutrients so that he can produce his own manure and compost. Recycling is important, and for their cover crops, VOE collects the seed and re-uses it.

## Certifying bodies

One of the complexities of producing a list of Biodynamic producers is that, similarly to organized religions, there are many flavours or streams of Biodynamics. Added to this, many growers take a "pick-and-mix" attitude, implementing some aspects of mainstream Biodynamics but omitting others. For wine-growers in Europe, there are two main certifying bodies: Demeter and Biodyvin. Demeter is the larger of the two and covers all forms of agriculture, with a rigorous set of hoops for growers to jump through. Biodyvin is a newer organization set up especially for wine-growers, with its own rules; Olivier Humbrecht is the current president. Some practitioners prefer not to belong to any certifying body. One such unofficial Biodynamicist is Dominique Lafon. "For me, Biodynamics is a tool," he says. He regards Biodyvin with some scepticism, as a "machine to promote Biodynamics in a commercial way".

## Bringing together Biodynamics and science

By now you will probably have some idea about the nature of Biodynamics. You'll probably also be surprised that I'd want to make any attempt to bring Biodynamics and science together; surely they are using such a different language and stem from such different fundamental world views that there simply isn't a way for scientists to begin to enter into a dialogue with Biodynamic practitioners. But I think there is – if we are prepared to strip Biodynamics down into its component parts and then consider or test the efficacy of its various aspects.

Michel Chapoutier, in France's Rhône Valley, began farming Biodynamically in 1991. All 250 hectares of Chapoutier's Rhône vineyards are now farmed this way, making him the largest Biodynamic wine-grower in France by some distance. Unlike many practitioners, he thinks that understanding the science behind Biodynamics is important. "Biodynamic culture has an interesting future if we have an open attitude to fundamental science," he says. Chapoutier suggests that, unless the observations of the effects of Biodynamics are underpinned by a theoretical scientific understanding, Biodynamics is in danger of becoming a sect. To this end, he is keen to uncover the scientific explanations behind the various treatments. "Steiner had the genius of finding a great idea," he explains, "but he is considered so highly that people think he got everything right, even the details. People like Steiner are good with big ideas, but not so good with the details."

Certainly, a scientific underpinning to Biodynamics would aid its acceptance by people currently deterred by its rather esoteric, cultish image. This, however, would probably be seen as undesirable by many practitioners of Biodynamics; to them, conventional science only offers a limited perspective on the natural world. However, scientific respectability could improve the take-up of Biodynamics dramatically.

Rigorous research on Biodynamics faces a number of obstacles, though. Firstly, because Biodynamics sees the whole farm as a single "organism", the idea of separate, adjacent plots being farmed by different methods in a trial-type scenario doesn't really fit. A second difficulty is persuading research-funding agencies to pay for these studies. Professor John Reganold, a scientist at the Washington State University (Pullman) and one of the leading authorities on

"Proper studies have been carried out, and generally they seem to suggest that Biodynamics (or at least part of the system) really does work. In 1993, Reganold and colleagues compared the performance of Biodynamic and conventional farms in New Zealand, and published their report in the leading scientific journal *Science*. They found that the Biodynamic farms had significantly higher soil quality, with more organic matter content and microbial activity."

| A selected list of Biodynamic producers | |
| --- | --- |
| Country | Producer |
| FRANCE<br>Burgundy | Domaines de Comtes Lafon, Leflaive, Leroy, Pierre Morey, Domaine de la Romanée-Conti (in part), Trapet |
| Alsace | Marcel Deiss, Pierre Frick, Kreydenweiss, Ostertag, Weinbach, Zind-Humbrecht |
| Loire | Clos Roche Blanche (Touraine), Coulée de Serrant (Savennières), Huët (Vouvray) |
| Champagne | Jean-Pierre Fleury, Leclapart, Jacques Selosse |
| Bordeaux | Falfas (Côtes du Bourg), La Tour-Figeac (St-Emilion) |
| Rhône | Chapoutier, Marcoux |
| Provence | Domaine Sainte-Anne (Bandol) |
| ITALY | Nuova Cappellata (Piedmont), Trinchero (Piedmont) |
| CHILE | Antiyal |
| USA | Ceago, Frey |
| AUSTRALIA | Robinvale |
| NEW ZEALAND | Millton (Gisborne) |

organic agriculture, told me that some of his research proposals have been vetoed by funding agencies because they have contained the word "Biodynamics". "Many scientists won't even look at Biodynamics," he reports.

Despite these problems, proper studies have been carried out, and generally they seem to suggest that Biodynamics (or at least part of the system) really does work. In 1993, Reganold and colleagues compared the performance of Biodynamic and conventional farms in New Zealand, and published their report in the leading scientific journal *Science*. They found that the Biodynamic farms had significantly higher soil quality, with more organic matter content and microbial activity. Then, in 1995, Reganold published a review of the different studies that have examined Biodynamics and have met basic standards for scientific credibility. The conclusion was that Biodynamic systems had better soil quality, lower crop yields, and equal or greater net returns per hectare than their conventional counterparts. But what could the mechanism be? A tantalizing clue is offered by some experiments carried out by a graduate student of Reganold's, Lynne Carpenter-Boggs, on the effects of Biodynamic preparations on compost development. In an experimental setting, Biodynamically treated composts showed higher temperatures, faster maturation, and more nitrate than composts that had received a placebo inoculation. Reganold is clearly impressed. "Of all the farm systems that I've seen, Biodynamics is probably the most holistic," he admits.

In May 2002, the results of a twenty-one-year study comparing organic and Biodynamic farming with conventional agriculture were published, also in *Science*. A group of Swiss researchers, led by Paul Mäder of the Research Institute of Organic Agriculture, showed that while Biodynamic farming resulted in slightly lower yields, it outperformed conventional and organic systems in almost every other case. The Biodynamic plots showed higher biodiversity and more soil microbes, and more efficient resource utilization by this microbial community.

More recently, Reganold published the results of a long-term, replicated

## The different Biodynamic preparations

| Preparation* | Contents | Mode of application |
|---|---|---|
| 500 | Cow manure fermented in a cow horn, which is then buried and overwinters in the soil | Sprayed on the soil typically at a rate of 60g/ha in 34 litres of water |
| 501 | Ground quartz (silica) mixed with rainwater and packed in a cow horn, buried in spring, then dug up in autumn | Sprayed on the crop plants |
| 502 | Flower heads of yarrow fermented in a stag's bladder | Applied to compost along with preparations 503–507. Together these control the breakdown of the manures and compost, helping to make trace elements more available to the plant |
| 503 | Flower heads of camomile fermented in the soil | Applied to compost |
| 504 | Stinging nettle tea | Applied to compost. Nettle tea is also sometimes sprayed on weak or low-vigour vines |
| 505 | Oak bark fermented in the skull of a domestic animal | Applied to compost |
| 506 | Flower heads of dandelion fermented in cow mesentery | Applied to compost |
| 507 | Juice from valerian flowers | Applied to compost |
| 508 | Tea prepared from horsetail plant (*Equisetum*) | Used as a spray to counter fungal diseases |

"We can tentatively conclude that Biodynamics seems to work when tested scientifically, albeit not as dramatically as many would claim. But this is a qualified endorsement; we still don't know exactly which elements of the Biodynamic system are contributing the efficacy."

study on a 4.9-hectare Merlot vineyard near Ukiah, California. Beginning in 1996, the vineyard was split into eight management blocks, and these blocks were randomized to either Biodynamic or organic farming. The goal of this study was to see whether Biodynamics had any efficacy beyond conventional organics. All management practices were the same except for the additions of the Biodynamic preparations. No differences were seen in soil quality over the first six years, and no change was seen in a range of other measures, including nutrient analysis of leaf tissues, cluster weight, berry size, and yield per vine. However, there were some differences. Ratios of yield-to-pruning weight in years 2001–03 indicated that the Biodynamic vines had ideal balance, while the control vines were slightly overcropped. Biodynamically treated wine grapes had significantly higher tannins in 2002, and higher (but not significantly so) tannins, phenols, and anthocyanins in 2003. Not a dramatic improvement over organics, by any means, although this is just one study in one vineyard area; the results might have been different in a region where a different set of environmental pressures exist in the vineyard.

Aside from these reports published in mainstream scientific literature, several practitioners of Biodynamics have also tried to test its effectiveness in a scientific way, although the experiments have frequently lacked the rigour to be convincing. The question remains: if these studies have been carried out carefully enough, why weren't they submitted to proper journals to undergo the peer-review process? This would have added greatly to their credibility.

So, we can tentatively conclude that Biodynamics seems to work when tested scientifically, albeit not as dramatically as many would claim. But this is a qualified endorsement; we still don't know exactly which elements of the Biodynamic system are contributing the efficacy, and because it works to a degree, this doesn't lend validity to the mechanistic assumptions of practitioners. From a scientific perspective, some elements associated with Biodynamics, such as the use of specially prepared composts, are much more likely to have benefit than others. Composting could increase microbial diversity, and some of the foliar sprays could have a scientifically explicable effect; they are likely to possess biological activity. I doubt that dynamization of preparations has any benefit, and like many scientists I'm sceptical about the use of serial homeopathic dilutions, which would probably only serve to reduce efficacy. Practices that go along with Biodynamics, such as allowing limited weed growth, could have benefits in terms of creating competition to keep vegetative growth in check, or attracting beneficial predators of vine pests. There's likely also a large placebo element; as wine-growers adopt Biodynamics, they are entering into a philosophical system that acts as a framework to help them maintain a careful approach in the vineyard.

Despite the odd and seemingly anti-science nature of some of its practices, Biodynamics certainly merits further scientific study. By and large, wine-growers operating within this rather unusual philosophical framework are making interesting, personality-filled wines: something the world desperately needs more of. And the limited scientific studies that have so far addressed Biodynamics have come down in its favour. Yet it's an open question as to exactly how Biodynamics has its effects, and by extension it is therefore unclear which elements of its theory need to be adopted by *vignerons* in order for them to accrue any benefits. This is something that could be tested. Where the difficulty remains is that while much of Biodynamic practice is so esoteric and has such a "pseudoscience" ring to it, mainstream scientists are afraid to be associated with it, and they would find it very difficult to get adequate funding to do the research that is needed.

# 9 PRD and regulated deficit irrigation

Partial root drying (PRD) is a brilliant idea: a good example of a concept developed in the laboratory and then applied to real-world agriculture. While the credit for the hard work spent developing PRD in the field must go to Australian viticulturalists, the theory underpinning this practice is largely British. It would be fair to say that the UK hasn't made many significant contributions to viticulture, but the concept of PRD – now one of the buzz subjects in wine science – was devised in laboratory experiments carried out at the University of Lancaster in the late 1980s. Initially, this work had nothing to do with grape vines. According to Lancaster's Dr. Mark Bacon, the research was "purely for the academic pursuit of understanding how plants communicate information regarding the soil-water status from the roots to the shoots". The chief focus of these studies was the plant hormone abscisic acid (ABA), and we'll need to understand a bit about ABA if we're going to appreciate how PRD works. It's actually a really interesting story.

## ABA

ABA is one of a group of chemicals known as plant hormones, or, in some circles, as plant-growth regulators. The core members of this group are auxin (first discovered back in the 1920s), cytokinin, gibberellin, ethylene (unusual, because it's a gas), and ABA. Other molecules, such as brassinosteroids, have made recent bids to be admitted to the hormone club, but we'll ignore those for now. These hormones are responsible for coordinating plant growth by acting as signalling molecules. Sent from one part of the plant to another, they give each cell instructions on how to behave and grow. An obvious example of this signalling is what happens if you prune a rose bush, fruit tree or vine; by cutting off the growing tip, the loss of the hormone signalling from this tip causes dormant lateral shoots to become active, and they grow out. Until fairly recently, researchers used to ascribe one or more functions to each hormone, but now it is becoming clear that hormone signalling pathways aren't arranged in a linear fashion but in a complex network of interactions, dubbed hormone "cross-talk". This makes it complex to unravel the precise roles of each, but recent progress in molecular genetics is proving extremely helpful in spurring this field on.

What do we need to know about ABA? It is actually a bit of a "negative hormone", meaning it usually pops up when things are going wrong. In particular, when plants are stressed, the first thing they do is make ABA. One of the most threatening stresses affecting plants is drought. During conditions of water stress, ABA is synthesized by the roots – the first bit of the plant to experience the drought – and sent to the shoots and leaves. This alerts the aerial bits of the plant to the fact that hard times are on the way, and they stop growing and close the small pores, called stomata, in the leaves. Stomata are important; while they allow in the gases needed for photosynthesis, they also leak out precious water vapour. As a result, the plant makes a calculation – if things are too hot and dry, it will simply close stomata, shut up shop and stop growing, because the risk of water loss then outweighs any benefit from continuing to grow. Even though vines are adapted to warm climates, in very hot summers they'll stop growth at the warmest times of day – as occurred widely in the European summer heatwave of 2003 – retarding development. The French term for this heat-induced shut-down is *blocage*. Paradoxically, therefore, periods of extreme high temperatures during the growing season can actually slow vine development, because photosynthesis has to stop.

Researchers were keen to show that it is the roots that are producing these drought signals, and not the shoot itself responding to water stress, and also that ABA is the chief hormone involved. They set about this in two ways. First, they showed that shoots stop growing before the development of decreased water potentials in the aerial parts of the plant. Thus a long-distance signal, rather than reduced shoot-water availability, is mediating this response. Secondly, they used what is known as a "split-pot system". In this elegant work, the root system of a single plant was divided and put into two separate pots. The scientists showed that by watering one pot and letting the other dry out, shoot growth was stunted, even though the plant – in this case a young apple tree – actually had enough water. This simple manipulation showed that the plant had been tricked into thinking it was stressed. Removal of the roots in contact with the dry soil also removed the growth inhibition, confirming that this signal was indeed coming from the water-stressed root system. Further research has identified ABA as the chief culprit in this root-to-shoot signalling, although it doesn't act alone. "Cytokinins, ethylene, and ABA have all been shown to play a role," says Bacon.

Although this split-pot system was initially just an experimental tool to prove a theory, it didn't take long for others to realize its potential commercial usefulness. However, as someone who grew up watching the UK science show *Tomorrow's World* in the 1970s and early 1980s, I'm aware of the gulf between clever inventions and things that are actually useful or feasible in practice. With PRD, this translation between lab and field is where the real work is being done.

**RIGHT** A diagram illustrating the principles of PRD.

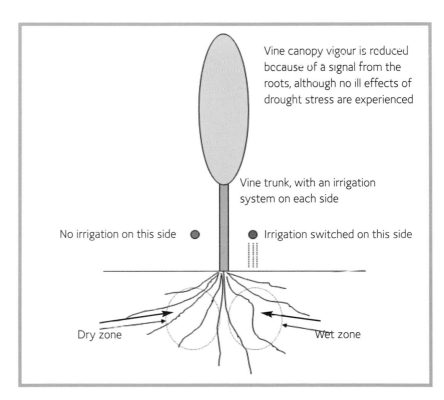

Vine canopy vigour is reduced because of a signal from the roots, although no ill effects of drought stress are experienced

Vine trunk, with an irrigation system on each side

No irrigation on this side

Irrigation switched on this side

Dry zone

Wet zone

While the theory underlying PRD was devised by Brits, it took an Australian to apply it to grape vines. The Aussie in question was Brian Loveys, who coined the term PRD and put in a mammoth amount of developmental work to make this idea practical in the vineyard. The potential benefits are clear. Grape vines, like many other plants, will choose to put their efforts into vegetative growth (making shoots and leaves) when conditions are benign. Give a grape vine plenty of water and nutrients, and it will happily produce luxuriant foliage, but relatively poor-quality grapes. Stress, on the other hand, encourages vines to invest in the future and concentrate their energies on fruit growth. The problem is, stress the vine too much and although fruit growth is the preferred option, the quality of this fruit will be compromised, and the vine might even die. Good vineyards – those producing the highest-quality fruit – tend to be those which allow the vine just enough water at the right time in the growing season. Grape-vine vigour is the enemy of wine quality.

Along these lines, an influential research study was carried out in the 1980s by French researcher Gérard Seguin. He conducted a survey of the properties of the soils in the Bordeaux region, and concluded that it was the drainage properties of the soil affecting the availability of water that mattered most. The soil's physical properties regulating the water supply to the vine are all-important in determining wine quality. Seguin maintained that the best terroirs are those where the soils are free-draining, with a water table that is high enough to ensure a regular supply of water to the vine roots, but which then recedes a good deal on *veraison* (when the berries change colour) so that vegetative growth stops and the vine concentrates its energies on fruit-ripening. Of course, if you are not blessed with such a terroir, then there's not much you can do about it. But what you can do is to try to implement viticultural interventions that aim to make your terroir as favourable as possible. And if you are irrigating, then you have some degree of control over water availability, which, according to Seguin, is probably the key vineyard factor influencing wine quality.

**BELOW** Vertically shoot-positioned vine with drip irrigation, in Portugal's Dão region. This sort of irrigation system can be used for RDI (*see* page 81), but for PRD two irrigation systems are needed, one on each side of the trellis.

# Regulated deficit irrigation (RDI)

One technique that has attempted to replicate the change in the vine's water supply is called regulated deficit irrigation (RDI). It sounds simple enough in theory: just reduce or cut irrigation at the right point and you get an increase in fruit quality. It's an artificial attempt to replicate the ideal conditions identified by Seguin for high-quality grape production.

In practice, it's more complex. You need to know exactly how much water deficit the vines are experiencing or things can go wrong. The benefit of this technique is that it is relatively simple to apply; it can be used in any irrigated vineyard and without the need for expensive modifications. Experience with RDI has shown that it works best if the water supply is cut just after flowering and berry set, but then restored at *veraison*. In some ways, this seems a little at odds with the results of Seguin's study; perhaps this has something to do with the climate differences between Atlantic-influenced Bordeaux and hot areas where irrigation is typically practised.

RDI has been particularly successful in Australia. According to Dr. Michael McCarthy, one of the pioneers of the technique, "RDI is probably the most rapidly adopted bit of new management that we have seen for a long time, starting with no industry awareness of it in the early 1990s to something like fifty per cent adoption now in irrigated vineyards in Australia."

## Partial root drying

PRD is more complicated than regulated deficit irrigation (RDI; *see* above), but from a scientific perspective it is perhaps more elegant, and has the potential to be more effective. Because physical separation of a vine's root system isn't feasible in the vineyard, the split-root system is created by use of a dual-drip system that irrigates either side of the vine. The irrigation regime is then switched from one side to the other at intervals of seven to fourteen days. This allows the root system to dry out enough for it to signal to the shoot and leaf system that there's some water stress, but not enough for damage to occur. This switching also ensures repeated bursts of signalling from the root that help keep canopy growth restricted. The watered roots on one of the sides maintain an adequate supply to the vine so it can still function, but because of the root signalling, vigour is reduced, water use is decreased, and potentially the grape quality is enhanced.

The chief benefit of PRD is the reduced water use. "Most users of PRD would do so because of the documented improvement in water-use efficiency," says Brian Loveys of Australia's CSIRO (*see* page 35). This doesn't sound too glamorous, but in fact it's a critical issue because in vineyard areas where irrigation is practised, water is scarce, and is likely to prove a limiting factor for viticulture in hot climates. This is a situation that is likely to get worse in the future, with increasing competition for water resources and a predicted rise in global average temperatures (*see* page 40).

Whether or not PRD actually creates better wines is still controversial. "The question of wine quality is much more difficult," agrees Loveys. "Grape quality has so many different components, some of which are certainly altered by deficit irrigation methods." He has done some research, as yet unpublished, which shows that PRD changes the types of anthocyanins in red grapes, and that some flavour compounds, including trimethyldihydronaphthalene, β-damascenone, β-ionone, and are also influenced positively. Experimental wines made by his group from PRD-irrigated vines also show improved flavour characteristics.

Moving away from grapes for a moment, experiments by the UK's University of Lancaster group on tomatoes have demonstrated measurable positive effects of PRD methods. In these studies, PRD caused a significant reduction in vegetative mass of the tomato plants (leaves and shoots), but not the fruit. The tomatoes produced were smaller, but twenty-one per cent more concentrated as determined by total soluble solid measurements. A commercial

"The concept of chemical isolation of the fruit – that the root signal doesn't actually reach the fruit – is potentially a good explanation for why the grapes carry on developing normally, even though shoot growth has largely stopped"

taste-test panel expressed a marginal preference for the PRD-grown fruit, describing them as "sweeter", "riper", "more tangy", and "less bitter". The most impressive statistic was that the water use efficiency (WUE) was increased by ninety-three per cent during the ripening period.

## Mechanisms

So how does PRD operate? Its physiological basis is still being worked out. As already mentioned, ABA seems to have a key role, by travelling from the roots to the shoots and telling them to stop growing. But why does ABA reduce shoot growth and not fruit growth? "PRD may have some effect on fruit growth, but in wine grapes, even though they may be smaller, the overall effect on yield is minimal, or not apparent," explains Mark Bacon. "There is some feeling that fruit may be relatively isolated from the vegetative part of the plant, in respect of xylem connections and function." As explained on page 15, the xylem is part of the conduction system of the plant, transmitting water and various solutes from the roots to the shoots. The other component of this system is the phloem, which conducts nutrients such as the sugars produced by photosynthesis. "After *veraison*, all water to the fruit is provided by the phloem, not the xylem," continues Bacon. "As signals like ABA travel in the xylem, the hypothesis goes that signal transport to fruit is much reduced." He adds that this will require a lot more work to unravel in detail, but the concept of chemical isolation of the fruit – that the root signal doesn't actually reach the fruit – is potentially a good explanation for why the grapes carry on developing normally, even though shoot growth has largely stopped.

A second mechanism for improved fruit quality is that PRD may alter the way a plant distributes its nutrient resources. One of the important physiological

**BELOW** Spray irrigation in the Constantia region of South Africa, here occurring late in the growing season in February.

processes in plants is how carbohydrates, produced by photosynthesis in the leaves, are partitioned to various parts of the plant, a topic which is known as source-sink relationships. Under normal irrigation conditions, when there is a steady supply of water, the actively growing shoots act as what is called a "sink", taking more of the carbohydrates than the fruit. There is some evidence that the reduced growth of the shoot system means that its sink strength is reduced, so that more of the resources are then allocated to the fruit. In tomatoes, developing side shoots are the main competing sink for carbohydrates, and if their growth is curtailed then resources are likely to be redirected towards the fruit. That's why when you grow tomatoes it's a good idea to nip the side shoots out. The same probably applies for grape vines – the shoot stops growing and its strength as a sink is reduced relative to the still-developing grapes. This is also the proposed mechanism for the effectiveness of RDI (*see* page 81).

### The role of irrigation

Of course, PRD is only possible where irrigation is practised. You can't do it in areas that have significant growing season rainfall, or where irrigation is against the rules, so this excludes many of the classical European wine-growing regions. However, the theory behind it has been applied by Bart Arnst, viticulturalist at Seresin Estate, in unirrigated vineyards in New Zealand's Marlborough region. He has begun a system of alternate mowing between vine rows, such that one half of a vine's roots will face competition from the cover crop at a time. It's an interesting implementation of the PRD theory.

One further obstacle towards take-up of PRD exists: the requirement for a dual-irrigation system. "PRD is proving complex to implement on large vineyards because of the complexity of, in effect, running an extra irrigation system," reports Michael McCarthy. He is hoping that by using subsurface drip irrigation for RDI, he'll be able to achieve the same water savings as PRD but without the complexity of the dual-irrigation system. "I now prefer the terminology 'strategic irrigation management' to encompass both PRD and RDI," he says.

### PRD around the world

It's early days, but how far have these sorts of technologies spread? In Australia, "Most of the major wine companies would have tested or implemented PRD and/or RDI," says Brian Loveys. "We are also aware of fairly significant use of PRD in California, Spain, and South America."

From what has been shown so far, it does seem that these deficit irrigation strategies are an important new tool in viticulture. However, there are dissenting voices. "You should be aware that there is a school of thought, coming mostly from the USA, that there are no benefits of PRD over and above those achievable through other techniques that reduce irrigation amounts relative to what has become industry practice," reports Loveys. "This is not surprising, as all these techniques rely on the stimulation of the same natural stress-response mechanisms of the plant. We believe that PRD offers a safer and more reliable way of achieving the desired result of improved water use efficiency."

Of course, it may well be that PRD will yield improved grape quality as well as improved water-use efficiency. "In any event," Loveys concludes, "what the debate has done is show that it is often possible to grow a commercial crop of grapes with considerably less water than would have been considered necessary a decade ago." It's not the most glamorous of conclusions, but perhaps, considering the growing urgency of efficient water use, it's the most important one.

# 10 Pruning, trellising systems, and canopy management

The grape vine is a bit of a freeloader. It has adopted a growth strategy where it can't be bothered to support itself and relies on others instead. If you like, it's the benefit cheat of the plant world. In nature, plants are in competition for two sets of resources: those from the earth and those from the sky. In most environments the latter is the key one – the struggle for enough light to drive photosynthesis and hence food production. Trees often win this battle by getting their leaves ten metres (thirty-plus feet) or more from the ground, but to do this they have to spend years slowly building a woody trunk with enough mechanical strength to support this elevated growth habit. Grape vines, like other climbers, have seized the opportunity to make the most of this third-party effort; they realized that, by climbing, they could save themselves the bother of a self-supporting stem. Not having to develop supporting girth permits rapid growth, so grape vines are experts at growing up other plants until they break through to uncompeted-for light on the outside of the canopy of their hosts.

The growth habit of the vine is finely tuned to this lifestyle. Shoot structure is simple, with each node having the capacity to produce tendrils or flower buds opposite each leaf. Gripping to the host plant via these tendrils, the shoots grow rapidly towards the light, seeking the gaps in the canopy. Where the vine breaks through to sunlight, tendrils are discarded in favour of flowers, resulting in fruit production. At the other end of the vine, the roots are capable of growing deeply, eking out water and mineral resources in competition with the pre-existing root system of the host plant. The science of viticulture attempts to manipulate vines to get them to produce good yields of high-quality fruit. It takes into account the natural growth habit of the vine and tweaks it to suit the context of the vineyard. Because vines are climbers, this usually involves some means of support for the freeloading vine to grown on. It's an area where good controlled scientific experiments are rare, in part because of the immense difficulty in doing them. The way vineyards look today is a reflection of tradition, trial and error, guesswork, specific environmental constraints, and convenience. As a result, vineyards across the world's wine-growing regions differ markedly in their appearance. This chapter sets out to discuss some of the scientific considerations that shape the way that vines are pruned, trellised, and managed.

## Viticultural goals
The holy grail of viticulture is to get high yields of high-quality grapes with minimum cost in terms of vineyard labour and inputs. Invariably, a compromise is involved – sometimes yield must be sacrificed for quality; sometimes it's the other way round. Good viticulture also takes into account the economic objectives of the wine that's going to be made from the crop. Vineyards are managed to produce grapes of appropriate quality and at the right yield, for the right cost.

**TOP LEFT** Spur-pruned bilateral cordon de Royat just after pruning, in France's Southern Rhône. *Figure courtesy of Château La Borie*

**TOP RIGHT** A similarly pruned cordon de Royat vine early in the growing season, from Portugal's Dão region.

**BOTTOM LEFT** Individually staked, cane-pruned vine in Germany's Mosel-Saar-Ruwer at harvest time. Canes are bent over in an arch and tied to the stake in a *Doppelbogen* arrangement (*see* page 91).
*Photo courtesy of Peter Ruhberg, www.winepage.de*

**BOTTOM RIGHT** Individually staked vines are also common in France's Northern Rhône region. This example is from Cornas.

When starting a vineyard from scratch, several key choices need to be made. These include choosing the appropriate variety, vine spacing, trellising method, and making decisions about irrigation, pruning, and canopy management. Making the right choice is important, because the vines will have a productive life span of twenty years or more. This sort of time-scale makes innovation based on experimentation tricky, so in already established vineyard areas people frequently copy the vineyard style of their neighbours. Often viticulturalists have to work within the confines of vineyards that have already been planted, in which case there is limited room for modification. The following sections give a brief overview of some of the scientific principles behind trellising systems, pruning, and canopy-management decisions, and how these all affect wine quality.

Current viticultural thinking is that the control of vine vigour and fruit-zone light exposure is the key to successful vineyard management. Vigour is an

TOP LEFT Young vines trained on a high vertical shoot positioned (VSP) trellis (*see* page 89) in Portugal's Dão region.

TOP RIGHT Vines on a high VSP trellis in the Pic St-Loup region of France's Languedoc.

BOTTOM LEFT Cane-pruned vines on a Scott Henry split-canopy trellising system. The two upper canes provide the upward-growing shoots while the lower cane shoots are trained downwards by movable supporting wires.

BOTTOM RIGHT The same vineyard midway through the growing season, showing the downward and upward growing canopy.

important element of viticulture. If the vine is growing actively all through the season, developing a huge, dense canopy, then the actively growing shoots will represent a powerful sink for the vine's resources that will inhibit the sugar accumulation that normally occurs during the fruit-ripening phase. The immediate result is delayed fruit development and reduced quality, but also of importance is the effect of the profuse canopy in shading the inside-growing shoots. This is because light is of crucial importance for bud fertility. In the fertile regions of the shoots (next year's canes), grape vines have uncommitted bud primordia that can form either tendrils or flowers, and because the development of these buds takes two seasons, it is the light that the fruiting canes received in the preceding season that determines their fertility in the current year. This is understandable, and makes sense for a grape vine in the wild, where it will be growing on trees; it only wants to make fruit where the shoots poke out through

TOP LEFT Gobelet (bush) vines in Châteauneuf-du-Pape, France.

TOP RIGHT An ancient vine from a Barossa vineyard in Australia, planted on its roots in 1843. This vine at Langmeil is still productive and is currently pruned to canes (or "rods"), with renewal spurs.

BOTTOM LEFT Vines in the Barossa displaying a permanent cordon pruned to two-bud spurs.

BOTTOM RIGHT A mechanically pruned ("bushed") vine in the Clare Valley, Australia. The blades leave numerous short spurs on the permanent cordons.

the host canopy into the light. In addition, shaded grapes may maintain high levels of vegetal-tasting methoxypryazines, which are undesirable in most wines and are dissipated through light exposure. In support of these ideas, precision-viticulture studies have emphasized that, in many wine regions, the areas of vineyards that produce the highest-quality grapes are those with the lowest vigour. Shaded canopies have another drawback: they increase the risk of disease.

Another key to successful viticulture is getting grape flavour development (known as phenolic or physiological maturity) to coincide with sugar maturity. In warmer regions, the risk is that by the time the grapes have reached flavour maturity, the sugar levels are very high, resulting in overly alcoholic wines. This is a major problem in many New World wine regions. In cooler areas, flavour maturity occurs at much lower sugar levels, and the challenge is getting enough sugar maturity before the fruit loses its photosynthetic capability or autumn rains set in.

With trellising systems and canopy management there is no one-size-fits-all solution. Viticultural methods have to be adapted to local conditions, and while the general principles remain the same, factors such as soil fertility, climate, water availability, grape variety, and skill and availability of vineyard workers should be taken into account in the consideration of the most suitable management choices.

### Pruning

Pruning is an intervention that aims to improve vine fertility, encourage optimum canopy development, and regulate crop load in line with the quality objectives of the grower. Pruning can seem a little complex for those unfamiliar with it, so here is my attempt to present a digestible introduction. There are two different styles of pruning, both widely used: spur pruning and cane pruning.

Cane pruning involves selecting one or two (rarely more) shoots from the previous season's growth and cutting them back to between, say, six and fifteen buds. These then form the basis for the following year's growth when they are tied down horizontally. A renewal spur is also left for generating new canes. Typically, with cane-pruned vines, the only permanent vine growth is a vertical trunk. The actual practice of cane pruning is more challenging than spur pruning and is usually employed with varieties that have low fruitfulness in basal buds, and

| Some common viticultural terms | |
|---|---|
| **Term** | **Definition** |
| Basal leaf removal | This is done to expose the fruiting zone, allowing access to light and disease-preventing air circulation. |
| Cane | The shoot of a grape vine that is one season old and has become woody, and which can either be cut back to spurs (up to four buds) or canes (typically six to fifteen buds) for the following season's growth. Canes are also sometimes called "rods" although in may cases "rod refers to a shoot intermediate in length between a cane and a spur". |
| Cordon | The woody framework of the vine extending from the top of the trunk. A cordon-trained vine has a trunk terminating in one or more cordons, which are then spur pruned. |
| Head training | Where the head of the trunk is pruned to either spurs (gobelet system) or canes (e.g. guyot). |
| Hedging | Also known as shoot tipping, this involves cutting back excessive growth at the top and sides of the canopy midway through the growing season. The aim is to leave enough leaves to ripen the fruit, while preventing excess growth that will lead to shading and competition for resources with the fruit. A balanced vine will typically have two fruit clusters and fifteen leaf nodes on each shoot. |
| Shoot | Green growth arising from a bud. |
| Spur | A short cane cut back to between one and four buds to provide the following season's shoots. |
| Trunk | The main, permanent vertical growth of the vine which supports the canes or cordons. |

where the vineyard workers are up to the task. Results can be very good. It's ideal for cooler climates and certain varieties where basal buds have low fruitfulness.

Spur pruning involves cutting the previous season's growth back fairly drastically to just a few (up to five, but more normally two or three) buds. These will be borne on a more substantial permanent vine structure, usually consisting of a trunk plus horizontal cordons. Spur pruning is technically much simpler and requires less skill on behalf of vineyard workers. It can be part mechanized by using mechanical pre-pruning (sometimes called "bushing") that may then be tidied up by hand.

Minimal or mechanical pruning is a relatively recent development. This involves no real pruning – just cutting the vine's growth back rather crudely using mechanical means. It makes a bit of a mess of the vineyard, but proponents claim that after a couple of years the vine gets into balance and produces good yields, with small bunches of grapes all over the canopy, rather than clustered in a fruiting zone. This is therefore only compatible with mechanical harvesting. It is used in situations where manual vineyard labour isn't practical or economically feasible, and only really works in warm climates. A variation on the theme is mechanical cutting back of vine growth, which is then tidied up by vineyard workers manually. This is evidently only going to work for spur-pruned vines.

## Trellising and canopy management

There is a confusing array of different trellising styles, some traditional artifacts, no doubt, but others each with their own advantages in specific situations. Trellis systems are a vital part of the canopy-management tool kit.

Canopy-management techniques are aimed at achieving optimum leaf and fruit exposure to sun, while reducing the risk of disease, and pushing the quality-to-yield ratio as far as possible. Open canopies help prevent disease in two ways: they allow better spray penetration and also better air circulation, with faster drying out times. Canopy-management strategies aim to get the vine into some sort of balance, and they have been particularly successful in situations of high-vine vigour, often caused by fertile soils and irrigation. The modern canopy-management techniques that involve, for example, split-canopy trellising systems such as the Smart-Dyson, are not, however, of much value in low-vigour sites such as the major vineyard areas in the classic Old World regions.

Viticulturalist Richard Smart's work has been particularly influential in this area. He dubs the traditional canopy-adjustment techniques of trimming, shoot thinning, and leaf removal in the fruit zone as "band-aid viticulture", because they are interventions that have to be reapplied annually. His solution is to alter the trellising technique to increase canopy surface area and decrease canopy density: a once-only intervention. In particular, the use of high vertical shoot positioning (VSP) systems and divided canopies (such as the Smart-Dyson and Scott Henry trellising systems) have been effective means of getting highly vigorous vines into balance. The basis of this work is to manage the vine vigour, achieving optimum leaf-to-fruit ratio. Smart considers this to be as important a consideration as the traditional vineyard currency of yield.

I asked viticultural consultant David Booth, who currently works in Portugal, about his views on canopy management. "I think it is probably one of the most important tools we have," he responded. "But I do have a very broad definition, much more than just putting up technically advanced trellis systems. My definition encompasses a range of vineyard management practices, including winter pruning, shoot thinning, shoot positioning, leaf thinning, and hedging.

The skilled viticulturalist should be able to look at the soil profile (pre-planting) at any particular site and anticipate future vine vigour. Then he or she can make a series of decisions about trellis system, spacing, and rootstock. A high VSP is probably the easiest to manage and I reckon this should be the natural first choice. The more advanced trellis systems are for when the anticipated vine vigour is so high that you have doubts about your ability to accommodate the growth within the VSP, or several years after planting, you realize you have blown it and underestimated vine vigour and need to modify the existing trellis. My first choice for divided-canopy systems is Smart-Dyson, since it is easy to manage, does not require wide rows, and is easy to machine-harvest."

Booth adds, "A key factor to think about in canopy light environment is not just sunlight striking bunches, but also leaves shading other bunches, which has negative implications for wine quality for reasons that are not understood, but probably have a lot to do with potassium balance."

### The dogmatic approaches

There are two dogmas in viticulture that are worth addressing here. One is that reduced yield equals higher grape quality (and vice versa); the other that old vines produce better wines. The scientific basis behind each of these assertions is not entirely clear. Evidently, it is possible to lower grape quality by means of excessive yields. And in classic Old World regions, which are typically low-vigour sites, reducing yields by pruning canes short does have the effect of raising quality, to a degree. But in higher-vigour, irrigated vineyards in warm regions, pruning short will not result in a vine that is in balance, and no quality gain is likely to be seen. In such high-vigour situations, moving to a split-canopy system often has the effect of bringing the vine into balance, raising yields and improving quality at the same time.

The second dogma is that old vines produce better wines. It is repeated so often that it is suspected there must be some truth in it. If it is indeed the case, what is the scientific explanation? One suggestion is that it has to do with the amount of overwintering perennial wood on the vine. Some researchers have noted that training systems with more perennial wood, and thus more carbohydrate storage area during the dormant period, produce better wines. Older vines tend to have more perennial wood, and this could be to their advantage. However, a more likely explanation is the one offered to me by David Booth. "Young vines are harder to manage because they are less buffered against any environmental stresses," he says. "But as you know, they can give great quality, probably because they are naturally low vigour (small root system) and have good leaf and bunch exposure. Old vines are also naturally low in vigour, due to wood disease and exhaustion of nutrients. I reckon the problem is more in the middle years, especially in high-vigour soils with inadequate trellising systems; then you get the classic shading problems."

I asked him whether it is possible to increase yield and maintain or even improve quality by viticultural interventions such as canopy management. "Sure," he replied, "but only really in the case that I have just mentioned of the middle-aged, vigorous vine on the high-capacity site. These sites are more common than you might think. Look for the small, yellowing leaves in the inside of the canopy as an indication of leaf shading. A full-on trellis conversion may be the solution, but I tend to work first with competitive cover crops, nutrition, irrigation management, leaf pulling, and shoot thinning. As you might have figured out by now, there is no silver bullet – just a raft of tools that often need to be used in conjunction."

"There are two dogmas in viticulture that are worth addressing here. One is that reduced yield equals higher grape quality (and vice versa); the other that old vines produce better wines. The scientific basis behind each of these assertions is not entirely clear."

## An explanation of different trellising systems

| Training system | Definition |
| --- | --- |
| Gobelet | An old technique and probably the simplest. Spurs are arranged around the head of a trunk or short arms coming from the top of the trunk. This is only really used in warm, dry climates in low-vigour situations. It doesn't need any support trellising, but shading of fruiting zones can be a problem. Popular in Mediterranean regions. Known in the New World as the bush vine (or head-trained in USA); in Italy it is called the *alberello*. |
| Guyot | One of the most popular cane-pruned systems, with a single or double cane layered horizontally from the head of a trunk. One or two renewal spurs are also left. Simple and effective. Particularly suited to Old World, low-vigour vineyards. |
| Cordon de Royat | Simple spur-pruned system, usually with a unilateral cordon spreading from a low trunk. Variations on the theme include a double cordon. Again, simple and effective. |
| Vertical shoot positioning (VSP) | Widely adopted system where the shoots are trained vertically upwards in summer, held in place by foliage wires. Leads to relatively tall canopies, and is suitable for mechanization. A good option for most sites. |
| Scott Henry | A split-canopy trellising system where the shoots are separated and divided into upwards and downwards growing systems, held in place by foliage wires. It is useful for high-vigour situations and is suitable for both spur and cane pruning. The advantage is lower disease pressure, improved grape quality, and higher yields. Looks like a wall of vines in practice, growing from the ground to two metres (6.5 feet) high. |
| Smart-Dyson | Developed by Richard Smart and John Dyson, this is a variant of the Scott Henry trellis, with curtains trained up and down from just one cordon. Popularized by the influential work of Smart, the world's foremost flying viticulturalist. |
| Doppelbogen | The "double bow" system for Riesling vines common in the Mosel-Saar-Ruwer region of Germany, where each vine is singly staked and two canes are bent round into a bow shape (*see* photograph, bottom left, page 85). Single-staked vines are also found in France's Northern Rhône. This sort of system is adapted for steep slopes where any other sort of trellising would be impractical. |
| Eventail | French term for "fan". A cordon system with a number of arms arising from a short trunk, each bearing a short cane. Popular in Chablis and also used in Champagne. |
| Geneva double curtain | A rather complicated split-canopy system, with cordons grown high on two parallel horizontal trellising wires, with the shoots bending down. A variation on this theme is the lyre system that is relatively common in Austria, but here the split canopies have upward-growing shoots, and angle outwards slightly. Both are hindered by the fact that they require wider rows and complicated trellising systems. |
| Tendone | Italian term for the arbour or pergola system common in parts of Italy (Veneto), Portugal (Vinho Verde), Argentina, and Chile. Vines are trained high off the ground on a series of wooden frames. They look pretty, and yields can be heroic, but fruit shading is a problem and quality suffers as a result. They are hard to work, too. Of all trellising systems, this replicates most closely the growth of the vine in the wild. |

# Section Two
# In the winery

# 11 Naturalness in wine: how much manipulation is acceptable?

Wine can be made naturally; it almost makes itself. At its most simple, the process of making wine involves harvesting grapes, sticking them into a vat, crushing them a bit, and letting them ferment. When fermentation is complete, separate the solid matter from the liquid and you have wine. But winemakers almost always add things to their wine. There are several reasons for this, some of them better than others, and this leads to a thorny question that's at the heart of many of the most passionate debates in winemaking circles: just how much manipulation is acceptable?

There's no simple answer to this question. It's a grey area and any attempt to prescribe permissible levels of manipulation is a line-drawing exercise. But just because it is difficult to make these sorts of distinctions doesn't mean that we shouldn't try to make them. Wine laws exist in virtually all wine-producing regions or countries which outline the type of manipulation that is acceptable and the type that is not. Some wine regulations are stricter than others. To get an understanding of the issues involved, let's consider four different positions and assess their strengths and weaknesses.

## 1. Add anything

Should a wine be judged purely on how it tastes? Is drinking wine just a sensory experience? Some people argue that this is, indeed, the case. If it is, then there are no real reasons to prohibit additives at all. The answer is in the glass, and if there are ways of making wine taste "better", then by rights they should be allowed. The weakness of this position is that it ignores the fact that wine is a discretionary purchase. Certainly, fine wine is something that people buy partly because it isn't manufactured – the grapes aren't just seen as the raw materials that act as a starting point in the manufacturing process. Grapes, as we have seen, have a connection to the soil as well as to individual vineyards. Part of the appeal of wine is that it is a natural product rich in culture, and its image will suffer if any kind of manipulation is allowed without scruples.

## 2. Add nothing

The idea of adding nothing at all to wine is an extreme position for one reason: sulphur dioxide. Sulphur dioxide ($SO_2$) is intrinsic to winemaking because it's hard to make good-quality wine without it. It plays a vital role as an antioxidant and also as a microbicide, preventing the growth of harmful bacteria and rogue yeasts at different stages – it is added during winemaking and at bottling. Some winemakers bravely attempt to make $SO_2$-free wines for the sake of naturalness or for health reasons, but it needs to be borne in mind that $SO_2$ is itself produced naturally during fermentation in non-negligible amounts anyway. *See* page 115 for a full discussion of this subject.

## 3. Add as little as possible

This is a laudable position for the reason mentioned earlier: that wine is perceived by consumers as a natural product, and this is part of its appeal. A sensible winemaking policy is only to add something if not adding it is going to compromise wine quality, and then only add as little as possible. It's tough to make good wine with no $SO_2$, but the effects of any additions can be maximized by smart use. Acid additions might be needed in warm climates. This raises a question about other sorts of wine manipulation.

For centuries, oak barrels have been used to make wine, and the use of them is uncontroversial partly because they are traditional. The use of new-oak barrels certainly would count as an additive manipulation because they contribute important flavour components to the wine. Smart barrel use is a vital component of the winemaking process for the majority of fine wines, and it's hard to imagine doing without them. But consider what might happen if they'd never been used for wine and someone tried introducing them now – there would probably be a bit of an outcry in certain circles. This raises the question of whether it is hypocritical to allow barrel use but exclude newer, high-tech manipulations such as micro-oxygenation and reverse osmosis (RO), each of which are given their own chapters in this book (chapters 12 and 14, respectively).

On balance, the case for accepting older, traditional manipulations and avoiding newer ones does have a sound basis: that of preserving product integrity in the eyes of consumers. The add-as-little-as-possible school would no doubt object to newer high-tech manipulations, although at a stretch it could be argued that alcohol reduction by RO would prevent excessive alcohol levels from compromising wine quality – and thus should be allowed.

## 4. The compromise

The final position in our debate would be to permit some manipulations but not those which could be deemed as "cheating". Openness and honesty are the key words here – *i.e.* adding most things is okay as long as their use is disclosed, and wine laws don't outlaw them.

So where should the line be drawn? A strong argument could be made for banning manipulations such as non-traditional chemical flavourings, but allowing winemakers access to other techniques if they choose to use them. I can't see anyone seriously arguing that fruit flavourings or non-wine fruits should be used to make wine and the substance still be allowed to be labelled as wine. On the other hand, this more relaxed view would permit RO and micro-oxygenation. These technologies are, like any other technologies, merely tools, and tools can be used well or they can be used badly. What counts is *how well* the tools are used – not whether or not they are used.

## Historically speaking

An interesting perspective on the wine-manipulation debate is offered by Clark Smith, of the California company Vinovation (*see* "Who is using micro-oxygenation?", page 98). "Our impression of the weirdness of any given technology alters daily, especially these days," he says. "An Egyptian winemaker would comprehend a nineteenth-century cellar better than a nineteenth-century *vigneron* would recognize even the most primitive winery today. "But none of us wants to give back our electric lights, our refrigeration systems or our freeze-dried yeast, or trade in our stainless steel. And consumers accept such innovations without thought, because they now appear in our kitchens."

# Magma: taking natural wine to the limit

Frank Cornelissen is a Belgian who has begun a new winery on the slopes of Mount Etna in Sicily. It is one of the most unique and unusual projects I've yet encountered in the wine world. After working as a merchant, he decided to make wines with a more natural approach – without any treatments in the vineyard, winemaking or bottling.

Cornelissen identified the northern slopes of Mount Etna as a place where this dream could be realized. His estate consists of 5.5 hectares, of which, 2.5 are planted with ungrafted vines grown in the classic, free-standing *alberello* (gobelet) system. The remainder are given over to olive trees, fruit trees and bush. "I strive to abandon monoculture in order to avoid the classic diseases, and have already intermixed the existing vineyards with various trees and plants," he says.

The top wine is Magma, made from old Nerello Mascalese vines (fifty to eighty years old) from the highest parts of the vineyard. Two other reds are made, and a white is planned. All wines are produced in a strictly non-interventionalist way, fermented and aged according to ancient traditions in terracotta amphorae in the ground in the cellar. Frank's aim is to avoid all treatments whatsoever in the vineyard, which he succeeded in doing in 2001, although he had to use a little Bordeaux mixture in 2002 and 2003. In the winery, no additions are made: the wines are made without any $SO_2$. Long macerations are used, with the grape mass only removed after malolactic fermentation.

The use of amphorae is a fascinating practice. Amphorae allow the wine to breathe a little, but don't give the tannins of wood, nor do they alter colour. The evaporation rate from a 400-litre amphora is about the same as from a 2,000- or 3,000-litre vat; a 250-litre amphora is like that from a 1,500-litre vat, and a 100-litre amphora is like that from a barrique.

How do the wines taste? They were actually fantastic: unusual, but compelling. I think the wine world needs people like Frank Cornelissen to push at the boundaries of what is possible. No, I don't expect other producers to give up using $SO_2$ and vineyard treatments. Nonetheless, what Cornelissen is doing with Magma will help others ask deeper questions about their own wines, which can only be a good thing.

## Conclusion

Ultimately, a relationship of trust exists between winemakers and consumers. I feel that where manipulations are used, they should be declared, and then consumers can choose which wines they want to purchase on this basis. If they want a wine that's totally natural, with no $SO_2$ added, then that's fine. But if they want a wine from a producer who uses as little manipulation as possible, this is also fine. Alternatively, if they don't mind how the wine was made and only care about the taste, that's their choice also. I suspect that many consumers would be surprised by the degree of manipulation that does take place with some wines, because the popular conception is that wine is a relatively "natural", additive-free product.

As stated above, the various means for manipulating wines are just tools; as such they can be used wisely, used badly, or not at all. Whether or not the use of these tools is justified is a decision that can't be made globally and enshrined in legislation. Would you rather have a flawed natural wine when a simple manipulation would have eliminated the fault? It's a difficult, multilayered question (for example, what is "flawed" in the context of a wine?). That's why I would advocate a policy of freedom on the part of the winemaker, coupled with honesty about disclosing to the consumer the sort of "manipulation", if any, that is used.

It is possible to argue that different categories of wines should be treated differently. While manipulation might be necessary to help out a commodity wine made from less than perfect grapes, there's less of a case for using more manipulation than is absolutely necessary for fine wines. Rules are important to preserve wine integrity and protect consumers from fakes, but they should be implemented locally rather than globally. Some manipulations, such as adding chemicals as flavouring agents (whether they occur naturally in the wine or not), are indefensible, and should be banned altogether.

# 12 Micro-oxygenation

One high-tech manipulation that is currently the focus of much attention is something called micro-oxygenation (or microbullage, as it is sometimes known). The principle behind it is quite simple. It's a winemaking technique for adding very low levels of oxygen to a developing wine over an extended period. Small "microbubbles" of oxygen are fed through a special ceramic device placed at the bottom of the fermentation tank. The tank needs to be quite tall to do this effectively, and the flow rate can be carefully controlled so that the oxygen dissolves into the wine completely before it reaches the top. The idea is that it allows winemakers to simulate the slow, controlled oxidation of barrel-ageing in wines that are kept in stainless-steel tanks.

The apparatus involved was developed in the early 1990s by Madiran winemaker Patrick Ducournau. Producers in this region in France's southwest experienced problems when they started putting their Tannat-based wines into stainless-steel tanks. Tannat is a red grape that has a tendency to be tough and tannic; without the softening benefits of oak-ageing, it can be quite uncompromising. Ducournau first employed micro-oxygenation commercially in 1991, and set up a company, Oenodev, which now offers this technology worldwide.

It's a near-miraculous technique, if the claims of its proponents are to be believed. Among other things, micro-oxygenation is supposed to build optimum structure, reduce herbaceous or vegetal characters, provide colour stability, stabilize reductive qualities, and increase the suppleness or roundedness of the wine. Robert Paul of Wine Network Consulting in Australia, a company providing micro-oxygenation facilities to around thirty wineries, claims that "treated wines can gain a more savoury, structured palate". Randall Grahm of California's Bonny Doon is an enthusiastic supporter of micro-oxygenation. He asserts that "microbullage, if practised appropriately, is the most useful tool for the mastery of *élevage*".

However, there are conflicting ideas about what micro-oxygenation actually achieves. A popular notion is that it makes red wines drink well earlier. This is largely based on the huge commercial success of the branded wines from Australian company Rosemount, which was in part attributed to the fact that micro-oxygenation allowed its reds to come to market in the same year as production. According to Robert Paul, "The technique is very successful, but the hardest part is convincing people that it is not about softening wines to make them drinkable earlier." Apparently, it's a bit of a paradox. As Paul explains, "The treated wines are more apparently rounded. I would argue that this is because they are better wines fundamentally – they have better balance, stability, and structure and are cleaner, with more apparent fruit."

On a trip to Portugal a couple of years ago, I mentioned to winemaker David Baverstock that I was researching micro-oxygenation. He suddenly became quite animated, clearly excited by this technology. "We're doing quite a bit of micro-ox in the Alentejo," he said, "particularly with Monte Velho [a commercial label of Herdade de Esperão, where he is winemaker]." Baverstock claims that it gets rid of a lot of the "green tannins" and softens the wines. He tends to use this technique with the more commercial wines, and has employed it in the past at Quinta de la Rosa in the Douro, with the company's second wine. "There's always some fruit that is never quite as good as the top stuff," he says, "perhaps from younger vineyards or from less well-controlled growers." He uses micro-oxygenation in conjunction with different sorts of oak chips matched to the type of the wine.

## Why and how micro-oxygenation is used

There seem to be two common motivations for the use of micro-oxygenation. Firstly, it is a useful remedial technique for removing unwanted green characters or sulphides from red wines (*see* chapter 16). Secondly, there is a cost saving. Instead of using expensive barrels for mid-range wines, it's possible to produce the same effects with micro-oxygenation in combination with barrel staves or oak chips in tank. The micro-oxygenation adds the structure to the wine, while the oak chips or staves add the wood flavour.

But for all the scientific claims made by its proponents, micro-oxygenation is still a bit of a black art, based on trial and error rather than precise knowledge of the underlying mechanisms. At the University of California at Davis, Roger Boulton, who is a professor of oenology and chemical engineering, expresses some reservations in this regard. "The chemical effects are likely to be several," he explains, "but there are no independent scientific measurements of the changes – mostly supplier claims and selected satisfied testimonials. There is little indication that the proponents of this treatment have developed a strong understanding of the changes occurring, and there are both short-term and longer-term results that cannot be predicted. In terms of science, treatments that are shrouded in secrecy, selective results, and 'proprietary' methods will have little scientific acceptance until they can be independently reproduced and validated. There is little evidence that 'micro-oxidation' has come close to a scientific method – and it seems that some people prefer it that way."

Ken Fugelsang of California State University agrees that a lot of scientific uncertainty surrounds the technique. "More people are using micro-oxygenation," he says, "but we still clearly don't understand the full potential impact on wine. It produces a more aged structure in young wines, but what impact does this have as wine goes into bottle?" Not all red wines adapt well to this technique. "It is highly dependent on the natural structure of the wine before the process starts," Fugelsang adds. "It is potentially dangerous for a light wine; it could oxidize it rather than build up structure."

## Who is using micro-oxygenation?

Clark Smith of Vinovation, the company which is the French-owned Oenodev's representative in the USA, suggests that the use of micro-oxygenation is pretty widespread in the wine world, with Chile leading the field.

"Chile has perhaps only 120 wineries," Smith says, "but some eighty of these use micro-oxygenation, or at least own the equipment." According to Smith, in California, all of the enormous Central Valley producers are currently using micro-oxygenation techniques, and of the ultra-premium North Coast wineries, perhaps as many as one-third are at least experimenting with it.

In addition to these producers in California and Chile, Smith estimates that around five per cent of wine producers in France and Australia are also using the techniques.

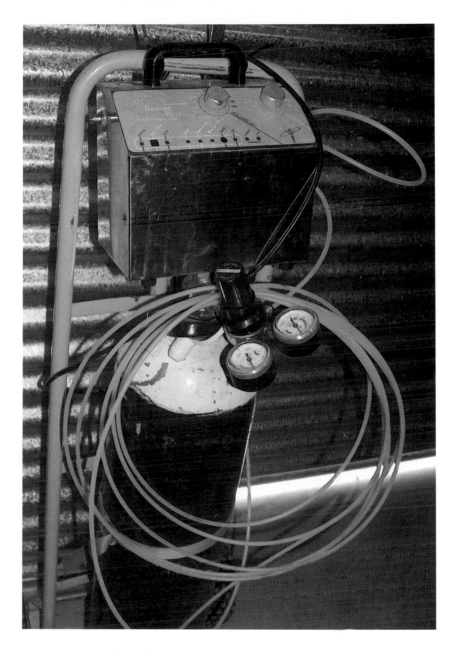

## A more in-depth view

Vinovation's Clark Smith (*see* box, page 98) outlines his explanations for the
chemical changes caused by micro-oxygenation. He refers to this technique
as a tool for "integrated tannin management", which involves the use of oxygen
for building tannin structure in red wines, and then harmonizing these wines
during the ageing process. "It's like making a tannin soufflé," he explains, the
implication being that it is a process of some complexity that's difficult to do
right, but worth it when it works. Smith says that to understand the use of
introduced oxygen in wine properly, it is necessary to look at its impact at
various stages in a wine's evolution. The first exposure, hyper-oxygenation,
is done prior to fermentation where it is needed. It is the opposite of micro-
oxygenation, because it causes tannins to drop out of the must, thus decreasing
the polyphenol content of the wine. This is typically used in white wines such
as Riesling and Champagne.

"Although micro-oxygenation is quite a new technique, the enthusiasm with which winemakers have adopted it suggests that there must be something to it, even though the exact details of the underlying science aren't actually clear yet."

The second type of exposure is macro-oxygenation, which can be used during fermentation to boost yeast health. "During fermentation, it is the yeasts that take up almost all the oxygen, not the phenolics," says Smith. "There is growing evidence that oxygen applied at the right time can help fermentation proceed." Reasonably large amounts can be added at this time without too much risk. Immediately after alcoholic fermentation is an important time to begin the third exposure, micro-oxygenation, for the purpose of building structure. At this stage, the goal is to encourage the phenolic compounds present to polymerize. The added oxygen is thought to oxidize ethanol to acetaldehyde, which then encourages this polymerization process. Relatively high levels of oxygen can be safely added at this stage because the excess aldehyde produced can be consumed during malolactic fermentation. This also has the effect of fixing colour, as the anthocyanins form complexes with the tannins. It is important that $SO_2$ isn't added prior to micro-oxygenation because this inhibits the structurization effects.

### From structure to harmony

This "structurization process" can continue during and after malolactic fermentation, but to a much lesser extent, and far smaller levels of oxygen can be added during these phases. The next stage is harmonization, when the wine, with its enhanced structure, begins to settle down, develop aromatic complexity, shed any vegetal characteristics, and generally grow up a bit. It's the wine's teenage years, if you like; it has gone through its growth spurt and now it needs to become civilized and responsible. This process can take place either in tank or barrel. It is a critical stage in the wine's development, and the only way to assess the progress of the wine is by tasting, paying particular attention to the characteristics of the tannins. This is tricky, and requires some experience. Too much oxygen exposure and the tannins will turn hard and drying; too little, and reduction characters might appear. As Smith points out, "We don't have instrumental measures for running micro-oxygenation."

## The future of micro-oxygenation

Although micro-oxygenation is quite a new technique, the enthusiasm with which winemakers have adopted it suggests that there must be something to it, even though the exact details of the underlying science aren't actually clear yet. Personally, I like the concept of integrated tannin management, beginning in the vineyard and carrying through into the winery. As soon as the science catches up with the technological push, micro-oxygenation looks set to become an established, mainstream technique throughout the winemaking world.

I'll conclude with Randall Grahm's ringing endorsement. "I am continually amazed at how misunderstood this technique is, even by some extremely competent members of the trade," he says. "It is an extremely useful tool to enable a winemaker to master long *cuvaisons* [the period of time grape juice is kept in contact with the skins and seeds during fermentation], so as not to extract excessive bitterness in the wine, to soften tannins, and preserve colour. Microbullage, if practised appropriately, is the most useful tool for the mastery of *élevage*. It is an extremely powerful lens that enables a winemaker to observe whereabouts in the developmental life cycle his wine might be, and when is just the moment to put the wine into bottle. I would liken microbullage to the advent of temperature control in fermentation, perhaps a technology that was considered 'unnatural' at one point, but [one that] is now largely considered indispensable."

# 13 Barrels and the impact of oak on wine

Barrels were probably the earliest form of wine technology, and their use is still vital in the production of many of today's wine styles. Despite their importance in the winemaking process, the positive effects of barrels were probably discovered providentially. They just happened to be the best way of storing and transporting liquids, and until the advent of epoxy-lined cement and stainless-steel tanks, winemakers lacked alternatives. However, oak's accidental association with wine has been a critical one. The majority of fine red wines are dependent on oak barrels for a vital component of their flavour, as are a good number of whites. Without oak, wine would be quite different. Even where older, larger barrels, which don't have such a direct flavour impact, are used, their ability to allow exposure of the contents to small amounts of oxygen is important in the development of the wine. In this chapter we focus on the science of barrels and their role in the élevage (literally the "breeding" or "upbringing") of wine.

## Oak

Let's begin our discussion with a slightly tangential biological perspective. Taking a somewhat simplistic conceptual view, there are four basic organisms which are crucial to wine production: two microbes and two woody plants. The microbes are the yeast *Saccharomyces* and the lactic-acid bacterium *Oenococcus*. The two plants are the grape vine *Vitis vinifera* and the oak tree, genus *Quercus*. Of these, two are essential for all wine styles (grapes from the grape vine and yeast), while red wines and some whites need lactic-acid bacteria, and many red and white styles wouldn't be possible without the use of oak.

The oak genus *Quercus* can be split into many hundreds of species. Of these, there are four that are principally relevant to wine, three of which are used to make barrels (*Quercus alba, Quercus sessiliflora,* and *Quercus robur*), and one of which makes corks (*Quercus suber*). *Quercus robur* also goes under the name *Quercus pedunculata*, while *Quercus petraea* is a synonym for *Quercus sessiliflora*. Taxonomy is a confusing branch of science.

Why then is oak so good for barrel construction? It is strong yet still relatively easy to work. It also has the capacity to make containers that are watertight. Its wood is rich in structures known as tyloses. Wood is mostly composed of large, open, water-conducting vessels, known as the xylem vessels, which travel up the trunk. The tyloses are outgrowths from neighbouring cells that block the xylem vessels. American oak is particularly rich in these structures, which mean that the wood can be sawn in a number of planes and still be impermeable, while French oak has fewer tyloses and thus has to be split in specific planes in order to make watertight staves. But perhaps most significantly, oak facilitates and is also directly involved in chemical interactions with wine that can have positive effects on its flavour and structure. That explains why, in this technological age, barrels still haven't been replaced in the cellar.

## How barrels affect wine

I remember the first time I sampled through the barrels in a producer's cellar. I was struck by the differences among samples of the same lot of wine that differed only in the barrels in which they were being aged. These barrels varied in their toast level, manufacturer, and source of oak. For those who use them, the choice of barrel is an important winemaking decision, and skilled producers will be as fussy about the barrels they use as they are about the condition of their grapes. There are several factors that influence the way that barrels affect wine flavour.

### The tree

Typically, oaks used in barrel production are classified on the basis of their geographic origin. The first and most important distinction is between French and American oak. As stated earlier, the American oak is a separate species (*Q. alba*) which possesses quite different characteristics to those of the two French species (*Q. robur* and *Q. sessiliflora*). Within the category of French oak, further subdivisions are made according to the forest region, which closely (but not completely) correlate with the species used. The situation is further complicated by the fact that each cooper has his or her own house style, and the characteristics of the staves will differ according to factors such as age of tree, the part of the trunk they were taken from, the seasoning process, and the amount of toast. This interplay among oak species, environment, and human intervention makes the science of barrels almost as complex as that of the viticultural and winemaking processes.

RIGHT *Quercus robur,* one of the two species of oak treees used in barrel manufacture.
*Picture courtesy of Garden World Images*

| Different species of oak used in barrel production | | |
| --- | --- | --- |
| **Oak species** | **Geographic origin*** | **General characteristics** |
| *Quercus robur,* known as pedunculate oak | French forests, principally in Limousin, Burgundy, and the South of France | High extractable polyphenol content; makes wines that are more structured, less aromatic |
| *Quercus sessiflora,* known as sessile oak | French forests, principally in the central and Vosges region | Contributes more aroma and less structure |
| *Quercus alba,* known as white oak | America | Low phenol content, very high concentration of aromatic substances** |

\* The three most commonly encountered French barrel styles are Nevers, Alliers, and Tronçais. These encompass the wood from these areas, but are also terms used to "type" wood from other regions.

\*\* American oak has extremely high concentrations of oak lactones. For example, a study by Pascal Chatonnet showed that French sessile oak gave concentrations of $\beta$-methyl-$\gamma$-octalactone of 77 $\mu$g/litre, French pedunculate 16 $\mu$g/litre while American oak delivered a whopping 158 $\mu$g/litre (a microgram, $\mu$g, is one millionth of a gram).

## Cooperage

Coopers are interested in the central part of the tree trunk – the dead, tough heartwood that is also known as "stavewood". This part of the trunk is split along something called "medullary rays", which are horizontal structures that run radially through the wood. Splitting is essential for French oak; if it were sawn, it would become porous (*see* page 101). As mentioned previously, American oak can be sawn because of the presence of tyloses – the structures that block the vertical-running fibres of the wood at regular intervals. The splitting continues until single staves are produced. The fact that French oak must be split while American oak can be sawn explains in part why French barrels are more expensive than their American counterparts. The "house style", or the method of producing staves, of various coopers is probably the most significant factor influencing the effect of the barrel on the wine.

## Seasoning

Before oak is used for barrel construction it must be seasoned. This is carried out in order to bring the humidity levels of the wood into line with the environment it will be used in, and also to allow some important chemical modifications to occur. The seasoning process typically takes two or three years, depending on the thickness of the staves. Seasoning is a bit of a balancing act; you need to leave the wood just long enough, but not too long. Seasoning normally takes place outdoors, and results in a number of changes to the wood: ellagitannins (otherwise known as ellagic acid) are reduced, as are levels of bitter-tasting compounds called coumarins (*see* table on page 105). At the same time, there is an increase in some aromatic components such as eugenol. It is also possible (not to mention considerably cheaper and quicker) to age staves artificially in ovens, but the drawback to this process is that the important chemical changes don't occur. As a consequence, the oak staves have fewer aromatic properties and more bitter compounds, which will be leached into the wine as it ages.

### Toasting

The barrel-manufacturing process involves heating the staves over a brazier so that they can be bent into shape. Somewhat fortuitously, this slight charring (referred to as "toasting"), coupled with the chemical properties of the wood, means that the interaction of the wine with the inside of a new barrel imparts pronounced flavour characteristics to the wine. When used appropriately, new barrels can have a significant beneficial impact on the wine that is aged in them. These are summarized in the table opposite.

### Micro-oxygenation the traditional way

Barrels don't just impart flavour directly. Another equally important but less talked-about effect of ageing wine in barrels is that this allows a very slight and controlled exposure to oxygen. Normally, winemakers do all they can to avoid exposing their wines to air, but in this case the low-level oxidation that barrels permit is beneficial to the structure and character of many wines.

Wines stored in average-sized barrels (around 225 litres) typically receive between about twenty and forty milligrams of dissolved oxygen per litre per year, but this is difficult to measure, precisely because some is consumed by ellagitannins in the oak. Some oxygen passes through the wood itself; the majority passes through gaps between the staves, and the remainder comes through the bunghole. This low-level exposure to oxygen has a number of important effects. Colour is intensified because of reactions between tannins and anthocyanins (*see* page 185), and tannins are typically softened by polymerization, which eventually causes them to precipitate out of the wine. But in the shorter term, barrels can help build a wine's structure in much the same way that micro-oxygenation does (*see* chapter 12).

**BELOW** A cooper toasting barrels over a fire.
*Photo courtesy of Jason Lowe*

| The beneficial effects of barrels on wine | | |
|---|---|---|
| **Flavour compound** | **Characteristics** | **Influence of manufacturing** |
| Lactones | The most important oak-derived flavours in wine are *cis* and *trans* isomers of β-methyl-γ-octalactone, known as the oak lactones. On their own, these oak lactones smell coconutty, but in wine they can smell quite oaky, too. The *cis* isomer is described as having an earthy, herbaceous character as well as the coconut, while the *trans* adds spice to its coconut aromas. | Seasoning barrels affects the ratio of *cis* to *trans* forms of oak lactone, and toasting is thought to reduce overall lactone levels. American oak contains much higher lactone concentrations. |
| Vanillin | The main aroma component of natural vanilla. This is present in significant quantities in oak wood. Vanillin contributes significantly to the aroma of oaked wines. If wine is actually fermented in oak barrels, yeast metabolism reduces the vanillin concentration by turning it into the odourless vanillic alcohol. Thus, barrel-fermented wines smell less oaky than wines fermented in tank and then transferred to barrel, even though the former have been in oak for longer. | Levels can be increased by toasting, but decrease at high toast levels. |
| Guaiacol | Guaiacol and the related 4-methylguaiacol have a char-like, smoky aroma; 4-methylguiacol is also described as spicy. | Formed by degradation of the wood component lignin during toasting, and thus increased at high toast levels. |
| Eugenol | With a clove-like smell, this is the main volatile phenol associated with wood. The related isoeugenol smells similar. | Increased during the seasoning process, and reported to increase during toasting. |
| Furfural, 5-methylfurfural | These are both produced by the heat-induced degradation of sugars and carbohydrates. They have caramel and butterscotch aromas, with a hint of almond. | Made when carbohydrates in the wood are degraded by the heat of the toasting process. |
| Ellagitannins | Tannins absorbed by the wine from the wood are known as ellagitannins. Capable of modifying the structure of the wine, as well as combining with anthocyanins and increasing colour. They have an astringent taste. Ellagitannins belong to a class known as hydrolyzable tannins. | Their concentration decreases at high toasting levels. |
| Coumarins | Derivatives of cinnamic acids, present in oaked wine at low concentrations, but which still affect flavour; their glycosides are bitter and their aglycones acidic. | |

"Not everyone likes or wants the flavour imprint that new-oak barrels stamp on a wine. While certain styles of wine possess the substance to absorb flavour compounds from new oak without being dominated by them, many wines are best aged in second-, third- or even fourth-use barrels. This is because older barrels impart progressively less flavour to wine."

## Testing barrel influence

Some companies, such as California's ETS Laboratories, are now offering analytical techniques that will allow winemakers to test the performance of barrels by analyzing their chemical imprint. To explain the results in ways that winemakers can visualize, they use a graphical representation known as a radar plot. Dr. Eric Hervé of ETS gave me an example to explain how they do this.

"Imagine that a winemaker wants a better understanding of how barrels from various origins influence the aroma of one of his top-end wines," he said. "The trial is simple: the same lot of wine is aged in groups of barrels from various coopers, with various specifications (*e.g.* toast level). During the ageing, the wine is tasted and analyzed. We report concentrations of oak aroma compounds for each sample in micrograms per litre (μg/L). Winemakers can then build a database for future reference and comparison. We also generate a 'radar plot' for each sample by comparing concentrations found versus the 'trial average' (the mathematical average of concentrations found in all samples from the trial). This allows us to see immediately what aroma compounds are below or above average, and therefore if associated aroma descriptors are likely to be less or more intense, compared to the other wines in this trial."

### How radar analysis works

An example of such a plot is shown in the diagram on page 107, which depicts an ETS "radar" analysis of oak flavour impact on wine. "In this particular example," Dr. Hervé explains, "a Chardonnay aged in medium-plus toast barrels from a cooper 'D', is presented. Fresh oak/coconut markers (or indicators) are slightly below average; vanilla and clove markers are close to average; sweet/butterscotch markers are considerably higher; while smoke compounds are only slightly higher. This tells us that, with those particular barrels, the cooper managed to increase greatly wood caramelization products (providing 'sweetness', 'roundness', and 'creaminess' to wines), while keeping any degradation of desirable 'coconut' compounds to a minimum, and not making too much of the 'smoke' compounds. This is generally the goal of a medium-plus toasting, but trials like this one show that 'cooper's styles' vary greatly.

"Results of such trials," Hervé concludes, "help winemakers in designing final blends, adapting their barrel-ageing practices, making barrel-purchase decisions, and so forth. The analysis itself is a high-tech tool we offer them

**BELOW** The old, *left*, and the new, *right*, from Niepoort in Portugal's Douro region.

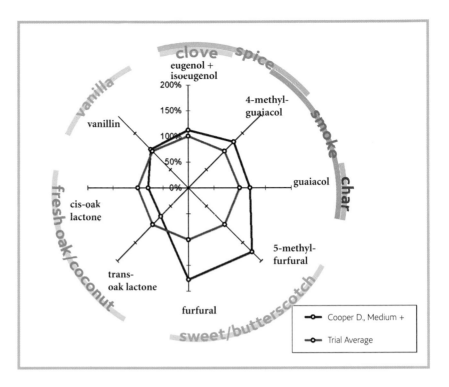

in order to fine-tune their wines' style." In this way it is possible to compare barrels from different coopers, different species of oak, and even with different toast levels. A strong relationship of trust has to exist between winemakers and their barrel suppliers, because once wine has gone into a bad or unsuitable barrel, it is too late to reverse the decision.

But this sort of analytic technique is only likely to describe a small fraction of oak-imparted wine flavour compounds. Do these sorts of analyses measure all the significant molecular contributions of barrels, or just a few? I asked Hervé about this. "Although the compounds we measure are widely considered the main contributors to the oak flavour, there are many others that may play a role in wine," he responded. "Luckily, most of these compounds belong to a 'family' of related compounds (same origin and similar odours), and measuring only one or two molecules gives a good idea of the 'family' as a whole." He continues: "This is the concept of 'indicator compounds'. One good example is the volatile phenols family; degradation of oak lignin by heat gives hundreds of these molecules, several of them playing a sensory role in wine, in synergy. Measuring only the two most important ones (guaiacol and 4-methylguaiacol), however, proves to be a very reliable indicator of the 'smoky' character in wines."

## Older barrels

Not everyone likes or wants the flavour imprint that new-oak barrels stamp on a wine. While certain styles of wine possess the substance to absorb flavour compounds from new oak without being dominated by them, many wines are best aged in second-, third- or even fourth-use barrels. This is because older barrels impart progressively less flavour to wine, but they still allow the controlled oxygen exposure that is important for resolving a wine's structural elements.

## Alternatives to barrels

Despite all their obvious charms, barrels are expensive. Oak chips, staves, and even liquid oak extract have been used to give cheaper wines some oak complexity and flavour. The results are mixed, and rarely replicate the characteristic imprint of barrels.

However, the use of oak alternatives suspended in tanks during fermentation of red wines at least offers a means of adding some barrel-fermentation character to red wine. Usually barrel fermentation isn't possible for reds due to the fact that they are fermented on their skins, and oak interaction is usually restricted to the post-alcoholic fermentation period. The addition of these various "oak substitutes" may present some interesting options for experimentation by winemakers. It could, for example, increase structure development and enhance colour stability.

In addition, there is the relatively new technique of micro-oxygenation, which aims to replicate the slow oxygen exposure wine experiences in barrel; this is the subject of chapter 12.

Older barrels, however, don't come without hygiene issues. While it is possible (and important) to clean barrels between uses, it is impossible to sterilize them. If they harbour any spoilage organisms such as *Brettanomyces* (*see* chapter 18), then there is virtually no way to remove the potential inoculum because of the porous nature of the wood – there's always somewhere for the bugs to hide. Even so, these barrels can still be used, but they need to be monitored very carefully.

## Conclusions

In this briefest of reviews, I have touched on the importance of barrels in the winemaking process, and discussed some of the significant effects they have on wine flavour and structure. It is clear that this is a complicated, multifaceted subject. However, the availability of non-invasive, analytical techniques for examining the potential of barrels will allow winemakers to make a more informed decision as to which oak sources and *tonnelleries* (cooperages) will best suit their wines. Any conscientious winemaker is taking a huge gamble if he or she isn't meticulous about the provenance of the barrels used.

**RIGHT** The barrel room at Thelema, Stellenbosch, South Africa.

# 14 Reverse osmosis, spinning cones, and evaporators: alcohol reduction and must concentration

Clark Smith is a controversial figure. He comes across as articulate, shrewd, and at times very funny. But while to some people he's an inspired innovator, to others he's the devil incarnate. Why? It's because his company, Vinovation, is the leading pioneer of a technique known as reverse osmosis that is increasingly being used worldwide as the latest high-tech tool in the winemaker's arsenal. To traditionalists, these reverse osmosis machines represent a very real threat to the "soul" of wine itself. This chapter takes a close look at reverse osmosis and the related technologies of spinning cones and vacuum concentration. I'll look at how widespread the use of these techniques is, and try to assess whether they are compatible with fine-wine production.

A key concept underlying Smith's message is that grape phenolic maturity is independent of sugar levels. So, while grape-sugar accumulation and acid respiration are dependent on climate, the colour, aroma synthesis, and tannin evolution occur at more or less the same rate wherever grapes are grown. So in warm regions a big problem is that rapid accumulation of sugars can impose a premature harvest, even though the grapes have not reached phenolic maturity.

The traditional compromise has been that if you want to pick grapes at optimum flavour maturity, you have to tolerate excessively high alcohol levels that are often to the detriment of wine quality. In cool climates the problem is quite different. For producers in the classic European wine regions, achieving phenolic ripeness often means leaving grapes to hang well into the onset of the autumn rains, risking dilution. Vinovation's reverse-osmosis technology offers solutions to both problems. Too much alcohol? You can remove it from the finished wine. Grapes got rained on? You can concentrate the must before fermentation.

## How osmosis works

So how does reverse osmosis work? You may remember the principle of osmosis from school science lessons. If two liquids are separated by a semi-permeable membrane, water flows across the membrane from the more concentrated to the less concentrated solution. Not what you want to do with wine, of course – the must or finished wine would get more dilute. The answer, or part of it, is to increase the pressure of the more concentrated solution, which reverses the flow. It's not quite as simple as this, though.

As the pore size of the filter membrane decreases to the levels needed for wine applications, dissolved molecules begin to foul it, making it unusable. The key to the success of reverse osmosis is the use of what is known as tangential or cross-flow filtration; instead of the flow being pushed through the filter, the process mimics the blood capillaries in the kidney by directing the flow *across* the

"There are currently three key uses for reverse osmosis: removing water from grape must, removing alcohol or volatile acidity from a finished wine, and a more recent development which removes 4-ethylphenol – a major contributor to the negative flavour impact of *Brettanomyces* – from finished wine."

filter. As a consequence, the turbulent fluid flow keeps the filter clean. Yes, a lot of energy is wasted just keeping this membrane from getting clogged up, but it works.

There are currently three key uses for this technique: removing water from grape must, removing alcohol or volatile acidity from a finished wine, and a more recent development is the possibility of removing 4-ethylphenol – a contributor to the negative flavour impact of *Brettanomyces* (*see* chapter 18) – from finished wine. This has led some researchers to joke that various consulting companies will first give you a brett problem in your wine by encouraging the use of micro-oxygenation, and then offer to clean the wine up for you with reverse osmosis.

## Alcohol reduction

If you grow grapes in a hot climate you usually have to make a compromise with the time of harvest. Pick too soon and you'll have ideal sugar levels but poor phenolic ripeness (flavour maturity). Wait for optimum phenolic ripeness and the sugar levels could be so high that the wines will be overly alcoholic. This problem is on the increase. A preference for richer, riper styles of wines may shoulder some of the blame, but so does global warming. In many regions it is getting tough to make wines with alcohol levels that don't impair the quality of the wine.

Not to worry, though. Vinovation can run your wine through a reverse osmosis machine. This takes out a colourless, flavourless permeate that consists of water, alcohol, and an undissociated form of acetic acid. The important stuff is all left in a substance known as the retentate. Then the alcohol is distilled off and the water added back to create a lower-alcohol wine. This can then be used as a blending component to mix back with the untreated wine to create a series of test wines at different alcohol levels, ideally separated by 0.1 per cent increments.

**BELOW** Schematic representation of the reverse osmosis process.
*Picture courtesy of Vinovation*

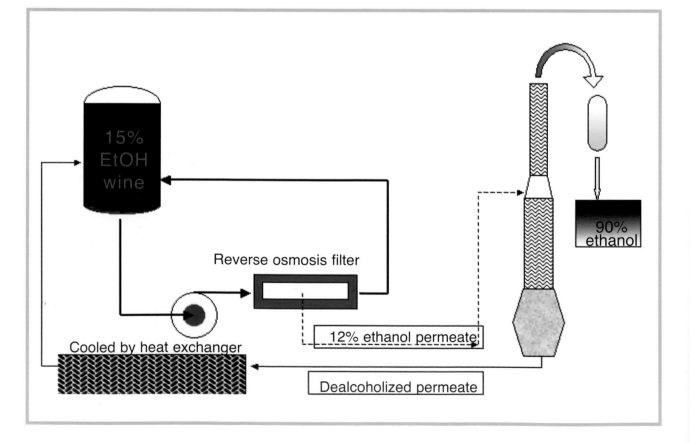

# Wine-flavour chemistry

How do wines treated in this way compare with control wines in terms of wine-flavour chemistry? Clearly, more independent work is called for here, a sentiment shared by Roger Boulton, professor of oenology and chemical engineering at the UC Davis: "There are no independent published reports of the sensory effects of this treatment compared to a control," he explains, "only proprietary claims and selective testimonials. There is no published example of a side-by-side comparison across several wines." It should be added that the use of cross-flow filtration for reducing alcohol levels in wine is not new; it has been trialled since the mid-1980s. But it is only in recent years that it has been the focus of much attention.

The next stage is tasting these samples to pick out the wines that taste the best. These points of balance are known as the "sweet spots". "We never see a normal distribution of preference," says Smith. "It's like the tuning of a chord." Sweet-spot determination is nicely illustrated by a fascinating collaborative project between Vinovation and California State University in Fresno. In 1999, the oenology students made a wine from Central Valley Syrah grapes. A quarter of this wine, which weighed in at a heady eighteen degrees of alcohol (it's hot in the Central Valley), was sent to Vinovation, which reduced the alcohol level to 10.1 degrees by reverse osmosis. Using this as a blending component, trial wines were made at 0.1 degrees of alcohol increments from the control of eighteen degrees down to 12.8. Twenty-two judges assessed these wines and came up with four points of "harmonious balance": at 13.35, 13.75, 14.35, and 15 degrees of alcohol. These wines were then sold commercially in a pack of five (the four sweet-spot wines plus the original eighteen-degree wine). I've not tasted them for myself, but I've heard two independent reports from people who have, and who were quite impressed.

## Spinning cones

An alternative technique for alcohol reduction is the spinning-cone column. Quite different in principle, this separates different volatile fractions from the wine by means of centrifugal force and vacuum. These fractions are then blended back once the alcohol has been removed. ConeTech is the US company that developed this technology, which is now being exported elsewhere. Because of the high cost of the machinery, this is a service industry.

**RIGHT** A reverse osmosis machine.
*Picture courtesy of Vinovation*

While these manipulation technologies sound horribly interventionist and the stuff of science fiction, they are becoming quite common in California. I asked Smith how many wineries use either reverse osmosis or spinning cones. "I'm guessing about 500 wineries, which is about half the state," he says. Vinovation is now looking to other markets: "We're just beginning in Australia and South Africa". Interestingly, while he cannot name names, Smith claims that it is mostly high-end wineries that are using these techniques. "It's the only way to get consistent phenolic maturity and true harmonious balance," he says.

The time-honoured method of reducing alcohol levels in wines is adding water to high-sugar musts – the "hose-pipe" method. This is, of course, illegal, but it is widely practised. The drawback is that it dilutes all components of the wine. Some winemakers use reverse osmosis to remove the water and alcohol from wine, and then add back water that has no connection with the grapes; this is cheaper than distilling the permeate or using low-Baumé juice, but it is still illegal. Legal alcohol loss can occur when wines are fermented in small, open tanks, as the alcohol simply burns off. Reductions of around one degree are talked about.

## Must concentration

Reverse osmosis has also found a home in the classic wine regions of Europe. Here the problem is that harvest often coincides with the onset of rainy autumnal weather. If it rains during harvest, you can end up with a dilute wine, and many potentially good vintages are ruined this way. "In Bordeaux," Smith explains, "true ripeness often means grapes hanging into the rain. Reverse osmosis can squeeze this rain back out in order to obtain flavour concentration and alcohol balance." He points out that the widely used "traditional" technique of chaptalization ignores this dilution and corrects just the alcohol imbalance with added sugar.

One problem with using reverse osmosis for must concentration is that the technique requires clarified juice to avoid fouling the filtration device, so the smaller the amount to be concentrated, the better. This is a factor limiting uptake of the technology for red wines, because not everyone wants to clarify grape must prior to fermentation. A modern reverse-osmosis machine operating at 1,500psi can concentrate just a portion of the must to forty-two Brix, which can then be used for blending.

## Reverse osmosis in Australia

Some confusion surrounds the status of reverse osmosis in Australia. According to some people I have spoken with, the rules allow winemakers to remove water and alcohol, but add back what is termed low-Baumé juice. In California, winemakers must add back the water that is removed along with the alcohol by cross-flow filtration, after a distillation process that then removes the alcohol. This seems a rather symbolic point, but it does mean that reverse osmosis is a subtractive rather than an additive process, taking something out but not adding anything that wasn't there in the first place. The loop is intact.

In Australia, the rules seem to be a little more flexible. Winemakers can replace the permeate removed from the wine with water evaporated from juice; this water is the "low-Baumé juice". The

let-off that prevents this being regarded as outright naughtiness by the purists is that the water involved would once have been inside a grape in the appropriate appellation, and thus carries its appellation with it. It saves having to bother with stills and all the rules and restrictions that distilling alcohol carries with it.

However, other Australian commentators have suggested to me that this is not the case. There is a strong recommendation by the official committee dealing with label integrity that a wine component must retain at least eight degrees of alcohol (or sugar equivalent to eight degrees potential alcohol) for it to be considered wine, unless the reverse-osmosis loop is kept intact and water derived from permeate distillation is added back to the wine. This illustrates the complexity of adapting rules to new technologies.

## Vacuum distillation

An alternative method of removing water from the must is vacuum distillation. These concentrators heat the must to temperatures of around 25–30°C (77–86°F) under vacuum, and can treat from ten to eighty hectolitres of must per hour, with an evaporation capacity of 150–1,200 hectolitres. These machines have been popular in the past, and their use preceded that of reverse osmosis. However, they have drawbacks. The heating of the must can introduce aroma losses and apparently a butterscotch, caramelly character to the fruit, and they are much more expensive than reverse-osmosis machines. One point worth mentioning is that the must usually has to be heated to temperatures above those claimed by machine manufacturers. To work one of these devices at 25°C (77°F) requires a vacuum of around eight-five per cent, which is hard to achieve. Industry people have said that many of the machines need must at 45°C (113°F) to work effectively, which could substantially change its character.

## Correcting and concentration

So far so good. In principle the use of reverse osmosis or vacuum distillation to remove excess water from the must is just a correction of a vintage anomaly, with the winemaker removing the rainwater that would have diluted the wine. But the problem is that, in a market dominated by critics who award high scores to super-concentrated wines, the temptation to do a little more than just remove the rainwater is strong, even if there are drawbacks. In effect, they aren't a million miles away from the technique of *saignée*, which aims to increase the ratio of juice to skins in red-wine fermentation by bleeding off some juice after a brief maceration.

I haven't yet mentioned the concentration of finished wines by reverse osmosis. This has been tried, but it is not widely legal. Richard Gibson, previously with Southcorp but now running Scorpex consultancy, recalls trials with dilute Riverland fruit. At forty-per-cent reduction, the wine became really interesting, with various aromatic compounds reaching threshold level. At sixty per cent, it was what he mischievously referred to as a "Grange blender". There are two potential drawbacks with this technique. First, the wine must be sound to start with; any unripe or vegetal characters will be concentrated along with positive flavour components. Second, it is subtractive and there is a loss of volume, which may not be economic in certain circumstances.

## Uses and abuses

Must concentration by reverse osmosis or vacuum distillation is allowed in the EU, but regulations limit its use to a twenty-degree-maximum volume decrease and a two-degree-maximum volume alcohol potential increase. It's illegal to chaptalize and concentrate the same batch of wine. Even so, it is possible to make a super-concentrated wine that may be difficult to distinguish from one produced by the more traditional route of low yields, good vineyard sites, and careful fruit selection.

How widespread is the use of must concentration? It's hard to get an accurate picture, because companies which supply these services are unwilling to name names, and most properties that own machines don't tend to advertise it. I've spoken to quite a few people, and the only clear answer I can get is "more than you might think". James Lawther, an expert commentator on the Bordeaux scene, reckons there are over sixty reverse-osmosis machines in operation in the region, and about double that number of vacuum concentrators. There are also a

**ABOVE** A distilling column used in the reverse-osmosis process.
*Picture courtesy of Vinovation*

"In principle, the use of reverse osmosis or vacuum distillation to remove excess water from the must is just a correction of a vintage anomaly, with the winemaker removing the rainwater that would have diluted the wine."

number of contract companies that offer reverse osmosis, all of which are pretty busy at harvest time. Must concentration is also being practised in Burgundy, but on a much smaller scale.

Elsewhere in Europe, the picture is one of a technical revolution in the offing. In Germany, over 100 wineries have experimented with must concentration, mainly in Baden and the southern areas. Must concentration is easier to achieve with white wines, because juice clarification prior to fermentation isn't as problematic as in reds. In Italy, there are reverse-osmosis machines in Piedmont, Tuscany, and Alto Adige. It seems that things are just beginning in Spain, although reverse osmosis doesn't yet appear to have reached Portugal.

## Is alcohol reduction a sin?

Let's get philosophical now. The crucial question regarding these interventions is whether they are appropriate or honest manipulations for making quality wines. In other words, is it cheating? As Clark Smith puts it, "Today the central debate about reverse osmosis and other high-tech wine-production innovations is not about whether they work; it is about whether winemakers will go to hell if they use them. Now it is largely taken for granted that these techniques work – in the same way that procreative ability is a side issue in assessing one's daughter's suitors."

Californian winemaker Randall Grahm makes an important point here. He thinks technological intervention is a question of context. "If a producer makes a *vin d'appellation*," he says, "then there is an implicit contract that he or she enters into, effectively promising to produce a wine of some degree of *typicité*, which I suppose would also include the characteristics of the vintage. If that producer utilizes certain techniques to wipe out vintage characteristics, even though he or she is perhaps producing a wine that most punters would prefer, I believe that winemaker is acting in bad faith. If a winemaker is producing a *vin de table, vino da tavola* or New World wine, I think that a different set of criteria apply. The contract is simply with the consumer: to make the best wine possible – namely a wine that will offer the consumer vinous *jouissance*."

Personally, I'm much more comfortable with the idea of alcohol reduction in New World wines than the use of must concentration in the classic European regions. As Grahm puts it, "There are some great old-vine vineyards in the New World that were planted in areas that are perhaps too warm for the grapes to arrive at optimal flavour/alcohol balance. One makes a better wine by picking the grapes riper and taking a little alcohol out of them than by picking them earlier."

Others are less accepting. When I quizzed Ernst Loosen, of Weingut Dr. Loosen in Germany's Mosel, about the increased use of must concentrators, he was quite clear in his opposition. "It's an awful development. How far can we go before wine becomes artificial?" Loosen believes that, increasingly, as machines are taking over, wines are losing their individualism. "It's already starting to get boring, with all these over-extracted wines that lack any edges," he adds.

In the meantime, open discussion of these issues can only be a good thing. Consumers must be kept informed so that they can participate in the debate about how much "intervention" is acceptable in the wines they are buying. In this respect, Smith is critical of wine writers, whom he believes have generally failed to educate consumers properly. "There's a major disconnection between what's being done to improve wine quality and what wine writers choose to tell consumers," he explains. "They are protecting the notion of wine; they feel that if we tell people what is really going on, then the mystery will go away."

# 15 Sulphur dioxide

Sulphur dioxide: it's one of the most frequently discussed, yet simultaneously one of the most frequently misunderstood issues in winemaking. Winemakers, merchants, writers, and even consumers talk about it constantly, but with the exception of the first group mentioned above, I suspect that most don't have a clear understanding of the issues involved. It's undoubtedly a technical sort of subject that fits firmly into the category of the chemistry of winemaking, but I'm going to try to keep this chapter readable and interesting without sacrificing depth of content. Sulphur dioxide is an important subject, so it's a good idea to have a decent grasp of the issues relating to its use.

First, I'll look at why sulphur dioxide ($SO_2$) is such an important component of winemaking and how it acts as a "chemical custodian" of wine quality. Then I'll turn to the important subject of how $SO_2$ can best be used, and why it is generally not a good idea to use too much or too little of it. Finally, and perhaps most interestingly, I'll report on some brave souls who, opposed to any sort of winemaking additives at all, have tried to make wines with very little or even no added $SO_2$.

## Free and bound forms

The key to understanding the effects of $SO_2$ is the ratio between its free and bound forms. When $SO_2$ is added to a wine, it dissolves, and some of it reacts with other chemical components in the wine to become "bound". This bound fraction is effectively lost to the winemaker (at least temporarily) because it has insignificant antioxidant and antimicrobial properties. Various compounds present in wine, such as ethanal (acetaldehyde), ketonic acids, sugars, and dicarbonyl group molecules, are responsible for this reaction.

Winemakers routinely measure total $SO_2$ and free $SO_2$, with the difference between the two being the amount existing as the bound form. Importantly, an equilibrium occurs between the free and bound forms, so that as free $SO_2$ is used up, some more may be released from the bound fraction. It's slightly more complicated than this, however. Some of the bound $SO_2$ is locked in irreversibly; the remainder is releasable. And of the free portion, most of it exists as the relatively inactive bisulphite anion ($HSO_3^-$), with just a small amount left as active molecular $SO_2$. To make this a little more understandable, I've summarized these ideas in a pie chart on the following page.

### The importance of pH

One of the key factors affecting the function of $SO_2$ is pH. For the benefit of those who have long forgotten their school chemistry lessons, pH is a measure of how acidic or alkaline a solution is (technically it relates to the concentration of hydrogen ions in solution). A pH of seven is neutral, and below and above this figure, the solution is progressively more acidic or alkaline, respectively. Thus a wine with a lower pH is more acidic. All wines are acidic (with a pH of less than seven), but some are more acidic than others. The pH is important here in two respects. Firstly, at higher pH levels, more total SO$_2$ is needed to get the same level of free SO$_2$. Secondly, SO$_2$ is more effective – that is, it actually works better – at a lower pH, so as well as having more of the useful free form for the same addition, what you have works better as well. It's a double benefit.

## How sulphur dioxide works in wine

The most useful attribute of the wonder molecule is that it protects wine against oxidation. Professor Roger Boulton of the UC Davis explains, "as a wine is exposed to oxygen, the key initial reaction is the oxidation of monomeric phenols with a special reactive group to form hydrogen peroxide. The peroxide can be consumed by a number of other reactions, either being quenched by tannins and other phenols, or the formation of acetaldehyde by reaction with ethanol." Boulton points out that the assertion that SO$_2$ is "protecting" wine from oxidation is technically incorrect. "There is a general misconception that SO$_2$ will protect against oxidation," he explains. "Its rate of reaction with oxygen is so slow that it cannot compete for the oxygen and stop the phenol oxidation. While it does compete for the peroxide formed, its main role is binding up the aldehyde formed, so that we do not smell the oxidation product."

The second type of oxidation that occurs in wine is caused by enzymes known as oxidases, which speed up oxidation reactions drastically. These enzymes are present in damaged or rotten grapes, so where these are likely to be present it is especially important to use sufficient SO$_2$. Winemakers should therefore use grapes that are as clean as possible, with the absolute minimum of fungal damage. It follows that sweet wines made from botrytized grapes need substantially higher levels of SO$_2$ to protect them against oxidation. Significantly, botrytized wines are also very high in compounds which bind free SO$_2$, with the result that winemakers can end up adding enormous levels and still not have significant free SO$_2$.

BELOW Pie chart showing a typical distribution of total sulphur dioxide in wine. The SO$_2$ is typically separated into bound and free pools, each of which consists of two different fractions.

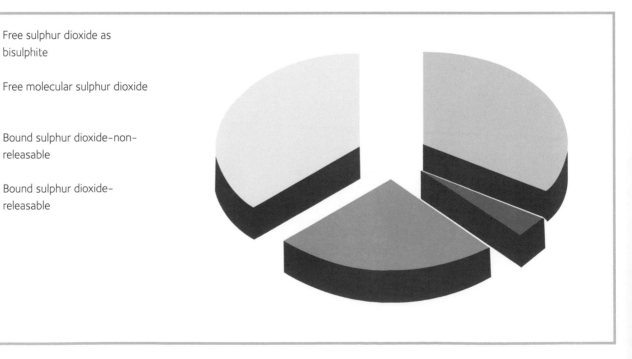

Free sulphur dioxide as bisulphite

Free molecular sulphur dioxide

Bound sulphur dioxide-non-releasable

Bound sulphur dioxide-releasable

White wines generally need higher levels of $SO_2$ than reds to protect them from oxidation. This is because red wines are richer in polyphenolic compounds, which give the wine a natural level of defence against oxidation. White wines that have been handled reductively (that is, protected against oxygen exposure through the use of stainless steel and inert gases in the winemaking process) are especially vulnerable to oxidation, and need careful protecting.

The ageing of wine is what is known as a "reductive" process. It works properly in the absence of oxygen, which is why a good tight seal by the closure, whether a cork or a screwcap, is important. While there's some debate about whether tiny traces of oxygen might be needed to ensure optimum evolution of wine in the bottle, it is universally recognized that any significant influx of oxygen will rapidly oxidize the wine – that is, the oxygen will combine chemically with compounds present, negatively affecting the flavour. Interesting data has come from the Australian Wine Research Institute's (AWRI) ongoing closure trial, which has tracked the performance of a number of different closure types over time, using a Semillon wine as the test subject. This has shown that the critical level of free $SO_2$ is 10mg/litre at the particular pH of this wine (3.1). When $SO_2$ levels have dropped below this, test bottles are rated high in the attribute "oxidized" by the sensory analysis panel, but this trait is much less common in bottles exceeding this level. Peter Godden of the AWRI has also calculated this critical point for some of the problem wines he has seen. "It is very pH-dependent," he reports, "and we saw one wine in which it was 15mg/litre; that is, bottles below this level were rated exponentially higher for oxidation during sensory analysis, which correlated strongly with brown colour."

But $SO_2$ is also microbicidal. It prevents the growth of – and, at high enough concentrations, kills – fungi (yeasts) and bacteria. Usefully, $SO_2$ is more active against bacteria than yeasts, so by getting the concentration right, winemakers can inhibit growth of bad bugs while allowing good yeasts to do their work. $SO_2$ is usually still added to the crushed grapes in wild yeast fermentations; while it kills some of the natural yeasts present on grape skins, the stronger strains survive, and thus are selected preferentially. Sweet wines and unfiltered red wines are at higher risk of rogue microbial growth, so with these it is especially important that correct $SO_2$ addition is practised.

It follows from all this that if you don't use enough $SO_2$ in your winemaking, you run the dual risks of oxidized wine, and off-flavours and aromas from unwanted microbial growth, together with potentially considerable bottle variation.

## Best practice in sulphur dioxide usage

While this might encourage some winemakers to bung in more $SO_2$ just to be on the safe side, Godden suggests that the best way to ensure wine quality is not to use more $SO_2$, but to use it more cleverly. His idea is that the key measurement for winemakers is not the free $SO_2$ level, but the ratio of free to bound $SO_2$. That is, the key to effective $SO_2$ usage is getting the ratio of free to bound $SO_2$ as high as possible, in order to maximize the benefits of the amount added. He sent me data gathered by the AWRI Analytical Service on a typical cross section of Australian wines, which shows that in a range of reds, free $SO_2$ has been steadily increasing in recent years, while the total $SO_2$ has actually been decreasing. Thus, the ratio of free to total $SO_2$ has improved. "I consider the use of the ratio of free to total $SO_2$ as one of the most useful quality-control measures during

"If you don't use enough $SO_2$ in your winemaking, you run the dual risks of oxidized wine, and off-flavours and aromas from unwanted microbial growth, together with potentially considerable bottle variation."

Sulphur dioxide acts as a guardian of wine quality in two ways. Firstly, and most importantly, it protects the wine from oxidation. Secondly, it acts as an antimicrobial agent, preventing the growth of unwanted spoilage bugs in the wine. Peter Godden of the Australian Wine Research Institute (AWRI) describes $SO_2$ as a "magical substance" because it has these effects at very low concentrations. "We're mostly talking about a maximum of 150 parts per million (150mg/litre) and much less in most Australian wines," he explains. Godden showed data indicating that of a representative sample of Australian wines, at least seventy per cent have levels below 100mg/litre, and close to sixty per cent have 80mg/litre or less)

Correct use of $SO_2$ is a subject Godden and his colleagues of the AWRI Industry Services team have been advising Australian winemakers on quite a bit in recent years. "A wide range of the problems we see have relatively few root causes, and $SO_2$ use, or misuse, has been the most common," he says. He adds that since they began this work, data from the AWRI's commercial analytical service laboratory, which analyzes many thousands of Australian wines each year, indicates that things have improved noticeably.

winemaking," says Godden. He has similar data on Australian white wines, although he feels that there is probably some more room for improvement with these. How is a good ratio achieved? Starting with healthy grapes is important. Grapes suffering from rot have significantly higher levels of compounds that will bind $SO_2$, and enzymes that encourage oxidation. Judicious filtration, where necessary, will also help make $SO_2$ additions more effective by reducing microbial populations to a level where the $SO_2$ is more effective against them. General cleanliness in the winery is also helpful.

### Timing sulphur dioxide additions

Perhaps most important, however, are two critical winemaking interventions: (1) controlling turbidity by careful racking, fining, and filtration (if necessary); and (2) the timing and size of additions. There are three stages where wine is likely to be subject to considerable oxygen stress or the risk of bug growth: at crushing, at the end of malolactic fermentation (or alcoholic fermentation where malolactic is discouraged), and at bottling. At each of these points a healthy dollop of $SO_2$ is highly recommended. Crucially, for the same total addition, it is much more effective to add your $SO_2$ in fewer, relatively large doses, rather than in many small additions. In the latter case, you run the risk of never getting your free-$SO_2$ levels high enough for the chemical to do its job properly.

## Vins sans soufre: the quest for natural wine

So, if $SO_2$ is just about essential for winemaking, why would anyone want to do without it? There are two reasons. Firstly, because of the increasing concern people have about what they put into their bodies, they are anxious not to consume anything that has been chemically manipulated. To many people unaware of the issues, $SO_2$ use sounds like a gratuitous addition of unnecessary chemicals. This creates a potential market for "additive-free" wines. Secondly, there exists a band of passionate winemakers who see wine as a natural product. Eliminating $SO_2$ usage is viewed as the final hurdle in the quest for fully natural wines. The desire for naturalness runs strong; it's not just fringe winemakers who pursue this goal.

Nicolas Potel, who is making a name for himself as one of Burgundy's most dynamic négociants, has experimented with making $SO_2$-free wines. "I'm against any winemaking additives," he told me. So far, his experimentation has been confined to just a couple of barrels, but he was disappointed with the results. However, he may continue his trials, since his organic consultant is trying

to introduce him to a piece of rather unscientific-sounding technology (that Potel describes as a plastic pipe with a hole in it), which is claimed to alleviate the need for $SO_2$. Another Burgundian winemaker I quizzed, Claire Forestier of Domaine Bertagna, was less sympathetic to the idea of making wine without $SO_2$. "I think it's crazy," she said rather bluntly.

I then spoke at length to Joe Dressner, a wine importer in the USA who specializes in sourcing manipulation-free, natural wines from France. He doesn't think that there's a *sans soufre* ("without sulphur") movement as such, but feels that, in recent decades, there were intersecting circumstances which brought together people with an emphasis on making more natural wine. "People were using tons of chemicals and had stopped working their land," he explained. Part of this quest for natural wine has involved experimenting with non-sulphited wines.

## Markets for non-sulphited wines

In France, there is now a definite market for these wines. Posh Parisian wine shop Lavinia has a section devoted to *vins sans soufre*, which lists a couple of dozen wines. This market really began in the 1980s, with a circuit of wine bars in Paris which wanted to serve fresh wines with a purity of fruit to them. An instrumental figure in the trend has been Jacques Néauport, whose inspiration was the late Jules Chauvet – a négociant with an enquiring mind who tried out a number of novel ideas, including making wine without added sulphites. Néauport has consulted for a number of growers, (the first was Overnoy in the Jura), including Marcel Lapierre in Morgon. Néauport developed a vinification method involving carbonic maceration under very cold conditions. Catherine and Pierre Breton, Thierry Allemand, Jean Foillard, and Pierre Frick are others who work without $SO_2$ for at least some of their wines. A common claim is that wines made in this way have a greater purity of fruit and are aromatically more interesting – plus, if you overindulge, you are less likely to suffer a headache later. While there exist producers who are fanatical or religious about not using sulphur, Dressner suggests these are usually the less interesting ones. His growers who work *sans soufre* will often add a little at his request, because many of his customers don't have good enough storage to preserve the integrity of these rather fragile wines.

"If the drive to use lower levels of added $SO_2$ can be coupled with a better understanding of how this wonder molecule works, so that it can be used in smarter ways, as Peter Godden advocates, then everyone is likely to benefit."

Indeed, storage is the key problem with $SO_2$-free wines: they need to be kept below about 14°C (57.2°F) at all points in the supply chain. It's easy to see how this might be achieved by consumers buying their wines direct from a grower and putting them straight into a temperature-controlled cellar, but this degree of protection is hard to envisage in the modern retail environment. For this reason alone, even if $SO_2$-free wines were to prove sensorially superior (and many dispute this claim), it's unlikely they will ever become widespread. Other keys to successful no- or very low-$SO_2$ wines include using good-quality fruit, keeping a spotless winery, and employing a relatively oxidative winemaking style.

But it is not just in France where winemakers are toying with eliminating added $SO_2$. In Italy, a few isolated growers have tried it, including Stanko Radikon in Friuli, and newcomer Frank Cornelissen, who has a vineyard on Mount Etna, Sicily (*see* box, page 96). In the USA, Coturri and Frey are the best-known of a number of producers who specialize in $SO_2$-free winemaking. It must be pointed out, though, that even if no $SO_2$ is added during the winemaking process, there will still be some present in the wine; it's a by-product of fermentation, and yeasts produce small quantities of around 5–15mg/litre quite naturally, so the notion of a totally sulphite-free wine is illusory.

Why focus on what is, in many respects, a winemaking fringe of little commercial significance? Joe Dressner makes a good point. He thinks that the *sans soufre* producers have been more generally useful to the wine world, in that pushing the extreme has moved everyone along in the direction of using less $SO_2$ overall, and certainly less than some of the heroic levels that used to be applied in many parts of Europe. He likens these pioneers to those who have advocated unfiltered wines; while not everyone bottles unfiltered, these days, quality-minded winemakers will generally try not to filter unless it's really necessary. Now, if the drive to use lower levels of added $SO_2$ can be coupled with a better understanding of how this wonder molecule works, so that it can be used in smarter ways, as Peter Godden advocates, then everyone is likely to benefit.

## The effects of sulphur dioxide on health

Now we turn to the consumer's perspective. Is $SO_2$ healthy? Not completely, is the simple answer. $SO_2$ can cause adverse reactions in some asthmatics that can be dangerous at ingestion levels as low as 1mg/litre. For this reason, some doctors have even gone as far as suggesting that asthmatics should avoid wine altogether. For most people, it is probably fairly harmless at the levels used in winemaking, but anyone drinking wine on a regular basis is probably taking in more than medical experts recommend (although it could be debated that these levels are set a little low in the name of caution).

$SO_2$ levels in wine are subject to regulation by various authorities. The EU has set a maximum permitted level that varies with wine type from 160mg/litre (or parts per million) for dry red wines to 300mg/litre for sweet whites and 400mg/litre for botrytized wines. In Australia, regulations permit 250mg/litre for dry wines and 350mg/litre for those with more than 35 grams/litre residual sugar. In the USA, the maximum level allowed is similar, and any wine with more than 10mg/litre $SO_2$ (this level can be reached naturally even if no $SO_2$ is added) has to be labelled "contains sulfites". As an aside, the EU is planning soon to implement labelling laws that will make it compulsory for winemakers to declare any potential allergens and their concentrations on wine labels, including $SO_2$. On the basis of animal experiments, the World Health Organization has set the RDA (recommended daily allowance) of $SO_2$ at 0.7mg per kilogram bodyweight. Doing some simple sums, this would permit a 70kg (that's 11 stone or 154 pounds) human to take in 49mg $SO_2$ a day. Half a bottle of wine with an $SO_2$ level of 150mg/litre would provide 56mg of $SO_2$, thus exceeding the RDA.

Many people who suffer adverse reactions to wine, such as headaches and flushing, blame $SO_2$ – partly, one suspects, because it seems an obvious candidate as an added chemical substance. The issue of adverse wine reactions is a complex one, and the scientific literature offers few clear indications of the culpable compounds. However, many foodstuffs contain higher levels of sulphites than wine, with the worst offenders being dried fruits, which typically contain 1,000ppm – about ten times the level in wine.

# 16 Reduction: volatile sulphur compounds

While every winemaking expert I've consulted agrees that reduction is an important topic to cover, there's no doubting that the subject is highly technical. My goal here will be to make this rather specialized subject understandable to non-experts, while at the same time not shying away from the hard-core wine chemistry where it's necessary to the story.

"I feel that reduction is a key topic for the trade," says Sam Harrop, a winemaker at Domaine Matassa in Roussillon, France. Why? "Because there is a lot of confusion over just what it is. The term 'reduction' is used extensively in tastings, and I feel that in a lot of circumstances people don't really understand what it means." What, then, is a "reduced" wine, and what do people mean by "reduction character"? And firstly, what does the term "reduction" mean?

To start, some elementary chemistry. It's all about oxygen. "Reduction and oxidation are like Orient and Occident," explains Richard Gibson of Scorpex Wine Services, "opposites that depend on the relative absence of oxygen (reduction) and the relative presence of oxygen (oxidation)." The precise definition depends on measuring what is known as the redox potential, which compares the affinity of substances for electrons. According to Gibson, this measure is rarely carried out in wines.

Redox potential is measured in millivolts (mV). Typically, an aerated red wine will have a redox potential of 400–450mV, whereas storage in the absence of air for some time will reduce this to 200–250mV. If levels get as low as 150mV, then there is a danger that reduction problems can occur. Exposure to oxygen through winemaking practices such as racking, topping up barrels, and filtering increases the level of dissolved oxygen in the wine and increases the redox potential, which will then return to 200–300mV. The effect of oxygen exposure is more severe in white wines, which have a lower buffering capacity (their redox state will change more easily) than reds. Another variable here is the level of free sulphur dioxide in the wine, which as an antioxidant will act protectively by absorbing the oxygen. Yeast lees also scavenge oxygen and protect the wine in a similar fashion, helping to lower the redox potential.

In simpler terms, most people are familiar with the idea that if you expose wine to air (which contains oxygen), it becomes oxidized. And with the exception of just a few wines that are deliberately made in an oxidized style – such as madeira, *vin jaune*, and some sherries – this is a bad thing. Well, reduction is the opposite. "In wine," explains Gibson, "it is enough to say that a state of reduction applies when air is absent. Thus, when grape harvest, fermentation, maturation, and bottling are carried out without air contact or with lashings of antioxidant, reductive winemaking practices have been followed. In Australia, reductive winemaking has been central to the development of fruit-driven white styles with crisp palates. In reds, reductive winemaking tends to produce a 'tighter', more fruit-driven style. Brian Croser taught reductive winemaking in Australia at Riverina College in the late 1970s, and it has been central to the rise in Australian white-wine quality, especially for aromatic varieties."

## Volatile sulphur compounds and their effect on wine

So where is the catch? While keeping a wine away from oxygen is normally a good thing, reduction has a dark side. The danger is that it can encourage the development of reduced sulphur compounds, which have a significant effect on the flavour of wines, even at tiny concentrations. This results in what is described as a "reduced" or "reductive" character.

In fact, when most people use the term "reduction", they are actually referring to the presence of sulphur compounds. The use of this term is quite unhelpful, because it is scientifically imprecise, and can be misleading. "'Reduction' is a simplification, a language abuse," says Dominique Delteil, scientific director of the Institut Coopératif du Vin (ICV). "As often occurs in wine vocabulary, tasters have been willing to link sensory sensations to chemical or physical states without being sure whether they are real or not. Reduction is typical of this. I prefer to call this concept 'sulphur flavours' rather than 'reduction'."

"Sulphur flavours" are commonly associated with descriptors such as "burnt match", "garlic", "onion", "leek", or "rotten egg", according to the intensity and the culture of the tasters (how often they have met those aromas, how intense were they when the tasters built their references). These sulphur compounds still exist in oxidative conditions, and this leads to misunderstandings when they are then also described as "reduction". "As a winemaking consultant," says Delteil, "I have seen winemakers making technical mistakes because of this false concept. For example, some have continued to aerate an already oxidized wine because it had 'reduction' characters, so it was thought to need oxygen."

## The different sulphur compounds in wine

The main baddy here is hydrogen sulphide. "This is easily formed by yeast during fermentation, whenever there are stresses, including nutrient deficiency," explains Phil Spillman, winemaker with New Zealand's Villa Maria. "When a yeast cell finds its preferred nitrogen source (ammonium and amino acids) in limited supply, it can turn to the two sulphur-containing amino acids, liberating the sulphur in them as hydrogen sulphide. Winemakers find that many conditions of non-nutritional stress (*e.g.* temperature-change or dry-goods additions) can also cause yeast to produce hydrogen sulphide, so we usually add some diammonium phosphate (DAP, a yeast nutrient) whenever such conditions are encountered or imposed.

"Mercaptans are a group of larger, sulphur-containing molecules, which are formed slowly where hydrogen sulphide is not removed promptly," Spillman adds. "These compounds are more worrisome to winemakers because they are difficult to remove, so good winemaking practice includes protocols for removing hydrogen sulphide (by copper sulphate addition) before there is any chance for them to evolve into mercaptans."

Time to talk to an expert on wine flavour chemistry. Dr. Leigh Francis is a senior research chemist with the Australian Wine Research Institute (AWRI), and he has a particular interest in sensory analysis. I quizzed him about how he would define "reduced" in the context of wine tasting. "The word is usually reserved for aromas arising from what are presumed to be sulphur compounds," he explained. "Often tasters at the AWRI would have sufficient technical knowledge to be are aware of how particular sulphur compounds smell, and often use the chemical name rather than an evocative descriptor." Dr. Francis then described the descriptions of some of these compounds in sensory analysis work. "'Reduced' would encompass aromas such as: hydrogen sulphide (and only rarely would a taster go the extra step of delineating the aroma as 'rotten-egg gas' or similar); mercaptans or thiols – and for these aromas, tasters would define [them] with words such as cabbagey, rubbery, and burnt rubber, or sometimes a more general term would be used such as 'sulphidic', which would encompass both of the above, or 'struck flint'.

"There is at least one other specific sulphur compound that tasters are aware of, and this may sometimes be included in the term 'reduced': dimethyl sulphide (DMS), which has its own normally distinctive aroma of cooked vegetables, at high levels reminiscent of cooked corn or canned tomato, at lower levels similar to blackcurrant drink concentrate. Sometimes wines showing an apparent DMS aroma will have a 'reduced' stinky note as well."

In addition, Francis points to recent research carried out by Denis Dubourdieu and colleagues at the University of Bordeaux. "[The substances known as] 4-mercapto-4-methylpentan-2-one, 3-mercaptohexan-1-ol, and 3-mercaptohexyl acetate are relatively newly identified compounds responsible for the tropical fruit/passion-fruit aroma at particular concentrations, and cat's-urine aroma at higher levels. These compounds have been found in Sauvignon Blanc, but also in other white varieties, and even in red wines, where they probably don't provide a tropical-fruit aroma but may contribute to blackcurrant character. Work has been done to indicate that yeast strains will strongly influence the levels of these compounds during fermentation." And there's more. "Benzenemethanethiol has recently been implicated in smoky/gun-flint aromas, and oak-derived thiol compounds have been implicated in coffee-oak character," Francis adds.

Yet it's not a simple case of avoiding these reduced characters altogether. "Most commonly, reduced aromas would be considered a negative by our panellists, but not always," Francis explained, "and often our panellists are simply instructed to rate the intensity of particular attributes rather than give a quality judgement. Usually the term in a tasting note would indicate that a wine had a

## The winemaking tightrope: sulphur compounds and wine complexity

Scorpex's Richard Gibson states that, "Walking the tightrope between enough oxygen exposure to give wines complexity without reaching a level that causes apparent oxidation is one of winemaking's big challenges."

"Mastering reduction during the winemaking process and during ageing is the only way to protect the 'fruity' character of wines (red included)," says researcher and consultant Dr. Pascal Chatonnet. "Some oxygen is, of course, necessary to prevent any excess of reduction with synthesis of off-flavours. It is more difficult with red wines, because we need oxidation to promote the positive evolution of the tannins and colour stabilization, while at the same time knowing that a strong oxidative stress can destroy the original fruit."

Gibson emphasizes that it is important to use the right technique for the right wine. "Aromatic whites benefit from reductive winemaking, which allows the clear expression of the varietal character, unsullied by oxidation," he says. "The same

applies for lighter, fruit-driven white styles. Bigger reds need air during maturation, because the phenols absorb oxygen, which leads to polymerization and complexity." Gibson also thinks it is important to use the right technique at the right time. "Oxidative juice handling for whites is a pretty popular technique," he adds. "Grapes are picked without sulphur dioxide and the juice is processed with air contact. All the susceptible phenols polymerize and the juice goes a horrid brown. Ferment as normal; the phenols precipitate and the resultant wine is relatively free of phenolics. From then on handle the wine reductively."

Along similar lines, some red grapes are regarded as reductive (e.g. Syrah and Mourvèdre), and others as oxidative (e.g. Grenache, Pinot Noir). "For winemaking, some varieties are originally very reductive," says Pierre Perrin of Château de Beaucastel. "We have to give oxygen to them, but not as much as they need, to keep a little reduction for bottling. The varieties that are sensitive to oxygen are kept away from it."

'stinky' cabbagey/rubbery/sewerage note that, depending on the intensity, could render it faulty and unpleasant, but it may be only a slightly noticeable character. If the compound responsible is hydrogen sulphide, it can disappear with swirling the glass, and make a final decision more difficult for the taster." Researcher and consultant Dr. Pascal Chatonnet also sees reduction as a double-edged sword. "An excess of reduction can produce off-flavours coming from an excess of volatile sulphur compounds," he says. "But a good equilibrium permits the maintenance of some very sensitive aromatic products involved in the 'flowery' and 'fruity' character of young wines."

## Toying with reduction

It seems that, while the development of reduced sulphur compounds in wine is normally best avoided, there are some circumstances where they can contribute something positive. Indeed, some winemakers have deliberately set out to use reductive winemaking techniques to encourage the development of these compounds as complexing agents in their wines. This currently seems to be quite a hot topic in winemaking, although few research studies have addressed it directly.

According to James Healey, previously winemaker at Cloudy Bay, "toying with reduction is a risky business that requires a bit each of courage, experience, and knowledge mixed in appropriate portions. Reduction can be a very positive thing in certain wine types and not in others. For example: in Champagne, the bready/brioche character from ageing for a period on the lees is a result of a certain type of reduction in association with autolysis (self-destructive breaking down of structure) and liberation of the contents of yeast cells into the wine. The reductive characters from the fermentation of Chardonnay juice containing highish solid concentrations result in accentuated nuttiness and improved texture after ageing on the lees for some time. And the 'cat's pee' or sweaty character that develops during fermentation of Sauvignon Blanc from cooler climates is the result of a certain reduction-related compound. In fact, the sweaty character is so close to hydrogen sulphide that one must be careful that the sweat doesn't mask the sulphide in a young wine about to go into bottle. I have seen wines spoiled as a result of the sweat diminishing with time and sulphides becoming more evident. Obviously, the sweaty story could be seen as good reduction or bad reduction, depending upon your liking for Sauvignon."

Leigh Francis of the AWRI agrees that reduced characters aren't always negative. "Overall," he says, "as always with flavour chemistry and sensory properties, it is hard to be too definitive about negative/positive. A small amount of a particular character in a wine that has other fairly strong aroma attributes will likely be accepted and liked. It's when the aroma dominates that the [reduced sulphur] compounds could be considered negative, but this is probably the case with any aroma you can think of. Too much of a good thing can be too overwhelming, make the wine too simple and not attractive to drink much of. For sulphur compounds in general, it does seem, however, that when they're at very high concentrations, an unpleasant note becomes evident, no matter how pleasant they seem at lower levels, which is not the case for many other flavour compounds. It is likely that hydrogen sulfide will be negative, no matter what level."

Phil Spillman sums it up well. "In a broader sense," he says, "the hundreds of aroma, flavour, and tactile compounds that make up wine are in various states of reduction or oxidation. Both processes have a bad name in wine because the words are used to describe extremes. 'Reduced' is used to describe a wine that is generally

"'In a broader sense, the hundreds of aroma, flavour, and tactile compounds that make up wine are in various states of reduction or oxidation. Both processes have a bad name in wine because the words are used to describe extremes.'"

sulphidic, and 'oxidized' for one that is aldehydic. However, attractive compounds can also result from these processes." Spillman also has a specific suggestion for how reduction might combine with oak barrels to add complexity. "An oak compound, furfural, is reduced in wine to furfuryl alcohol, and I have heard conjecture that this compound can react with the old devil hydrogen sulphide to produce a compound that possesses a coffee-like aroma. Unfortunately, I am not aware of any literature that can substantiate this, but, as a winemaker, I am interested in playing around with such ideas in the pursuit of complexity. But all such exploration should occur in the early stages of wine production, well before bottling: a point at which all quality aspects should be well-refined."

## Sulphur characters can be good

Dominique Delteil gives two examples of how sulphur characters can be positive according to their context. "First," he says, "[consider] a very ripe Languedoc Syrah macerated to reach liquorice aromas, and then aged in oak. In that wine, hints of 'burnt match' could be very interesting from a sensory point of view. They will match the ripe fruit/vanilla style. Most wine-drinkers will appreciate that because those aromas are in a very sweet, aromatic environment, so they won't express as

## Managing sulphur-compound flavours in wine

How can the negative effects of sulphur compounds be managed? "By prevention," says Dominique Delteil. "For prevention, a minimum knowledge of the phenomenon is necessary." He explains the good practice he tries to develop in the wineries with which the Institut Coopératif du Vin (ICV) is working. "Sulphur compounds are produced by the yeast, either during its life or after its death," he says. "This is ninety-nine per cent of sulphur flavours. Those compounds are chemically extremely reactive, so what we identify with a word such as 'garlic' comes from yeast native molecules (molecules liberated by the yeast in the chemical form they have when they reach our sensory bulb), and from sulphur compounds that are made through different chemical reactions during fermentation and ageing. But almost everything comes from the yeast, so prevention is based on the yeast."

Delteil explains that avoiding the production of excessive sulphur compounds is a complex matter. "The key point is the yeast strain. There are huge differences between the different yeasts; that's true among the hundreds of selected oenological natural yeasts available today, and also among the indigenous yeasts. This is then amplified by the yeast nutrition – the second key point. The higher the sugar in the juice, the lower the natural content in complex nitrogen compounds (particularly amino acids), the higher the yeast stress, and the higher the risk of sulphur-compounds excess. Those conditions are typically found in the Mediterranean areas. Once the yeast strain and the nutrition are okay, oxygen will be an extra tool for the winemaker. If the first two key points are not managed, it is hazardous to manage the problem just with oxygen. Why? Stressed yeast cells produce sulphur compounds continually, and high-oxygen winemaking processes add oxygen once a day in reds and once or twice during the whole fermentation in white or rosé. The added oxygen arrives to find some already-stabilized sulphur compounds.

"The third key point is yeast management during ageing. Once a winemaker has made a fermentation without a sulphur problem, he must manage the risk due to dead yeast. Many practices are consistent. If one keeps a certain level of dead yeast (we call them light lees), it is recommended that they should be stirred regularly into the wine to avoid reductive zones in the tank or the barrel. Here, 'reductive' is used in its proper physico-chemical sense. This movement is the reason for the traditional stirring (bâtonnage) during ageing with lees. The right amount of oxygen is also important, either through the stirring, or through directly managed injections."

So, how should winemakers enhance the positive effects of sulphur compounds? "They should amplify the other positive characters in the wine," says Delteil. "That is, ripe aromas (fruity, spicy, vanilla, etc., according to the grape, the place, the style goals, the market goals) and round mouth-feel sensations. Among ripe aromas, sulphur flavours will express as mineral characters, and in the mouth they won't provoke too much dryness and bitterness in the after-taste." Why talk about mouth-feel? "Some common sense," Delteil says. "Volatile compounds that are aggressive to the olfactive bulb through the so-called ortho-olfaction (direct smell versus retro-olfaction) are not 100 per cent volatile. Most of the compounds (in quantity) stay in solution in the wine (at tasting temperature) and so will come into contact with the mouth, and will come across as aggressive, just as they are in the olfactive bulb. That impact of sulphur on mouth-feel is not often recognized and integrated in winemaking, although it is very important for consumers."

dominant. Second, [take] a cool-climate unripe Cabernet Sauvignon. Let's suppose that this wine has exactly (chemically speaking) the same amount of the sulphur compounds that gave the interesting light 'burnt match' in the above Syrah. In that wine, those chemicals will give a different sensation that the same taster will translate as 'leek', 'green bean', and eventually 'garlic'."

Delteil then provides two explanations: one from a sensory perspective and one from a chemical one. "Sensory answer: the same sensation (the molecules reaching the sensory bulb in the palate cavity) will produce different perceptions (neuro-sensorial unconscious feeling) and finally a different translation (the conscious expression, such as the pronounced word 'garlic') according to the other compounds reaching the sensory bulb at the same time. This phenomenon is very well-known in cooking. So some vegetal character in the unripe Cabernet will emphasize the sensation and translation. [In contrast], the ripe aromas of the Syrah make more acceptable and even interesting the same amount of chemical compounds. Chemical answer: recently there has been significant progress in understanding the chemistry of macromolecules in wine, particularly with the work carried out in the INRA research centre in Montpellier by Professor Moutonnet and his team. An interaction has been identified (non-classical chemical links between molecules) between volatile compounds and some polysaccharides from the grape, the yeast or the lactic-acid bacteria. It is also now known that ripe grapes release more macromolecules into the wine. So in our examples, maybe there was the same amount of sulphur compounds (from a classical, analytical, chemistry point of view) but the volatilities were different because of a higher macromolecule concentration in our ripe Syrah."

With the sorts of wines he is making in the Mediterranean regions from very ripe grapes, Delteil thinks that "It is interesting to manage sulphur characters closer to the razor's edge, once we are sure that we are managing the basic sulphur off-flavours risks." Oxygen is a useful tool in this sort of manipulation. "Once one gets the first level of security with yeast, nutrients, and so on with a lower amount of oxygen," he explains, "one can play around with the 'burnt-match' character. Working this way, one also helps preserve native fruit characters. So there is a double effect: hints of burnt match with rich, fresher fruit. If the wine is backed with very rich, ripe fruit, it is a style change that can be attractive. In hot-climate areas, it recalls the good characters of cooler areas (when they reach ripening!). It is trendy today not to push the natural, ripe Mediterranean style too far. Oak management is also a tool to complement ripeness with mineral/smoky/fresh-fruit characters."

## Deconstructing terroir?

Sam Harrop, of Domaine Matassa in France's Roussillon, has a fascinating idea, albeit one that may prove difficult to test. In chemical terms, minerality is an ill-defined quality in wine, but when it does occur, it is commonly explained as being a terroir character. Yet what if it is actually a consequence of reduction, caused by a combination of volatile sulphur compounds at low levels? "Wines from many of the best wine regions in France show mineral/reductive qualities," says Harrop. "Perhaps these qualities are derived in the winery and not the vineyard."

"I do believe that minerality and reduction are related," counters James Healey. "It could be a result of struggling ferments, coupled with nutrient deficiency/vine stress, but I don't think that this is why great white burgundy or Riesling achieve this character. I think these wines derive this character because

"In chemical terms, minerality is an ill-defined quality in wine, but when it does occur, it is commonly explained as being a terroir character. Yet what if it is actually a consequence of reduction, caused by a combination of volatile sulphur compounds at low levels?"

the producers understand how to get it from their vines and vinifications. I suppose that someone could fluke it from time to time, but there are many great producers that consistently hit the nail year after year."

Delteil agrees that flavours from sulphur compounds are often misidentified as terroir characters. He recounts his experience with a client in Friuli. "According to the commercial manager, the flinty character was too high in the wine even though they were applying classical prevention practices." Delteil looked to see how the flintiness could be reduced, and found that the best method was through amplifying the ripe-grape character. "It was a classical pendulum effect between ripe fruit and sulphur," he recalls, "and we now have an accepted level of flint hints for the market goal. I personally think that excessive sulphur characters are too often presented as a terroir expression (so nobody can say a word about it because it's terroir!), although they are misunderstanding the risks created by a situation, and the winemaker. And when one applies a better-adapted process, that famous terroir appears to be a luscious fruit source."

Richard Gibson is less sure about this effect on terroir characters. When I asked him about minerality and reduction, his response was, "You expect an Australian to answer this with a straight face? Minerality: this is a very difficult term to define." He continues, "I think terroir characters are unlikely to be a function of reduction. Reductive characters favour varietal expression. The situation in the south of France and Italy with Australian-style winemaking highlights this."

## Screwcap reduction

One reason why reduction is currently a hot topic is because of the increasing adoption of screwcaps. Because screwcaps provide a tighter seal than tree bark and synthetic corks, they encourage reduction. The potential hazards here were emphasized in the ongoing AWRI trial on closure types, where the Semillon wine used in the trial developed a rubbery, reductive taint after bottling with screwcaps.

This issue was recently addressed in a technical review from the AWRI, which confirmed that the aroma was due to chemical reactions of sulphur compounds in the reduced environment of the screwcap seal. Interestingly, this

## Sulphur-containing mercaptans (volatile thiols) and their importance in the aroma of Sauvignon Blanc wines

Dr. Catherine Peyrot des Gachons studied the aroma potential of Sauvignon Blanc for her PhD, and has demonstrated that two classes of compound are key. First, methoxypyrazines, which contribute herbaceous and green-pepper aromas; these decrease during maturation of the grapes. The other class of aroma compounds are the mercaptans: sulphur-containing compounds that also go under the name of volatile thiols. These are produced by yeasts acting on precursors, some of which are present in the must, others only in the grape skins. The precursor concentration in must is therefore increased by prolonged skin contact, but it is a complicated situation. Not all precursors are developed into thiols; the specific yeast strain has a significant effect; copper decreases the level of thiols by reacting with them, so care must be taken with copper sprays in the vineyard; malolactic fermentation depletes the citrous aromas of Sauvignon; and thiols and their precursors are sensitive to oxidation. Some of the thiols present in Sauvignon Blanc and their characteristics are detailed below:

| COMPOUND | DESCRIPTION |
| --- | --- |
| 4-mercapto-4-methylpentan-2-one | Boxwood, broom, eucalyptus, cat urine |
| 4-mercapto-4-methylpentan-2-ol | Citrous |
| 3-mercaptohexal-1-ol | Passion-fruit, grapefruit |
| 3-mercaptohexyl acetate | Boxwood, passion-fruit |
| Benzenemethanethiol | Smoke, flint stone |
| 2-furanemethanethiol* | Roast coffee |

* Only in wines fermented in new barrels

*Based on a table from Dr. Catherine Peyrot des Gachons*

smell didn't diminish over time. But this is by no means a consistent feature of screwcapped wines, and there are no solid data suggesting that this is more likely to be a problem with screwcaps than with natural cork. Even if negative reduced aromas turn out to be a general screwcap hazard, they could be eliminated by measures such as bottling with a bigger head-space, using less sulphur dioxide at bottling, avoiding ascorbic acid use (antioxidant), and taking care to eliminate sulphide compounds in the wine at bottling.

## Conclusions

So, lots of questions, few solid answers, and lots of room for further research. As we have seen, the chemistry of reduced sulphur compounds is fairly complicated, but an increased understanding of their evolution in wine would permit winemakers to manipulate their levels with a view to increasing complexity. There's even the tantalizing prospect that some of the "terroir-like" characters in Old World styles could be understood in terms of sulphur chemistry, and perhaps allow the production of more "terroir-like" New World styles.

There are several issues related to reduction which, because of space restrictions, I haven't touched on here. One is the role of micro-oxygenation, a technique that is becoming increasingly popular (*see* chapter 12). Could micro-oxygenation be used as a tool to eliminate reduction in situations where reduced sulphur compounds would be a problem, such as leaving white wines on their lees in the anaerobic confines of a tank? Then there is the vexed but crucial issue of the role of oxygen exposure in the development of fine wines in bottle over many years. Is there enough dissolved oxygen in the wine at bottling to support extended ageing? This is critical to the potential adoption of screwcaps for fine red wines.

This leads to a final – and crucial – question. Would a technically perfect wine be boring? Chemically, wine is bewilderingly complex. Is it the case that there exist components of wine which at low levels impart complexity, at higher levels are considered as faults, and vice versa? And how can winemakers walk the tightrope of encouraging the development of these factors, while avoiding faulty wines?

# 17 Microbes and wine: yeasts and lactic-acid bacteria

Yeasts don't get enough credit. When it comes to wine, grapes get all the glory. Yet without yeasts, which are unicellular fungi, all we'd have is grape juice. The choice of yeast, or indeed the decision of whether to use indigenous yeasts or cultured strains, is an important part of winemaking. Not only do yeasts convert sugar to alcohol, but they are also able to influence the flavour and aroma of the final wine. Of the estimated 1,000 or so volatile flavour compounds in wine, at least 400 are produced by yeast. Take some freshly crushed grape must; it doesn't smell of much. In contrast, the fermented wine is often rich in aroma and flavour, all thanks to the action of yeasts.

So we've agreed that yeasts are undervalued. This chapter seeks to redress the balance a bit, looking at their role in winemaking, and addressing the science of fermentation. I'll also cover the controversy that surrounds wild yeast ferments and the attempts to engineer beneficial traits into yeast strains by genetic modification. Tagged onto this will be a brief discussion about that other important microbiological influence on wine flavour: malolactic fermentation.

## Microbes and wine: some concepts

Until the nineteenth century, fermentation must have seemed a mysterious process to winemakers. It wasn't until the studies of Louis Pasteur in the latter half of that century that yeasts were shown to be directly responsible for converting the sugar in grape must into alcohol. Pasteur correctly surmised that particular yeasts could influence the flavour of the wine. As the late, great oenologist Emile Peynaud pointed out, "Before his time, good wine was merely the result of a succession of lucky accidents."

You can't see yeasts. Like bacteria, these unicellular fungi are far too small to spot with the naked eye. Humans are tremendously visually centred, and it is perhaps because of this that we've found it hard to understand and be comfortable with the microbial world that surrounds us. In medicine, this has no doubt contributed to the current antibiotic crisis. Because we are unable to appreciate that microbes are everywhere, the message that there are good bacteria as well as pathogenic ones has been hard to handle; we're much more comfortable with the idea that bugs are bad and we should zap them all. This attitude has encouraged the irresponsible overuse of antibiotics, and led to the development of widespread antibiotic resistance, now a major threat to human health.

So, before we get to the gritty details, it's worth taking a conceptual look at microbes in winemaking. Yeasts and bacteria are ever-present in wineries. Even in a spotlessly clean environment there is always some receptive surface, like a badly soldered joint in metal pipes, where microbes can hide. Barrels are particularly receptive to microbes because the structure of wood makes it almost impossible to sterilize. Because a potential source of inoculation is just about ubiquitous, all yeasts and bacteria need is the right sort of environment, and they will begin to grow.

> "The choice between native and cultured yeasts has opened up a philosophical divide between winemakers who want to bring fermentation under control, and those who prefer to leave things to nature. These days there's a loose sort of Old World-New World divide."

Grape must represents a sugar- and nutrient-rich medium that's ideal for the growth of certain microbes. As it ferments, it changes, and its suitability for one species or strain wanes as its suitability for another develops. Let's illustrate this in picture terms. Take the side of a mountain. At the base, vegetation is lush and plentiful; the environment here suits a wide variety of organisms. Move a short way up and the change in climate due to the higher altitude means that a different population of plants will prevail. This will continue up the mountainside, until conditions are such that, towards the summit, plants can no longer establish themselves. It's a bit like this in fermenting wine. Create the right conditions and you can select the population of organisms you want to be growing at that particular time. Winemakers tend to concentrate on eradicating rogue organisms from the winery, but they might be better off concentrating on ensuring that their musts and developing wines represent ideal habitats for the sorts of microbes they want to encourage, while at the same time not neglecting winery hygiene. To quote Emile Peynaud again, "The winemaker should imagine the whole surface of the winery and equipment as being lined with yeasts."

Microbes have short generation times; thus they can be fiercely competitive. If conditions suit one yeast or bacterium a little more than any others, it will rapidly outpace the competition and establish itself as the primary fermenting organism. Winemakers have to make sure that the musts they are working with give a competitive advantage to the sorts of bugs they'd like to see growing.

## Cultured or spontaneous fermentations?

So you have your grapes and want to make some wine. You want to start a fermentation. There are two approaches open to you. Traditionally, the only option would have been to crush the grapes and leave the yeasts already present to get on with it. This is known alternatively as a "spontaneous", "wild yeast", "indigenous yeast" or "native yeast" fermentation. Since the 1960s, with the ready availability of cultured strains of *Saccharomyces cerevisiae*, winemakers now have

## "Native" yeasts

Yeasts are widespread not only in the winery, but also in the vineyard. They spend winter in the upper layers of the soil, spreading to the vines during the growing season via aerial transmission and insect transfer. They colonize grape skins during the maturation phase, although they never reach very high levels on intact grapes. Contrary to popular opinion, the bloom on the surface of grape skins isn't made up of yeast populations, rather, a wax-like, scaly material that doesn't harbour many fungi.

Only a limited number of yeast species are present on grapes, the so-called "native" yeast populations. These include: *Rhodotorula*, the apiculate yeasts *Kloeckera apiculata* and its soporiferous form *Hanseniaspora uvarum* (the most common by far), and, to a lesser extent, *Metschnikowia pulcherrima*, *Candida famata*, *Candida stellata*, *Pichia membranefaciens*, *Pichia fermentans*, and *Hansenula anomola*. Also present may be potential spoilage organisms such as *Brettanomyces* (*see* chapter 18). It needs to be added that yeast nomenclature is rather a confusing

business, with various synonyms in common use for the same bug. This isn't surprising, because until the recent development of molecular methods for typing yeast strains and species, it was rather hard to tell all of them apart.

The main wine yeast, the alcohol-tolerant *Saccharomyces cerevisiae*, is rare in nature. Attempts to culture *S. cerevisiae* from the skins of grapes have proved unsuccessful. The only way its presence can be demonstrated is by taking grape samples and placing them in sterile bags, crushing them under aseptic conditions and seeing what happens, an experiment that has been performed in Bordeaux. At mid-fermentation, *S. cerevisiae*, which is undetectable on grape skins, represents almost all the yeasts isolated. In a few cases no *S. cerevisiae* is present and apiculate yeasts do the fermentation. Opinion still remains divided about whether *S. cerevisiae* originated in the vineyard or is actually a human introduction, crossing over to winemaking from its ancient and widespread use in baking and brewing.

the choice of inoculating the must with a starter culture of their preferred yeast. Estimates are that, worldwide, some eighty per cent of wine was still produced by spontaneous fermentation in the late 1990s, although this proportion may have shifted since then.

The choice between native and cultured yeasts has opened up a philosophical divide between winemakers who want to bring fermentation under control, and those who prefer to leave things to nature. These days there's a loose sort of Old World-New World divide, with the former largely preferring to use indigenous yeasts and the latter relying on cultured strains, although this divide is far from an absolute.

What happens during a spontaneous fermentation? Because the initial inoculum of yeasts from the winery environment and grape skins is quite low, things can take a while to get going. This introduces an element of risk. If bugs such as *Acetobacter* (the acetic-acid bacterium that turns wine to vinegar) establish themselves before the fermentative yeast species, then the wine will be at risk of spoilage. Also, there's no guarantee that the native yeasts that establish themselves will do a good job. Like *S. cerevisiae*, all various native yeasts exist in many different strains, some desirable, others not. With a spontaneous fermentation you take what you are given.

The early stages of these fermentations are typically dominated by *Kloeckera*, *Hanseniaspora*, and *Candida*. As the alcohol levels rise a little, they bow out and others such as *Cryptococcus*, *Kluyveromyces*, *Metschnikowia*, and *Pichia* step in to take their turn. It has been estimated that in an uninoculated ferment as many as twenty to thirty strains participate. But as alcohol levels reach four to six per cent, the native species can't take it, and the alcohol-tolerant *S. cerevisiae* will take things from there.

There are twists to this story, however. Most winemakers will add some $SO_2$ on crushing. This slants things in favour of *S. cerevisiae* and the more robust of the native species, eliminating some of the more dodgy wild yeasts and spoilage bacteria, which tend to be more sensitive to the microbicidal actions of $SO_2$. Temperature also affects the balance of yeast species in the fermentation. Cooler temperatures (below 14°C/57.2°F) favour wild yeasts such as *Kloeckera*, whereas higher temperatures shift things in favour of *S. cerevisiae*. Added to this, as harvest gets under way, the winery equipment will be a ready source of inoculum, and fermentations will get going a lot faster, with *S. cerevisiae* establishing itself sooner. Studies have shown that after a few days of harvest operations, half of yeasts isolated from the first pumping over of a spontaneously fermented red-grape tank are *S. cerevisiae*. Aside from the actual properties of the wild yeasts themselves, spontaneous ferments cause a delay to the onset of vigorous fermentation. This will allow oxygen to react with anthocyanins and other phenolics present in the must, enhancing colour stability, and accelerating phenolic polymerization.

## Weighing the risks of spontaneous fermentation

Why take the risk of a spontaneous wine fermentation? In many cases the motivation will be ideological – this is the traditional approach in certain areas and there is a reluctance to adopt alternative methods, or a disbelief in the integrity or efficacy of these alternative methods. Others do it for quality reasons: native yeasts are thought to produce wines with a fuller, rounder palate structure, and the ferments tend to be slower and cooler, burning off fewer aromatics. There is also a cost saving: cultured yeast has to be paid for.

It should be pointed out that, even where cultured strains of yeast are used, wine must is not a sterile medium, and even though a good dose of sulphur dioxide ($SO_2$) will kill off the more susceptible bacteria and yeasts already present, some indigenous strains will probably play a small role in the fermentation.

## An ideological divide: wild versus cultured yeasts

French winemaker Nicolas Joly sums up well the objection that some winemakers have to using cultured yeasts to initiate fermentation. "Re-yeasting is absurd," he says. "Natural yeast is marked by all the subtleties of the year. If you have been dumb enough to kill your yeast, you have lost something from that year." He's not alone. Many winemakers, particularly those in the classic European wine regions, see the use of cultured yeasts as unnecessary and even plain wrong. They argue that the native yeasts present in the vineyard are part of the terroir (see chapter 2). "We are very big fans of wild-yeast ferments," says Pierre Perrin, of Château de Beaucastel in France's Châteauneuf-du-Pape region. "It can be risky if the fermentation doesn't begin quickly. But if you do a *pied de cuve* [a small amount of must derived from previously picked grapes] two or three days before your first harvest day, you can mix this with your crop after a few days of maceration, and then the fermentation will go. The key is to have a fermentation departure that isn't too fast (which eliminates the maceration process) or too slow (which risks acetic problems)."

However, most New World winemakers, and a growing band of Old World producers, now initiate winemaking with cultured yeasts, seeing the subsequent control of fermentation parameters as the key to quality. The choice of specific yeast strain is also seen as an important winemaking decision, since the various properties of the yeast can be chosen to complement or add to the wine style being made. Yeast expert (and now managing director of the Australian Wine Research Institute (AWRI)) Isak "Sakkie" Pretorius points out that the outcome of spontaneous fermentation is highly unpredictable, and describes the risk involved as "potentially staggering".

I asked Rui Reguinga, a Portuguese consultant winemaker, about whether he preferred to use cultured or indigenous yeasts. "I always use cultured yeasts," he explained. "While we might lose a little *typicité*, with the cultured yeasts we see more of the potential of the variety. We have a correct fermentation that starts at the right time and finishes without problems. If things go well with wild yeasts, you have better *typicité*, but if you have bad yeasts, you have a problem." However, Reguinga doesn't see the choice of yeast strain as a way to alter the intrinsic characteristics of the wine. "We use neutral yeasts in order to achieve a successful fermentation without influencing the aroma," he adds. There are specific regional considerations that alter Reguinga's decision. With his work for Quinta dos Roques in the Dão region, he is dealing with a harvest time where there can be sudden changes of temperature. This unstable climate can make it problematic to get fermentation going. Additionally, there's an element of risk management, especially when you are dealing with large quantities of someone else's wine. "It is too much to play with 200,000 litres," admits Reguinga.

"Success with wild yeasts depends on the right combination of yeasts and cellar. On occasion the wine is more complex," says California State University professor Ken Fugelsang, "but in the majority of years, the dangers outweigh the

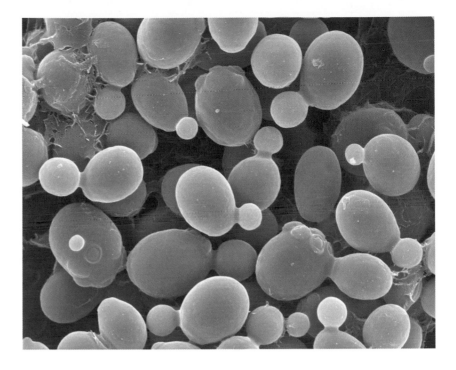

benefits." It is now even possible to buy commercial cocktails of wild yeasts plus cultured *S. cerevisiae*. "You do see the succession," says Fugelsang, who has used these experimentally. "*S. cerevisiae* doesn't take off immediately." How does he feel native-yeast ferments affect the wine? "They add mouth-feel and structure, with an interesting bouquet," he says, and points out that it is hard to separate the wild-yeast action from the fact that the native yeasts work slower, allowing oxygen to have more effect on the wine.

## Selecting for yeast strains: desirable properties

Yeasts do a whole lot more than just convert sugar into alcohol. They are responsible for the metabolic generation of many wine flavour compounds from precursors in the grape must. Because of this, the use of strains of cultured yeast with specific properties has become an important winemaking tool – although one that is not universally welcomed. Some traditional producers see this as a way of cheating.

Wine microbiologists see the development of yeast strains with enhanced abilities as an important goal in furthering wine quality. There are two ways of doing this. The first is by more "traditional" genetic techniques that don't involve the direct introduction of new genes. These include selection of variants (choosing the best of a range of natural genetic variants); mutation and selection (using a mutagen to increase the frequency of genetic variation and then selecting for those mutants with enhanced properties); hybridization (mixing together different species); and sphaeroplast fusion (a special way of joining yeast cells to produce progeny with enhanced properties). The second is by transformation: the precise introduction of new, specified genes into the genome of the yeast strain of interest. This is also known as genetic modification (GM).

Both have their benefits and drawbacks. If the trait of interest is polygenic (multiple genes are involved), then non-GM methods are the best way to select for this. However, they are less precise, and you run the risk of losing the

"Wine microbiologists see the development of yeast strains with enhanced abilities as an important goal in furthering wine quality."

| Goals for genetic improvement of wine-yeast strains | |
| --- | --- |
| Fermentation performance | Fermentations are often faster than optimum, so they are often controlled by lower temperatures. Sometimes, though, they are sluggish and can even become "stuck", with disastrous consequences for wine quality. Improved yeast strains could help here; targets include increased stress resistance, improved grape sugar and nitrogen uptake, resistance to high alcohol levels, and reduced foam formation. It would also be beneficial to have yeasts that can utilize nitrogen sources in wine that they currently don't (this would help avoid stuck fermentations), and for them to be resistant to toxins produced by wild-yeast strains. |
| Biological control of spoilage bugs | Spoilage microbes are a constant threat, and are countered by the addition of sulphur dioxide. A new development has been the use of antimicrobial peptides and enzymes as an alternative to chemical preservation. It would be ideal if these could be synthesized directly by yeasts. |
| Processing efficiency | The fining and clarification of wine is time- and resource-consuming, and risks removal of flavour components. Wouldn't it be great if yeasts could do this themselves? They could be engineered to secrete proteolytic and polysaccharolytic enzymes that would remove proteins and polysaccharides, which can form haze and clog filters. Another avenue of research is the regulated expression of flocculation genes; this would enable winemakers to encourage the yeast to enter into suspension for fermentation, and then settle quickly as a residue on completion. |
| Flavour and sensory qualities | Wine is a complex mixture of hundreds of different flavour compounds, many of which are synthesized by yeasts. Yeast-derived compounds can be both positive and negative in terms of flavour impact; evidently, yeasts should be selected for positive-flavour impact. Yeasts that possess colour- and aroma-liberating enzymes have been selected for, as have those producing ester-modifying enzymes. Elevated alcohol levels are becoming an increasing problem in many regions, and attempts have been made to produce yeasts that ferment to dryness at lower alcohol levels by diverting more sugar to glycerol production. Yeast strains are also being developed to adjust acid levels biologically. |
| Healthy properties | Sometimes wine contains elevated levels of undesirable compounds, such as ethyl carbamate and biogenic amines (*see* page 135). It is ideal to minimize these. Yeasts could also be developed with enhanced production of supposedly health-enhancing compounds such as resveratrol. |

beneficial traits of the starting yeast strains. GM methods are much more precise and elegant, but things get complicated if more than one gene is involved, and there is still the huge hurdle of public antipathy (*see* chapter 5). It is likely that both types of strategy will prove important.

What are some of the desirable properties that microbiologists would like to engineer into yeasts? There's a fairly long list, summarized in the table above.

It is clear that there is a lot of scope for the manipulation of yeast strains to enhance wine quality. However, such developments are unlikely to appeal to the traditional wine producers, who see the wild yeasts that dominate the early phases of spontaneous fermentations as part of their terroir, and an important factor in fine-wine production.

# Malolactic fermentation (MLF)

*Saccharomyces cerevisiae* isn't the only vital microbe in winemaking. Most red wines and some whites go through a secondary fermentation, known as malolactic fermentation (MLF). Carried out by lactic-acid bacteria, it involves transforming malic acid into lactic acid. Malic is stronger than lactic (*see* page 184), so this change softens the wine's acidity. It occurs after alcoholic fermentation is complete.

There are three genera of lactic-acid bacteria: *Oenococcus* (the most important), *Leuconostoc*, and *Pediococcus*. They are ubiquitous in all grape musts and wines, but can be problematic. They can generate off-flavours and turbidity (cloudiness) and have been reported to degrade components such as glycerol and tartaric acid into bitter substances and volatile acidity. Certain strains can produce significant levels of the biogenic amines histamine, tyramine, and putrescine (made from the degradation of amino acids). In red wines, the lactic-acid bacteria remains high after completion of MLF, and can make large amounts of these biogenic amines. Using selected starter cultures of bacteria that lack amino-acid decarboxylase activity and then sulphiting at the end of MLF are popular control strategies. Techniques now exist to test what sort of lactic-acid bacteria strains are occuring naturally. If they are the wrong sort, the winemaker can inoculate with cultured *Oenococcus* strains. If wines do not undergo MLF, lactic-acid bacteria can cause secondary fermentation in the bottle, with the formation of small bubbles of $CO_2$. MLF also effects the colour of red wines. The best strategy for colour stabilization seems to be to inoculate with lactic-acid bacteria at the end of alcoholic fermentation, and then allow MLF to proceed slowly at low temperature (10–14°C/50–57.2°F). MLF in barrel is now common for red wines. The wine is pressed and run off into barrel at the end of alcoholic fermentation; this is supposed to result in a better integration of oak, and a finer texture to the wine.

It would be simplistic to think that lactic-acid bacteria just metabolize malic acid. They are also likely to metabolize other organic acids (*e.g.* citric acid), sugars, and aromatic compounds present in much smaller quantities. MLF also produces ethyl lactate, which enhances the sensation of "body", and diacetyl, which can smell buttery at higher concentrations. The sensory impact of lactic-acid bacteria is thus of great importance. The possibility remains that, as with yeasts, the inoculation of wine with engineered strains of *Oenococcus oeni* could be exploited by winemakers.

Control of lactic-acid bacteria is fairly straightforward. They are sensitive to $SO_2$, and prefer high temperatures, so keeping temperatures down and maintaining decent free $SO_2$ concentrations is quite effective. Also, frequent racking deprives these bacteria of nutrient resources from the decomposition of yeast lees.

## Modified yeasts: a tool in the battle against rising alcohol levels?

One of the major problems facing winemakers in warm-climate regions is high alcohol levels. This has become more acute now that harvests are commonly dictated by phenolic ripeness rather than sugar levels. Is it possible to select for, or engineer yeasts that are less efficient at converting sugar to alcohol, possibly by making different end products from some of the sugar?

One proposal has been to make yeasts that still ferment to dryness, but which divert more of the sugar they use to glycerol, rather than alcohol. It sounds like a promising strategy, and it is one that has succeeded, to an extent. Yeasts with elevated levels of the glycerol-3-phosphate dehydrogenase (GPD) enzymes do make more glycerol, and this will result in wines with lower alcohol levels.

There are two main problems with this strategy as a way of countering high alcohol levels. First, there is a lack of consumer acceptance of wines made with genetically modified yeasts. Second, glycerol isn't a neutral flavour component in wine. Ramp up your glycerol levels and your wine will taste different. "Wines with elevated glycerol levels are peculiar in flavour presentation," says Ken Fugelsang. "To produce enough glycerol to reduce alcohol levels will make a red wine with a decidedly sweet finish." Back to the drawing board.

# 18 Brettanomyces

When Brian Fletcher, chief winemaker at Calatrasi in Sicily, found out I was writing on this subject, he couriered me a bottle of red wine. Labelled simply as *Brettanomyces*, it was a sample from Puglia that Fletcher had recently been sent by a producer there. So I opened it and poured a glass. Immediately, I got a whiff of animal sheds with some savoury, cheesy character. The palate was similarly animal-like, with a thin, metallic edge. Very rustic. Not undrinkable, but getting there, and a textbook example of a *Brettanomyces*-infected wine.

*Brettanomyces* is a yeast – that is, a unicellular type of fungus, not a bacterium – that is, a common spoilage organism in winemaking. It was first identified in the early 1900s in beer production, and its first observation in wine was in the 1950s. The goal of this chapter is to assess how much of a problem it is, what its effects are, and how it can be prevented. Finally, I'll look at the controversial issue of whether low levels of "brett", as it is widely known, can ever be a good thing, adding complexity to certain sorts of wines.

First, a dull but necessary paragraph to clear up a potential confusion. The name *Dekkera* is often used interchangeably with Brettanomyces. They are actually the same genus (this is the taxonomic group directly above "species"), with *Dekkera* being used for the ascospore-forming (sporogenous) form of this yeast, and *Brettanomyces* used for the non-spore-forming type. There are currently five recognized species of *Brettanomyces/Dekkera*: *B. nanus*, *B. bruxellensis*, *B. anomlaus*, *B. custersianus*, and *B. naardenensis* with a range of synonyms in common use. Of these, research indicates that *B. bruxellensis* is the most relevant to wine.

The microbiology of wine production is a complex business, which is covered in more depth elsewhere in this book. Freshly crushed grape juice provides an inviting habitat for a wide variety of microbes. This creates a competitive situation, and the species that can grow fastest in the prevailing condition become dominant. Initially, the yeast which is best suited to the high-sugar conditions dominate. However as the sugar levels drop and the alcohol levels rise, *Saccharomyces cerevisiae* takes over. As alcoholic fermentation finishes, the *S. cerevisiae* population decreases significantly. If, by this stage, the sugar and nutrient supplies are exhausted, that's the end of things, and the wine is stable. But if they aren't, this leaves the way open for spoilage bugs to develop; brett is one of the worst culprits here. Brett is a resourceful bug that can make use of a range of substrates, making it hard to control.

## Descriptors used to describe Brettanomyces characters

| | | | | |
|---|---|---|---|---|
| Ammonia | Barnyard | Horsy | Leathery | Sweaty |
| Mouse droppings | Stable | Medicinal | Wet dog | Cheesy |
| Manure | Smoky | Pharmaceutical | Rancid | Band-aid |
| Burnt beans | Spicy | | | |

## What does bretty wine taste and smell like?

Volatile phenols and fatty acids are the key molecules responsible for the olfactory defects in wines affected by *Brettanomyces*. According to Peter Godden of the Australian Wine Research Institute (AWRI), "The anecdotal dogma in this area is that 4-ethylphenol (4EP), isovaleric acid (IVA, also known as 3-methylbutyric acid), and 4-ethylguiacol (4EG) are the key molecules, in order of sensory importance." But he adds that he has seen variations in brett character in different bottles of the same wine. 4EP is the most prominent molecule in bretty wines, giving aromas of stables, barnyards, and sweaty saddles (apparently, but I must admit to never having smelled one). Its presence in wine is an almost certain indicator of a brett infection, and this is what most diagnostic labs test for to indicate the presence of brett. 4EG is a little more appealing, known for its smoky, spicy aromas. IVA, a volatile fatty acid, is known for its rancid, horsy aroma. Godden emphasizes that this is a complex area of study. "There is not much of a relationship between overall brett character and 4EP levels," he says, "and there are synergistic effects between the three most important sensory compounds."

As with other volatile odorants, people differ widely in their sensitivity to these molecules, and each individual shows a range of different thresholds (for example, the threshold for detecting an odorant differs from the threshold for recognition of the same odorant). Godden suggests that a

**BELOW** *Brettanomyces* cells as viewed under a light under microscope.
*Picture courtesy of ICV, France*

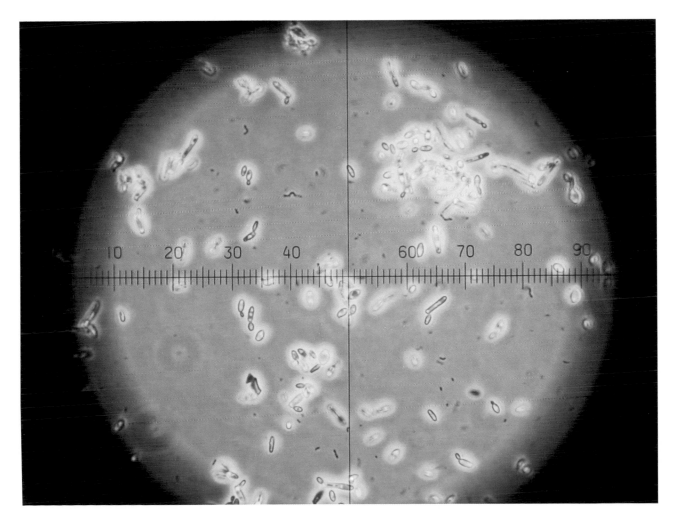

useful sensory threshold to use for 4EP is 425 μg/litre. At this concentration and beyond, a wine will typically be noticeably bretty. Below this concentration, the character of the wine may be changed but people won't, on average, recognize that this is due to 4EP. Pascal Chatonnet, who did pioneering work on the problem of brett in Bordeaux wines, found that 425 μg/litre of 4EP negatively affected the sensory property of the wines from this region that he tested. For 4EG, the thresholds were in the range of 100 μg/litre. But, specifying thresholds is an inexact science: these may be altered by the style of the wine, and the presence of other volatile compounds. Others have suggested levels as low as 300 μg/litre and even 150 μg/litre for 4EP.

Because the threshold for 4EP drops when 4EG is also present – and in brett-infected wine they typically occur together in a ratio of about 10:1 – this threshold is best calculated for a 10:1 mixture of 4EP and 4EG. In fact, the ratio of 4EP to 4EG varies among wines, although there is quite a good correlation overall. This ratio is fairly consistent for wines made from particular varieties or from particular regions, varying from 8:1 for wines from Bordeaux to 3:1 for Pinot Noir and 24:1 for Shiraz, where this has been tested. The speculation is that regional and varietal differences alter the composition of precursor compounds in the wines.

## How common is brett?

The short answer to this question is that brett is highly prevalent, and now represents an increasing problem, even in New World countries such as Australia. "We first started raising this as an issue five years ago," explains Peter Godden of the Australian Wine Research Institute (AWRI). "Since then, the AWRI has started a major project looking at *Brettanomyces*." As a scientist, Godden feels that for such an important issue, this is a relatively under-researched area. "There is a lot of conjecture," he says. "Anecdotal observations are very important, but we have to be careful with them because they can skew people's opinions."

Although *Brettanomyces* can and does occur with white wines, it is predominantly a red-wine problem. This is because red wines are far higher in polyphenol content, and they generally have a higher pH – both factors which encourage brett development for reasons that are outlined below.

With rising standards of winemaking worldwide, I was a little surprised to hear that brett is on the increase. There seem to be two contributing factors to this rise. First, there is the current trend for "natural" wines. "Minimalist winemaking is a perfect recipe for bretty wine," says Godden. "It's probable that the increase in *Brettanomyces* in the 1990s can be traced back to the winemaking fad to stop adding sulphur at crushing." Indeed, the most effective way of

## Compounds identified as contributing to Brettanomyces odours

| VOLOTILE PHENOLS | MEDIUM-CHAIN FATTY ACIDS | OTHERS |
| --- | --- | --- |
| 4-ethylphenol | octanoic acid | 2-phenylathenol |
| 4-ethylguaiacol | dodecanoic acid | isoamyl alcohol |
| | isobutyric acid | *cis*-2-nonenal |
| | isovaleric acid (3-methylbutyric acid) | *trans*-2-nonenal-damascenone |
| | 2-methylbutyric acid | ethyl decanoate |

"Diammonium phosphate (DAP) has been described as 'junk food' for yeasts – they'll use DAP in preference to amino acids, leaving them in the wine as a nitrogen source that encourages the growth of brett."

preventing brett is to maintain an adequate concentration of free $SO_2$ (*see* chapter 15). Randall Grahm of California's Bonny Doon comments, "If you are ideologically committed to no sulphitage at the crusher, this increases your chances of brett dramatically. Likewise, if you use low or no $SO_2$ in the *élevage* of the wines, this greatly increases the risk of brett." Preliminary studies by the AWRI have shown that there is a lot of genetic variability among the different *Brettanomyces* strains. This makes the correct use of sulphur an even more important issue. If it is added in small, regular doses, winemakers might unintentionally be selecting for $SO_2$-resistant strains of *Brettanomyces*, or to put it another way, super-brett strains that are then even harder to eliminate. So, timing and magnitude of $SO_2$ additions are important, as well as the actual concentrations. The best way to get rid of brett seems to be large $SO_2$ additions at strategic intervals.

The second contributing factor is the move towards making "international" styles of red wine, which are produced in an extracted style from super-ripe grapes. "These are higher in pH and richer in polyphenols," explains Grahm. The pH level is important, most likely through its role in modulating the effectiveness of any $SO_2$ additions. The higher the pH, the less effective the $SO_2$ and the more likely that *Brettanomyces* will grow. Polyphenol content is important because these compounds are the precursors for the volatile phenols largely responsible for bretty odours.

## When sugar isn't so sweet

A vital risk factor is the presence of residual sugars and nitrogen sources left over at the end of fermentation. With the gradual rise in alcohol levels in wine that has been happening over the past twenty years, the last bit of sugar commonly isn't being metabolized by the yeast. In France, Pascal Chatonnet reports that as little as 0.5g/l residual sugar is enough for *Brettanomyces* to grow to levels where it has a significant impact on the flavour profile of a wine. Godden suggests that one solution could be to try to keep the wines warm while they are being pressed.

As well as sugar, a nitrogen source is needed for *Brettanomyces* to grow. In fermenting wine, *Saccharomyces cerevisiae* uses amino acids as a nitrogen source. A recent winemaking trend has been to add diammonium phosphate (DAP) as a supplementary nitrogen source for yeasts, to reduce the risk of stuck fermentations. However, fewer than half of musts actually need this additive, and DAP has been described as "junk food" for yeasts – they will use DAP in preference to amino acids, leaving them in the wine as a nitrogen source that then encourages the growth of brett. Phenolic compounds are also a substrate for *Brettanomyces* growth.

The practice of using old barrels to mature wines is frequently touted as the main culprit of *Brettanomyces*. But according to Randall Grahm, this is not the whole story. "The received wisdom about old barrels being the great repository of brett, I think, is somewhat mythical and simplistic: dirty barrels equal dirty wines, QED. Since *Brettanomyces* is largely ubiquitous," he explains, "a rampant brett infection is often more a function of a large inoculum coming in on the grapes."

To gauge the extent of the current brett problem, Peter Godden and his colleagues recently completed a survey of Cabernet Sauvignon wines in five major regions of Australia. "If a consumer were to go out and buy a mixed

| Concentrations and ratios of 4EP, 4EG, and isovaleric acid in red wines used for the AWRI course | | | | | | |
|---|---|---|---|---|---|---|
| Variety | Number of wines | Mean 4EP (mg/l) | Mean 4EG (mg/l) | Mean ratio 4EP:4EG | Number of wines | Mean isovaleric acid (mg/l) |
| Cabernet Sauvignon | 33 | 771 | 76 | 14 | 30 | 1,264 |
| Nebbiolo | 14 | 368 | 49 | 9 | 13 | 1,155 |
| Pinot Noir | 13 | 120 | 50 | 3 | 11 | 718 |
| Shiraz | 19 | 495 | 37 | 24 | 16 | 929 |
| Total | 79 * | | | | 70 ** | |

* A total of 192 bottles were analyzed for 4-ethylphenol and 4-ethylguaiacol. Where multiple bottles of the same wine were analyzed, the mean result was used. Seven wines, which exhibited variability in the analytical results between bottles that fell outside of the uncertainty of measurement for the analytical method used, were excluded from the data.
** Seventy single bottles of different wines were analyzed for isovaleric acid concentration. *Table: courtesy of the AWRI*

dozen," he told me, "several bottles would have more than 425 μg/litre 4EP. If you drink wine regularly, you'll have come across a lot of brett." By the end of July 2003, 228 wines from the vintages 1996 to 2001 had been analyzed for 4EP and 4EG, but because of difficulties in sorting out the analytical method for IVA (*see* page 137), just twenty-five of the wines had been investigated for this latter compound. The results showed that the 4EP and 4EG levels were highly correlated, although neither level correlated with IVA concentrations.

Godden and his team at the AWRI have also studied the concentrations of brett flavour components in a range of varietal red wines used in their Advanced Wine Assessment Course in July 2003. Altogether, 192 bottles were analyzed for 4EP, 4EG, and IVA; the data are presented in the table above. The Cabernet Sauvignon wines seemed especially susceptible to brett. Average levels of both Cabernet Sauvignon and Shiraz wines were above threshold – a startling finding.

Before the 1990s, *Brettanomyces* was common in Bordeaux. The wines of several well-known classed growths were well-known for their distinctive "stink". This was almost certainly because of brett infections, but without the data (and most properties would understandably be reluctant to own up to this) I can't name any names. Since the early 1990s, however, brett has become much rarer, and this is mainly due to the groundbreaking work of Dr. Pascal Chatonnet. In 1995, Chatonnet published the results of a survey of 100 French wines, and showed that a staggering one-third of those tested had levels of volatile phenols above the perception threshold.

The conclusion seems to be that *Brettanomyces* is widespread, and that virtually every barrel of red wine has the potential to go bretty. Simply create the right environment for it, and you'll have a brett infection. Thus the key objective for winemakers who want to avoid bretty wines isn't to create a sterile winery, which will never happen, but rather to make sure that their barrels aren't a receptive environment for brett to grow in.

## Adding complexity?

Beaucastel has been widely acknowledged as one of the world's great wines over recent decades. Yet from Charles Collins's limited sampling (*see* the box "Brett, Mourvèdre or terroir? A case study" on page 142), coupled with individual tasters' experiences, it seems likely that some of the most successful past vintages of this wine have been marked by high levels of brett. This leads us to a critical – and fascinating – question: is brett ever a good thing? In small quantities, can it have a positive influence on certain styles of red wines?

If the results of surveys such as those of Chatonnet and Godden (*see* previous page) are to be extrapolated across all wines, it is likely that many wines with above-threshold levels of brett have received critical acclaim in the past and have been enjoyed by countless consumers. This leads to the conclusion that while most people wouldn't enjoy a really stinky wine, low levels of brett might not be a problem; indeed, a bit of brett might even add complexity to certain robust styles of wines.

Bob Cartwright, senior winemaker of Leeuwin Estate in Western Australia's Margaret River region, acknowledges that "a lot of winemakers like to have some brett as a complexing character. The question is, how much is too much?" Randall Grahm is undecided. "I suppose brett could theoretically add some complexity to a wine," he concedes. "But the problem is that, for now, this is not easily controllable." Pascal Chatonnet is opposed. He sees the problem of brett as a lack of fruit and loss of *typicité*. "If brett is able to grow in all the red wines of the planet – and this is the case –then all the wines will have the same odour, which is a pity."

Peter Godden is another who isn't keen on the idea. "My view is that if we could eliminate *Brettanomyces* altogether, then we would," he says. But Godden stressed that he wouldn't go so far as to say brett is always negative. "In tests where brett character has been added, it has a severe adverse effect on the palate. 4EG can be interesting and complexing and doesn't have the negative palate effect of 4EP, but with brett infection you get ten times as much 4EP than 4EG." The official AWRI position was, at the time of writing, as follows: "There is no evidence that any amount of 4EP in a wine is positive, and there is some evidence that even a small amount can be negative. Our aim, therefore, is to be able to understand and manage *Brettanomyces* to the point where winemakers could eliminate it if they wanted to, or allow 4EP to be formed in a controlled manner to the point where they considered it to be positive in their wines."

Richard Gibson, who previously worked for Southcorp but is now running a consultancy called Scorpex, takes up the theme. "There will be endless debate about whether a small amount of brett character enhances the complexity of a wine," he says. "Certainly, a little of the spicy character of 4EG may be preferable to cheesy IVA, so it is a case of *what* you get from brett, not only how much you get. But the key point for me is management and control. If you want a little, or if you want heaps, the key question remains the same: how can I manage my wines and winery environment to deliver the outcomes I want for my style, without threatening the quality of other wines in the cellar?"

## Taste tells

Winemaker Sam Harrop, a previous buyer with UK supermarket Marks & Spencer, who is now concentrating on producing his own wine (Domaine Matassa in France's Roussillon), conducted a fascinating tasting as part of his Master of Wine (MW) dissertation. He was interested in the contribution of brett to wines made from Syrah. To this end he convened a tasting of twenty-five leading Syrah-based wines, including notables such as Penfolds Grange 1990, Henschke's Hill of Grace 1996, Jaboulet's La Chapelle 1996, and Chave Hermitage 1997. A dozen or so participants from the wine trade (this author included) were asked to comment on the wines, and specify whether they detected any brett. After the tasting, samples of each wine were sent off for chemical analysis for 4EP and 4EG.

The results were telling. Although I don't have permission to specify in this book the exact levels found in individual wines, eleven of the twenty-five had above-threshold levels of 4EP (in excess of 425 µg/litre). Eighteen out of twenty-five had 4EP levels higher than 100 µg/litre and three had levels in excess of 2,000 µg/litre. Interestingly, the performance of tasters in detecting brett didn't correlate terribly well with actual levels. These striking results illustrate that brett certainly seems to be an element of the character of critically acclaimed Syrah-based red wines, and it would seem premature to dismiss brett altogether as a wine fault in all circumstances. The context seems to be important.

## Brett, Mourvèdre or terroir? A case study

*Brettanomyces* is a favourite topic for discussion among wine geeks, who'll often enter into lengthy debates about whether a certain wine is bretty or not. One wine that keeps cropping up in the context of these discussions is Château de Beaucastel, the highly regarded Châteauneuf-du-Pape estate. To some, the distinctive earthy, slightly animal-like characteristics of many past vintages of Beaucastel have reflected an expression of terroir, or even the high Mourvèdre content of this wine. Others think it's due to brett infection. Who is right?

Back in early 1998, Charles Collins, an American wine collector, became so frustrated with the endless discussions about Beaucastel and brett that he decided to try to get to the bottom of it for himself. He got hold of some scientific papers on the subject and did some cramming. "I realized that the presence of the compound 4EP is a virtually certain indicator of the presence of a brett infection," explains Collins. He contacted a laboratory which does testing for 4EP and sent them some Beaucastel from his cellar." I opted to test two of the most famous vintages: the 1989 and 1990," Collins told me. "These wines are supposed to represent what great Beaucastel is all about." He prepared the samples for shipment in sterilized glass 375ml bottles, and used fresh corks to seal them. The wines were labelled so that the lab had no clue as to their identity.

The results? According to Collins, there was "indisputable evidence that significant *Brettanomyces* infections occurred in both the 1989 and 1990 vintages of Beaucastel". Microscan and plating tests showed only small amounts of mostly dead brett cells, but the 4EP levels were 897 µg/litre for the 1989

and a whopping 3330 µg/litre for the 1990. Collins concludes, "If you personally like the smell of brett, none of this should dissuade you from buying and cellaring Beaucastel. You should, however, give up the myth that the odd flavours are due to terroir. They aren't."

"We believe in natural winegrowing and winemaking, and I must admit that this has led us to have serious debates with scientists spanning three generations," responds Beaucastel's Marc Perrin. "In the mid-1950s, for instance, our grandfather, Jacques Perrin, decided to stop using chemical pesticides or herbicides on the vineyard. At that time, when scientists were recommending the use of such chemicals for productivity or lobby reasons, that seemed crazy and impossible. Now, it seems that people have changed their mind, and more and more vineyards are turning organic.

"I could quote many more examples of opposition between a scientific vision of wine and our traditional/terroir-oriented philosophy of wine, and the subject of *Brettanomyces* is just one more," he explained. "There are certainly some *Brettanomyces* in every natural wine, because *Brettanomyces* is not a spoilage yeast (as many people think), but one of the yeasts that exist in winemaking. Some grapes, like Mourvèdre, are richer in 4EP 'precursors' than others, and we have a high percentage of these grapes in our vineyard. Of course, you can kill all natural yeasts, then use industrial yeast to start the fermentation, saturate the wine with $SO_2$, and then strongly filtrate your wine. There will then be no remaining yeasts, but also no taste and no *typicité*. That is the difference between natural wine and industrial wine, between craftsmanship and mass-market product."

## An ideal solution?

Randall Grahm has a novel suggestion, as usual. "It would," he says, "be very interesting if we could isolate a strain of *Brettanomyces* that worked in wine, depleting nutrients but producing very low levels of 4EP. In this way, one could inoculate one's wine with brett, much the same way as one inoculates one's wine with malolactic bacteria, thus depleting nutrients and rendering the wine safe from further microbial degradation." Richard Gibson of Scorpex echoes more revolutionary sentiments. "Currently, in Australia, the move is to eradicate brett," he explains. "However, with more understanding, management of brett may move to developing the ability to produce blenders with high proportions of the right brett compounds that could be used for judicious back blending, managed in a way that does not threaten the total winery environment with infection."

## Controlling brett

These suggestions bring us round to the topic of control of *Brettanomyces*. As we have already seen, maintaining high free-$SO_2$ levels is probably the most effective means of limiting brett growth. The pH level is an important factor here for two reasons: firstly, a lower pH increases the effectiveness of free $SO_2$, meaning that less is needed; and secondly, more $SO_2$ is likely to be in the free form at lower pH. Other preventive steps to control brett include completing fermentation so that there is no residual sugar left in the wine to act as a substrate, and maintaining lower temperatures in the barrel, vat or tank.

High grape-sugar levels are a risk factor for brett, because *Saccharomyces* yeasts are made to struggle to complete primary fermentations. Sam Harrop suggests that part of the problem may lie in the vineyard. "A winemaker who is serious about managing *Brettanomyces* should work his or her vineyards to achieve fruit maturity at lower levels of alcohol. This will support a healthy fermentation, reduce residual sugar content, and limit the possibility of *Brettanomyces* growth. In addition, fruit that is harvested at lower sugar levels will have lower natural pH levels, which aid greatly in managing *Brettanomyces* throughout the winemaking process by way of its relationship with $SO_2$."

Meanwhile, winemakers in Europe are hampered in their efforts to control *Brettanomyces* by the fact that dimethyl dicarbonate (DMDC, a compound also known commercially as Velcorin), which is widely used in the USA, is not allowed in European winemaking. This compound is an effective sterilant that works by deactivating enzymes in microbes, and while it is hazardous to apply, it is completely safe once in wine. A drawback, though, is the expense of the equipment needed for the application of DMDC. Any winemaker with access to DMDC can kill off any active *Brettanomyces* present, effectively stabilizing the wine before blending or bottling. In the absence of DMDC, filtration would seem to be a wise precaution for stabilizing wines at risk from brett before bottling. The down side is the possibility that filtration will also remove flavour compounds from the wine.

In any case, it is clear that, unless you are a winemaker who feels very lucky, playing with *Brettanomyces* necessitates having accurate tools for both its measurement and management. Not everyone, it must be remembered, wants to buy a wine that smells of sweaty saddles. Winemakers tend to be curious people prone to experimentation: for those with access to DMDC (and thus able to guarantee brett won't bloom in bottle), having the odd bretty barrel for use as a blending component would be interesting.

# 19 Corks, screwcaps, and alternative closures

I have to admit it – I'm a bit embarrassed about including a chapter on closures in a book on wine science. It's a subject that has nothing to do with wine itself, but instead the way it is packaged. So it seems a bit silly. In truth, however, it's a subject that impacts on the quality of wine significantly, and one that is a focus of intense debate in the wine trade. The issue at stake is the variability and high failure rate of cork-based closures, and whether alternatives such as synthetics or screwcaps would be a better way of sealing bottles. The goal of this chapter will be to review this rather complicated and potentially dull subject, focusing on the scientific data rather than the strongly held opinions and anecdotes that currently form the bulk of the discourse on closures.

## Cork: a remarkable natural substance

In the debate on closures, cork has frequently been cast as the baddy. It's the enemy. What's often forgotten is that it has remarkable natural properties. It may be highly unfashionable to say this, but cork is a gift from nature, ideally suited for sealing bottles. It comes from the bark of the cork oak, *Quercus suber*. This is an unusual and useful tree. If you stripped the bark of most trees, they would die, because you'd be removing the cambium, the cylinder of dividing cells just inside the bark that is responsible for new growth in the stems or trunks of woody perennials. The cork tree has such a thick bark that it can be stripped from mature trees without harming them. Unusually, cork trees have two cork cambium layers. The first, which has its origin in the epidermis, is removed when the tree is about twenty years old, and a new cork cambium is then formed a short distance below the site of the first. From then on, new cork tissue accumulates rapidly and can be harvested every nine to ten years, until the tree reaches a venerable old age of 150 or so.

The key to cork's mechanical properties is that it is formed of a honeycomb network of densely packed cells, whose walls have been "suberinized". The molecular composition of suberin is still a bit of a mystery. The latest view is that it is formed by a hydroxycinnamic acid-monolignon (poly)phenolic domain embedded in the cell wall, which is linked to a glycerol-based (poly)aliphatic domain located between the plasma membrane and the inner face of the cell wall. "Suberin" is therefore a term that should be used carefully, because it doesn't refer to a single molecular entity.

Suberinization also involves the deposition of a number of waxes in this inner-wall region. A wine cork consists of hundreds of millions of these suberinized cells, rendered inert and impermeable. Because these cells are filled with gas, the whole cork structure is compressible and elastic. Cork can be compressed to about half its width without losing flexibility, and it has the remarkable property of being able to be compressed in one dimension without increasing in another. It can resist moisture for decades, and will stay compressed, thus maintaining a seal, for equally long periods. Because of this composition and structure, cork is good at sealing wine bottles. A decent cork will provide a good seal for thirty years, possibly longer, allowing the wine to develop and mature. And despite the tightness of the seal that corks provide, it is relatively easy to extract them using one of a wide array of different designs of corkscrew. Added to this, taking the cork out has become a valued part of the tradition of wine. It may sound silly, but there's something special about uncorking a bottle. People like the process, and the fact that cork is a product of nature is seen as a positive attribute by many in today's environmentally conscious age.

## Cork's Achilles heel

But before you begin to wonder whether this chapter is actually an advertorial, paid for by the cork industry, let me try to put things in perspective. Cork does have an Achilles heel. As a natural substance it is variable, and is prone to failure. Most significantly, it harbours a contaminant that is able to spoil wine at fantastically low doses. Meet TCA, curse of the wine industry. TCA is the commonly used abbreviation for a chemical called 2,4,6-trichloroanisole. The dirty secret of the wine trade is that around one in twenty bottles of wine is ruined as soon as it is bottled by "cork taint", when a wine takes on a musty odour. The main culprit is TCA present in some corks, although other related anisoles have also been implicated in cases of musty taints. In extreme cases, it's hard to miss a "corked" wine – the mustiness can sometimes be overpowering. In other situations the taint is subtler, reducing the fruitiness of the wine, giving it a subdued aroma, usually with a faint whiff of damp cardboard or old cellars in the background.

**BELOW** Freshly harvested cork bark.
*Picture courtesy of Sabaté*

The problem with TCA is that it is incredibly potent; most people can detect it at concentrations as low as five parts per trillion (ppt, the same unit as nanograms [ng] per litre), and some are even more sensitive. This makes it hard to eradicate. To give you a better idea of this figure, it's equivalent to one second in sixty-four centuries. Where good data have been collected, the frequency of cork taint hovers around five per cent of bottles sealed this way – a rather contested figure, which we will address later.

## The origins of TCA

Where does TCA come from? It's a compound produced primarily by interaction between microbial metabolites and chlorine in the environment. The use of chlorine in washing steps in cork production was thought to contribute to this, but now that chlorine-based products have been replaced by alternatives such as hydrogen peroxide, cork taint is still with us, suggesting that an exogenous chlorine source may not be needed. Indeed, in a study published in the Wine Industry Journal in 1987, some researchers from Australian wine company Southcorp analyzed cork trees *in situ* from four regions of Portugal. They detected TCA in fifty-eight out of 120 trees analyzed. Microbes such as mould-forming fungi live in the small pores, called lenticels, that run throughout cork bark. The lenticels are areas of the cork where cells have divided faster than elsewhere, forming a looser structure that allows air through this otherwise impermeable barrier. They can be seen in corks as darker-coloured lines or

**BELOW** Cork: a brilliant but flawed natural substance.

# TCA in the winery

TCA taint doesn't just come from corks. In 2003, Gallo, one of the world's largest wine companies, admitted experiencing problems with endemic TCA in its Dry Creek winery in Sonoma, following an alert raised by the tasting panel of *Wine Spectator* magazine. The tasters noted off-flavours consistent with TCA in a large number of Gallo wines and sent two bottles of each of ten wines off for scientific testing by ETS Laboratories. All had detectable TCA levels, with an average concentration of 3ng/litre (ppt).

In response, Gallo also commissioned ETS to run tests, which showed that there was a problem with TCA in the Dry Creek winery. This produces some two million cases of wine annually, including many of Gallos's flagship Sonoma labels. Dr. Mary Wagner, Gallo's chief technology officer, was keen to downplay the scale of the contamination. "In our Sonoma cellars," she said, "a random lot of barrels of wine averaged 1.9ppt. These levels of TCA are so minute that, typically, only a few sophisticated palates can detect it. Note that one part per trillion is equivalent to one second in 320 centuries." Gallo decided not to withdraw any bottles for sale or destroy any wine. "TCA is not a health issue, and it is almost never a quality issue," added Dr. Wagner. "Perception of minute levels of TCA in the [*Wine Spectator*] article is not realistic for the consuming public."

Gallo isn't the first US winery to experience such problems. Boutique winery Hanzell discovered TCA in its winery in 2002, after another alert from the *Wine Spectator* tasting panel. Hanzell immediately stopped sales and abandoned its old winery, but following extensive consumer studies, the company decided to continue selling its 2000 Chardonnay and 1999 Pinot Noir, the two wines affected. This raises the question of commercially relevant taint. Is a trace of TCA that is detected only by professionals who are looking for it, in a controlled environment, something that wine producers should worry about for everyday wines?

imperfections. In addition, the processing steps used in making corks from sheets of barks may encourage fungal growth, and thus TCA production. Chloroanisoles can also be produced in the absence of microbes. All that is needed are the phenolic precursors, and a chlorine source. It is a complicated subject, but the take-home message is that TCA is endemic to cork.

It's likely that we are so sensitive to TCA for good reason; because it is often an indicator of fungal growth, it is a biologically relevant odour. Generally, we'd do well to steer clear of foods and drinks that have a whiff of TCA to them, because there is a chance that they will have been contaminated by potentially dangerous fungi. "Corked" wines, though, pose no danger to human health.

It needs to be emphasized that TCA isn't confined to corks, nor is it the only compound responsible for musty aromas. Off-odours are a major problem in the food industry. CAs, chloroanisoles other than TCA, are also potential contaminants, especially TeCA (2,3,4,6-tetrachloroanisole), which is detectable in wine at concentrations of 10ng/litre. A 2004 study by Pascal Chatonnet and colleagues identified a further potential musty contaminant: 2,4,6-tribromoanisole (TBA). This is what causes musty aromas in wine at concentrations of 4ng/litre, and is formed from its precursor TBP (tribromophenol). TBP is used as a pesticide inside buildings; barrels, corks, and plastics are all susceptible to TBA contamination from the environment in situations where TBP has been used: old wooden structures in particular. In support of this hypothesis, Chatonnet cites the results from the analysis of wines carried out by the Ontario Liquor Control Board (a monopoly state-owned supplier) on wines it intends to list. In 2002, 2,400 wines were tested. Of those that were considered to have a musty taint, only forty-nine per cent had significant levels of TCA (>2ng/litre). The other fifty-one per cent of tainted bottles may have been affected by other chloroanisoles, or TBA. Because these weren't tested for, we don't know how much influence they had. Several wineries have had problems with TCA or TBA contamination, resulting in large volumes of wines suffering from low-level musty taint (*see* box above). But all the indicators are that the vast majority of TCA taint is down to the cork.

# How common is cork taint?

The prevalence of cork taint is a subject that hasn't been addressed as often, or as scientifically, as you might think. The first large, systematic survey was carried out in the UK by the Wine and Spirit Association (WSA). It's worth reporting this in some detail, because it highlights the difficulty in setting up a scientific study involving a molecule such as TCA that is a potent contaminant at very low concentrations.

## The WSA musty taint survey

Back in May 1999, John Corbet-Milward of the WSA was in the audience at a panel debate on cork taint, held as part of that year's London Wine Trade Fair. "The mood in the audience was one of confusion and crossness," he recalls. "People were coming up with all sorts of figures, and there was no scientific basis to what was being said." Instead of this "internecine strife", as Corbet-Milward called it, he thought it would be much better for the trade as a whole to work together to help produce taint-free wine for the consumer. So, after discussions with several key companies from various parts of the supply chain, and a quick whip-round, the "WSA Musty Flavour Defects in Wine in the UK" survey was born. This survey involved a consortium of eighteen companies, including retailers, producers, wholesalers, and stopper manufacturers. Over the course of twelve months, from January 2001 to January 2002, data were collected on over 13,000 wines tasted by assessors in the contributing companies during the course of their work. The goal was to establish a "benchmarking baseline" to estimate the true level of musty defects in wines on the UK market.

Publication of the final report, in June 2002, provoked a storm of controversy, principally because the final quoted figure of verified musty taint prevalence was almost bizarrely low: just 0.7 per cent. "We were astounded to see such a low figure," says Warren Adamson, UK head of New Zealand's Villa Maria. "Everything we've seen, from show results to specific tastings, suggests the real figure is five to six per cent." Is the real rate of cork taint very much lower than many had previously suspected, or is the WSA survey flawed? The raw material for the study consisted of wines that "approved assessors" from nine of the participating companies tasted as part of their normal duties. The next stage

| Results of the WSA "Musty Flavour Defects in Wine in the UK" survey | | |
|---|---|---|
| | Number of samples | Number of samples as % of total samples |
| Total number of samples | 13,780 | 100.0 |
| Reported as musty (before verification) | 277 | 2.0 |
| Verified as musty | 94 | 0.7 |
| Other reported defects (*e.g.* oxidation) | 202 | 1.5 |
| Total samples with reported defects | 470* | 3.4 |
| * This number is reduced by nine as some samples exhibited more than one defect | | |

"People differ in their sensitivity to TCA; is a discerning consumer any less sensitive to TCA than the professional assessors in this survey?"

involved "verification" of suspected TCA taint. If wines were judged to have a "musty" taint by the assessors, the ullaged bottles were then resealed with the original closure and sent to one of two independent companies for verification. The final report doesn't mention the method of verification used by these labs, but when questioned they both confirmed that it was another round of sensory analysis; in each case, the wines were re-tasted by company staff within a week of receipt.

Remarkably, of the 277 samples identified by company assessors as musty, only thirty-four per cent were "verified" as musty. The report concludes, "It can be assumed from this that there was a significant degree of misclassification in terms of false positives, either in the form of other defects being wrongly reported as musty, or satisfactory samples being classified as musty." This discrepancy caused internal strife within the consortium itself. Intriguingly, the report tells us that, "One participant withdrew from the trial in October 2001, due to concerns over the disparity between tasters and verifiers." Initially, the WSA chose not to disclose the identity of this participant, but some digging around revealed that it was Oddbins which had opted out. Steve Daniel of Oddbins confirmed this. "Our major objection was methodology," he said, "specifically, the lack of scientific controls and how the wine was verified as musty."

The major problem was indeed the "huge discrepancy" between what was submitted as musty and what was found in the verification step. This led to a further disagreement that centred around the WSA's decision to focus solely on "commercially significant" mustiness. Samples with low-level taint might not come across as overtly musty, but could still be out of condition. Things came to a head at a public meeting of consortium members in June 2001, where the WSA was openly questioned by many members about the verification procedure, and in particular what had happened to the budget that was supposed to be in place for chemical analysis of submitted samples. The consortium was reassured that this was still in place. Subsequent to this meeting, it was deemed that the steps to rectify the verification problem, "weren't aggressive enough", and Oddbins eventually withdrew in October 2001. When questioned about the overall budget for the survey, the WSA's director, Quentin Rappoport, revealed that it was in the order of £30,000 – so it's hardly surprising that there wasn't any chemical analysis.

### Finding the fudge factors

Aside from the opaque verification process, Oddbins' criticism highlights one of a couple of fudge factors that could be in part responsible for the low final rate of taint claimed by the survey. The emphasis was on "defects considered to be at a level that is likely to be detected by a discerning consumer". According to Rappoport, "We were not measuring incidence [of cork taint] in terms of zero tolerance." This leads to an unanswerable question: what constitutes commercially significant musty taint? Who decides this? People differ in their sensitivity to TCA; is a discerning consumer any less sensitive to TCA than the professional assessors in this survey? What about low-level cork taint that introduces a very faint musty taint and strips the wine of its fruit?

A second fudge factor is the fact that the final rate of musty taint quoted by the report includes *all* closure types, not just the cork-based ones. Ironically, while the report studiously avoids using the term "cork taint", none of the 1,934 wines that were sealed with non-cork closures showed any mustiness – an important observation.

But the most damning criticism of the WSA's methodology comes from the findings of the Australian Wine Research Institute (AWRI). A single ten-minute phone conversation with the AWRI's Peter Godden was enough to expose the problems with the scientific design of this survey. There are two fundamental assumptions underlying the verification step in the WSA survey. The first is that TCA is sufficiently stable that musty taint detected by assessors will still be detectable by the verifying laboratories up to a week later, when the wines are retasted. The second is that TCA is readily detectable against a background of oxidation, which will have occurred between the first tasting and the retasting of the ullaged bottles. Godden thinks that both of these assumptions are false.

When the AWRI began its first closure survey three years ago, staff tested the stability of TCA in opened bottles of corked wine. "We tested ullaged bottles with a reasonably high level of TCA: 15ng/litre," Godden reports. "Ullaged bottles were recorked and left on a desk for two weeks. Just a trace of TCA was found; all the rest had been absorbed back into the cork." Godden thinks it is "quite probable" that most of the TCA in the musty wines submitted for verification could have been absorbed back into the cork. For this reason, in its studies the AWRI insists that samples to be tested for TCA later should be transferred after opening to all-glass containers (with ground-glass stoppers), or glass bottles with an aluminium foil barrier between the wine and the stopper. Plastic is no good because the TCA will all be absorbed by the plastic within a few days.

Godden also strongly disagrees that musty off-flavours will be readily detectable over the background of oxidation. "In the last six months," he says, "we have done a major investigation in an insurance case where there has been random bottle oxidation, in which we have investigated how oxidation affects the perception of TCA." The AWRI carried out sensory analysis of all the bottles, together with chemical analysis of the oxidized bottles. The conclusion? "Oxidation has a massive effect on the ability of experienced tasters to assess TCA. We expected the cork people to be touting these WSA results more," adds Godden. He guesses that the reason the pro-cork lobby hasn't done this is that they may suspect there is a problem with the study.

Where does this leave the WSA survey? First, it provides an explanation for the controversial discrepancy between the number of submitted musty samples and those that were verified as musty by the independent labs. Second, it means that the low quoted rate of musty taint of 0.7 per cent is anything but a "benchmark baseline". While credit is due to the WSA for initiating this survey in the first place, it is a shame that the poor study design meant that this turned out to be a largely wasted opportunity.

## AWRI data

Like many others, the AWRI's Peter Godden is convinced that the real level of cork taint is substantially higher than the 0.7 per cent claimed by the WSA study. Once or twice a year the AWRI runs a four-day course known as the Advanced Wine Assessment Course (AWAC) for potential wine-show judges. During these courses, a large number of bottles from around the world are opened, and because of the scientifically rigorous approach applied, this represents perhaps the best-verified assessment of the incidence of TCA in cork-sealed wines. Participants taste in silence and then discuss their results. For a bottle to be regarded as TCA-affected, fifteen per cent of participants must have identified the taint during their assessment. There is back-up to this sensory analysis in the form of chemical analysis by gas chromatography-mass spectrometry (GC-MS);

"Other interesting observations were that Australian wines were no more likely to be corked than those from France, for example, and that the taint rate was slightly higher in whites than in reds."

over the last three AWACs, all wines described as TCA-affected by the panel and then analyzed by GC-MS have proved to be TCA-tainted.

The results are striking. For the three AWACs held immediately prior to June 2003, 1,625 bottles sealed with cork were sampled; 6.46 per cent of these showed TCA taint. If statistical confidence limits are applied, then we can be ninety-nine per cent sure that if this sample is representative of all wines sealed with cork, then the real rate of taint is between five and 8.2 per cent. In fact, the sample here is skewed towards higher-priced wines, which would probably have been sealed with more expensive corks. It must be pointed out that there is no indication that taint rate bears any relationship to the price of the cork, though. Other interesting observations were that Australian wines were no more likely to be corked than those from France, for example, and that the taint rate was slightly higher in whites than in reds (suggesting that some low-level taint might have been more apparent in whites and went unnoticed in some reds).

### International Wine Challenge results

Each year, the International Wine Challenge is held in London. An enormous number of bottles are opened and tasted systematically by panels of trained tasters. Although a tally of cork-tainted bottles has been kept in previous years – in 2001, it was six per cent and in 2002, it was 4.6 per cent – in 2003, all cases of suspected mustiness were verified as cork taint by a "superjuror". The results were that, of 11,033 bottles sealed with natural corks, 4.9 per cent were considered to be corked. A further 2.79 per cent were faulty for other reasons. This figure tallies well with results from other surveys. The weakness of this sort of sampling is that it is likely either to flag false positives, or that low-level TCA contamination will be missed in some cases. Although there is no chemical analysis of the bottles judged to be affected, the scale of the sampling is impressive enough to make these useful results. From the data presented here, imperfect as it is, it seems that the incidence of cork taint is worryingly high at around five per cent, perhaps a little higher.

**RIGHT** George Fistonich of New Zealand's Villa Maria has shifted his entire production to screwcap, and is evidently no longer a fan of the cork.

*Picture courtesy of Villa Maria*

## IS CORK A NEUTRAL CLOSURE?

There's one further question about cork performance that isn't often addressed: are corks neutral in contact with wine? During the cork-manufacturing process there are steps – such as seasoning, boiling, and stabilizing the cork planks – which are designed to remove various tannic and phenolic compounds, rendering the cork as neutral as possible. The suberinized cork cells are relatively inert, but it is likely that the cork is not completely neutral, and will interact with the wine chemically, albeit to a rather limited extent. Data on this subject are scarce. This raises further questions. If corks aren't completely neutral, will wines that are normally aged with cork closures age differently with alternative closures? If so, is this positive or not? While this is unlikely, the possibility has been seized upon by the pro-cork lobby.

## FLAVOUR SCALPING BY CLOSURES

The process of "flavour scalping" is a problem in the food industry, where aroma components are absorbed by packaging. Aware from other studies that TCA could be absorbed from the wine by the cork, scientists at the AWRI investigated the potential flavour scalping of aromatic wine components by a range of closures. The wine used was a 1999 Semillon, spiked with the flavour compounds they wanted to study. Closure performance was compared with that of the same wine in a sealed glass ampoule. After two years, the concentrations of many of the flavour compounds had changed significantly, partly through absorption by the closures, but also via chemical modification independent of closure. Screwcaps didn't absorb any flavour compounds, performing similarly to the sealed glass ampoules. Relatively non-polar volatile compounds were absorbed by the corks, technical corks (part cork, part synthetic substance), and synthetic closures, while the more polar compounds weren't absorbed by any closures. Of these closures, technical corks absorbed a little more than the natural corks, and synthetics absorbed a lot more than either. The conclusion was that synthetic corks are responsible for considerable flavour scalping, and even natural corks are capable of absorbing certain wine-aroma components in limited amounts.

## Sensitivity to TCA taint

People differ in their sensitivity to TCA. In the AWRI's Advanced Wine Assessment Course, participants have been shown to differ quite widely in whether they can detect TCA, with some not spotting low-level taint, and a very few who can't detect it at any concentration. The AWRI's closure trial showed that even at concentrations as low as 1ng/litre (1ppt), trained tasters found that it suppressed the fruit characters of a Semillon wine by as much as forty per cent. Perhaps the most illuminating data on human sensitivity to TCA in wine came from a study commissioned by the cork manufacturer Sabaté (now called Oeneo Bouchage). This was rigorously conducted research, shedding light not only on the performance of a particular closure type (Sabaté's Altec), but also on the nature of human perception of TCA.

As well as making conventional corks, Sabaté's portfolio includes the Altec, a fully manufactured and standardized cork-based closure. Launched in 1995, it represented a novel approach to alternative closures. The problem it addressed was the dissatisfaction of wine producers with the performance of the inexpensive corks that they were using for their mass-market wines. Because of perceived consumer resistance to plastic corks and screwcaps (which is particularly strong in the French market), Sabaté devised a new manufacturing process that produced what is in effect a hybrid closure – part cork, part synthetic – that looks like a natural product. The manufacturing process for Altecs involves taking raw cork and fragmenting it into tiny particles. These are then sorted and most of the lignin – the hard, woody material that surrounds the lenticels (the tiny pores in the cork) – is discarded. This cork "flour" is then blended with proprietary polymer microspheres and the whole lot are stuck together with a binding agent. The resulting closures are consistent, and in theory they should have a lower risk of TCA taint than normal corks, because the lignin-rich material that surrounds the lenticels is considered to harbour the majority of the TCA contamination.

Initially, the Altec closure was tremendously successful. Sales were huge, and to date more than two billion bottles of wine have been sealed with them. But a

"After two years, the concentrations of many of the flavour compounds had changed significantly, partly through absorption by the closures, but also via chemical modification independent of closure. Screwcaps didn't absorb any flavour compounds, performing similarly to the sealed glass ampoules."

few years ago, reports began circulating that the Altec – which had initially been marketed as being taint-free – was causing unacceptably high levels of taint. The situation was particularly bad in the USA, where four wineries blamed Altec for tainting large numbers of their wines. These claims led to expensive legal action. Then, more bad news came from the results of the study conducted by the AWRI. This scientifically rigorous study monitored the performance of a number of closure types over time – including Altec. When the twenty-four-month results were published, they reported that each of the bottles sealed with Altec closures was found to have a TCA-like aroma, and follow-up chemical analysis found detectable levels of TCA in each of the Altec samples analyzed.

## Sabaté's response

Sabaté responded with a three-pronged strategy: firstly it instituted a new quality control standard for Altecs; secondly it devised a $CO_2$-extraction technique for the removal of TCA from the cork "flour"; thirdly it commissioned an impartial, wine-industry-led research programme to investigate actual and perceived TCA levels across a number of closures. This research involved two studies: one in the USA and one in the UK. The closures examined were the pre- and post-quality-control Altecs, and the new prototype Altecs made with their $CO_2$ extraction process (described in detail on pages 155–6). The UK branch of this research programme is of interest here, because it sheds light on the human perception of TCA. The strength of this study is that it is looking at real-life TCA taint; there is evidence to suggest that studies looking at TCA detection with spiked wines don't produce realistic results. Partially this is because of the low solubility of TCA in a water-based substance such as wine.

## Study methodology

Cube, the PR company which coordinated the UK study for Sabaté, convened a star-studded panel of fifteen wine-industry figures to participate in the trial. As well as helping to decide on the study methodology, the panel chose two wines from a selection available, one white and one red, which were then bottled using a variety of different closures. The procedure used for analysis was largely based on the methods used by the AWRI in its benchmark closure trial (*see* page 150). Chemical analysis of 2,600 bottles for TCA was carried out by the Campden and Chorleywood Food Research Organization (CCFRA), using solid-phase micro-extraction and gas chromatography-mass spectrometry (GC-MS) to a tolerance of 0.2ppt. Of these 2,600 bottles, 528 were also tasted by the panel of experts to compare the actual versus the perceived TCA occurrence. These tastings were spread over four sessions at three-monthly intervals. When the wines were tasted, CCFRA staff were on hand to take two samples from each bottle, which were then sealed in individual glass capsules with foil caps, transported to the lab, and analyzed with minimal delay. The raw data were passed on to an academic statistician, Russell Gerrard of the City of London University, for final analysis. While the results cheered Sabaté, in that they showed that the $CO_2$-extraction process is effective at removing TCA from the Altec closures, the more interesting data concerned the panel's ability to perceive TCA.

## Taster thresholds for TCA

At what level does TCA become a problem? Is there a threshold concentration below which it TCA undetectable by an individual taster, and above which it is identifiable? It would be extremely useful for the wine industry to identify a cut-

"At what level does TCA become a problem? Is there a threshold concentration below which TCA is undetectable by an individual taster, and above which it is identifiable? It would be extremely useful for the wine industry to identify a cut-off point above which TCA is problematic, and below which it can be safely ignored. Does such a threshold exist?"

off point above which TCA is problematic, and below which it can be safely ignored. Does such a threshold exist? In short, no. One of the significant, general findings from this study shows that the notion of a threshold for TCA is not tenable. Russell Gerrard, the statistician who analyzed the findings, says: "The proportion of bottles identified as containing TCA increases steadily as the measured TCA content increases, rather than jumping from a lower value to a higher as TCA content passes some cut-off point."

Gerrard's analysis reveals some interesting findings, summarized in the box below. Half of the tasters detect TCA when it is present at 1.2ppt in white wines and 2.5ppt in reds. Three-quarters detect it at 2.07ppt in whites and 3.93ppt in reds. But even in this expert group of tasters, there was over a ten per cent chance of them detecting TCA in red or white wines when none was present – a startling statistic. These figures correlate with other data on TCA detection and recognition from the WSA's Musty Flavour Defects in Wine survey (*see* pages 148–50). Although not a focus of the WSA's study, their report gives some measurements of the participants' sensory thresholds for TCA in white wine, for both detection (when participants could spot something was wrong with the wine) and recognition (when they could identify the flaw as TCA). The average values for these were 1.5ppt (range 0.5–10ppt) and 6.5 ppt (range 2.5–20ppt), respectively, for twenty-eight participants spread over two sessions.

What does this say about quality-control levels for TCA? Sabaté has set its batch quality-control level at 3.0ppt TCA for the Altecs. For white wines, the data suggest that a majority of tasters would report a wine with 3.0ppt TCA as tainted. For reds, it would be just over half. But tasters in this study were experts actively looking for TCA. The fact that clean wines were diagnosed as tainted over ten per cent of the time suggests an overzealousness in diagnosing slight differences in the samples as TCA, even when they were not detecting any mustiness. At each session, they were simultaneously assessing dozens of samples of the same two wines, so any differences would be immediately apparent. It would be interesting to see the study repeated using a range of different wines, and a non-expert group not actively looking for TCA.

| Chance of reporting TCA related to actual TCA content, aggregated over all tasters and closures | |
|---|---|
| **White wines** | **Red wines** |
| There is a greater than 10% chance of reporting TCA when there is none present | There is a greater than 10% chance of reporting TCA when there is none present |
| a 25% chance when TCA is at 0.35 ppt | a 25% chance when TCA is at 1.07 ppt |
| a 50% chance when TCA is at 1.20 ppt | a 50% chance when TCA is at 2.50 ppt |
| a 75% chance when TCA is at 2.07 ppt | a 75% chance when TCA is at 3.93 ppt |

THE DIFFERENCE BETWEEN WHITES AND REDS
Another interesting finding is that even expert tasters are significantly better at detecting TCA in white wines than red wines. Perhaps more surprising, though, is that the technical analysis indicated that white wines in this sample actually had more TCA than the reds. The underlying reason for this is a matter of speculation; it may be that there is some sort of chemical interaction between TCA and specific components of red wine. Nonetheless, it is an intriguing observation.

## Solving the cork-taint problem

There are three strategies for combating cork taint. First, eradicate TCA from natural corks, thus curing the cause of taint, and rescuing cork from an otherwise gloomy future. Second, manufacture synthetic, taint-free corks from alternative materials such as plastic, allowing wineries to keep their bottling lines and consumers their corkscrews. The third, which is more radical, is to ditch the concept of corks altogether and turn to different closures, such as screwcaps. We'll begin with attempts to salvage cork.

### Sabaté's Diamond process

Sabaté, the globe's second-largest cork manufacturer, has developed a sophisticated "cure" for cork taint. It's a process developed in conjunction with the Supercritical Fluids and Membranes laboratory of the Commissariat à l'Energie Atomique (CEA), a French government organization whose goals include the delightfully euphemistic "guaranteeing national independence by designing, manufacturing, and maintaining dissuasion tools". Named the "Diamond" process, it uses supercritical $CO_2$ for selective extraction of volatile compounds from cork. The first work on this process was initiated in 1997 and it was patented in 1999, the patent being shared by Guy Lumia and Christian Perre

# Can cork be saved from TCA?

As we have seen, cork has tremendous natural properties that make it suited to sealing wine bottles. It also has the advantage of being traditionally associated with wine, and being a "natural" product. People like corks when they aren't tainted with TCA. Yes, they are variable and sometimes let air in, causing the wine to oxidize, but this event is rare enough that if we could cure the TCA problem, most producers would be happy enough to stick with cork.

Two different potential strategies for dealing with TCA exist. The first is to prevent the TCA getting into the cork in the first place; the second is to remove it once it is there. As yet, no one has succeeded with the first strategy; because cork is natural and has lenticels that are open to the environment and allow microbes in, this may never be possible. So cork producers have instead concentrated on ways of getting TCA out of the cork.

This presents severe technical challenges, principally because it is a contaminant at minute concentrations, and to eradicate it requires some way of getting it out of the cork – an impermeable, watertight tissue. Any method invasive enough to get all the TCA out runs the risk of damaging the structure of the cork, impairing its physical properties. Nevertheless, the two leading manufacturers have both developed new techniques for dealing with TCA, which they hope will dramatically reduce its incidence in their products.

of the CEA, and Jean-Marie Aracil, Sabaté's head of R&D. Supercritical $CO_2$ is a difficult concept to explain in simple terms. If you pressurize a gas, at a certain point it becomes a liquid. If you then juggle the parameters of pressure and temperature, at a specific combination of these – known as the critical point – the interface between the two disappears, and you then have the penetration power of a gas and the extraction power of a liquid. For $CO_2$, this point is at 31.1°C (87.98°F) and seventy-three bars of pressure – a conveniently low temperature, even though the pressure is on the high side (seventy-three times atmospheric pressure). Other advantages of using $CO_2$ are that it is cheap and relatively environmentally friendly. The technique is already used to remove caffeine from coffee and by the perfume industry to extract fragrances. According to Jean-Marie Aracil, "The Diamond process shows an efficiency rate around ninety-seven per cent for TCA extraction."

Initially, the Diamond process was used to treat the cork "flour" that is the basis for Sabaté's Altec closure; to be blended later with polymer microspheres and stuck together with a binding agent. Wines sealed with prototype Diamond-treated Altecs showed no detectable TCA, either by sensory or chemical analysis, in a rigorous, independently conducted panel study carried out in the UK last year. So it looks like Diamond works. "For obvious reasons, Sabaté rejects any idea of offering a 'zero TCA' guarantee," says Aracil, "first of all because TCA can come from other sources than cork, and also because zero per cent doesn't exist from a scientific point of view." But he says that the maximum residual level of TCA is "between the quantification and detection limits of the analytical method: that is, between 0.2 and 0.5ppt".

Since then, significantly, the Diamond process has been extended to treating sheets of raw cork bark, which can then be used to produce what are effectively taint-free natural corks. "We had to face some difficulties with deformation in the early stages of our trials," reveals Aracil, "but we've since been able to optimize the parameters to get satisfactory results with cork planks." Tests show that the cleaning process does alter the mechanical properties of the cork, although not greatly. However, some uncertainty surrounds the capacity of these treated corks to retain a good seal for as long as their non-treated counterparts. This could be a major hindrance to their uptake by fine-wine producers whose wines evolve over decades.

The initial production capacity of treated corks at the CEA facility was small, at around 100,000 per year – sufficient only to supply test corks to

customers. Sabaté decided to implement the Diamond process on an industrial scale, but this has meant constructing a new factory in Extremadura, Spain, where the firm already has a facility. At the time of writing, the first commercial release of the Diamond-treated closures is anticipated within six months, but there is no date for the release of treated natural corks, because of continuing problems with deformation.

### Amorim's ROSA process

Amorim is the globe's largest cork producer. Carlos de Jesus is marketing and communications director. Initially, he was hired to look after investor relations, but as a polished communicator, he has rapidly found his way into this new post. "A great part of my mandate is to change the PR culture," he says. Indeed, many wine journalists have been infuriated by the communication style that cork companies have commonly adopted up till now, which has been largely to deny the existence of cork taint, and deflect attention from the topic by bringing in issues such as the protection of cork-forest ecology and consumer preference. "The traditional response has been to run for cover," agrees de Jesus, "[yet] when you are confronted with an overwhelming amount of evidence, you have to get your act together. The only way to move forward is to align our interest with the wine industry's and bring debate to a rational level." In terms of addressing taint by means of research and development, his view is that "we've done more in the last year and a half than in the previous thirty years."

I asked Antonio de Barros, Amorim's executive vice-president, about what the company is doing to tackle cork taint. "We became aware of the problem in 1978," he recalls, "and we've been trying to fight it ever since." He admits that, in the past, the industry tended to ignore cork taint. "The problem has become more apparent as wine has become more sophisticated and subtle," he says. "Over the last ten years we have been doing whatever is necessary to try to control the problem." De Barros notes that one of the key steps for Amorim has been to renew the R&D department, bringing in Professor Miguel Cabral as its head, "with a total focus on TCA control and removal".

Miguel Cabral told me of the three different approaches Amorim is taking to address the taint problem. "The first is a new boiling system that has been in place for a few years," he says. "It's completely different in several ways. Most significantly, the cork planks are extracted with boiling water, plank by plank; in the previous system, the planks were close together so extraction was not so easy." Linked to this system, Amorim has devised a process known as Convex (for "continuous volatile extraction"), by which all the volatiles present in the water during the boiling process are cleansed at the same time. Secondly, the company has incorporated chemical analysis for TCA into its quality control, involving gas chromatography-mass spectrometry/solid-phase microextraction (CG–MS/SPME). Amorim has five different machines. "We can do 400 analyses of cork soaks in twenty-four hours," reveals Cabral, "and the current threshold is 5ng/litre TCA for a soak of fifty corks." According to Cabral, half the volatiles from the soak would be expected to get into wine after fourteen months, so this threshold would correspond to a wine with a TCA level of 2.5ng/litre. How many batches of corks fail to meet this threshold? "An enormous amount of batches are clean," says Cabral, "then some have twenty to thirty per cent of bales [of cork] with above-threshold levels."

Thirdly, and most importantly, Amorim has developed a curative strategy. "We tried a few different approaches," reports Cabral, "but the best is ROSA." ROSA, which stands for "rate of optimal steam application", is a method of steam cleaning, claimed to significantly reduce TCA in the cork granules used to make

BELOW Making synthetic closures in the Nukorc factory, Adelaide: the one-piece extrusion process in action.

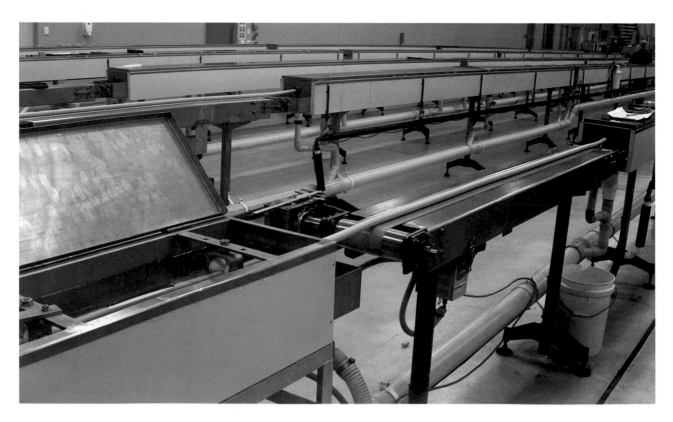

technical corks such as the hugely successful Twin Top. "We've asked two institutes to validate this independently," he reveals, "the Campden and Chorleywood Food Research Association (CCFRA), (which found an eighty per cent reduction), and Geisenheim, (which showed a seventy-five per cent reduction)." Amorim has invested in ROSA technology, which can also be used for disks and corks. "The reduction in TCA has been very good, but there has been high deformation – we had to change from a continuous to a batch system," says Cabral. At the moment, Amorim is testing at an industrial scale. "We have not achieved the same results, but we're not far off, with a sixty to seventy per cent reduction in TCA," he adds. "There is no problem with the mechanical performance of the treated corks." This raises a critical question. What effect will a sixty to seventy per cent TCA reduction in cork sheets have on the incidence of cork taint? Without proper data, this question is almost impossible to answer. This could be enough to lower TCA below threshold levels in those corks that are currently tainted, effectively eliminating taint. Alternatively, thirty to forty per cent of the current TCA level in those corks might still be enough to taint the wine.

### Better manufacturing practices

The cork companies may also be able to reduce taint levels simply by improving their manufacturing practices. During cork processing there are several stages where TCA-producing mould growth or cross-contamination could occur. The cork planks are left outside to season and dry for several months. Poor conditions here can encourage fungal growth. The planks are then boiled to improve their physical properties, remove tannins, and kill off any bugs. If the water isn't changed frequently or too many planks are boiled at once, then this may contribute to TCA contamination. After this, the planks are allowed to stabilize, which takes a week or two; if these wet planks are put in a warm warehouse, these conditions will encourage fungal growth. You'd expect that care and attention during these stages, coupled with a quality-control stage that involves chemical analysis, would lessen the prevalence of TCA taint.

I find these developments encouraging, but I'm not going to get carried away until I see treated, virtually taint-free corks rolling off production lines in numbers sufficient to bottle significant quantities of wine. There's always the danger that the added cost – both to the manufacturer and the producer – of eliminating TCA from cork will prove a barrier to the large-scale application of these techniques, even if they are proven to be effective. It's frustrating that when these techniques are applied to whole natural corks they cause limited but measurable changes to the physical properties of the corks. This would imply that before they are used to seal wines intended for long ageing, long-term trials may be needed. This could take decades.

## Alternative closures

So, if cork is flawed, what are the alternatives? The first choice for most winemakers would probably be a taint-free synthetic cork that could be used with existing bottling lines. Surprisingly, modern science hasn't been able to come up with a synthetic substance that fully shares cork's properties of elasticity and compressibility. While there are a number of synthetic corks on the market, the data provided in the following pages indicate that many of them they are only suitable for wines destined for immediate consumption (that is, within a year or two). The problem has been that the plastics used can't provide a seal equal to that of real cork, without being impossible to extract from the neck of the bottle. The result is that many synthetic corks have high oxygen transmission that is permeable enough to cause the wines to oxidize after a few years. They are fine for everyday wines, which are usually drunk soon after release; the vast majority of wines produced today fall into this category. The current state of the market is that, of a range of several different synthetics, three synthetic closures stand out. These are: Nomacork, Neocork, and Nukorc. All use an extrusion process, rather than injection moulding. The difference is that Nomacork and Neocork have a two-piece construction with an extruded core and a separate sleeve, whereas Nukorc is made by a single-extrusion process. These have the advantage of being inexpensive, visually attractive, and can also be used with existing bottling equipment However, while it looks like there is a future for synthetics, in the struggle against cork taint the attention has focused largely on the screwcap.

Screwcaps provide a pretty good seal – better than cork, in fact. And they are easy to open – you don't need a corkscrew; you just twist them off. Because they are manufactured and are not a natural substance, they provide a much more uniform seal than corks. Added to this, there are plenty of reports (*see* next section) of twenty-year-old screwcapped bottles being opened and the wine tasting fresh and lively. In effect, screwcaps are an old, proven technology, given a new lease of life.

So how come all wines aren't sealed with screwcaps? This is what a vocal element in the wine trade is calling for. There have been (and to some extent remain) three main problems. Firstly, screwcaps still have a "cheap" image in the minds of many consumers. People associate screwcaps with bargain-basement plonk. Some markets, particularly those in traditional European wine-producing countries, are highly resistant to alternative closures such as screwcaps, whereas others, such as Australia and New Zealand, are more receptive. However, consumer-poll evidence suggests that to a degree, this low-rent image is now changing. Secondly, people *like* corks. They're natural, they look and feel right, and the ritual of getting the corkscrew out is part and parcel of the wine-drinking experience. Thirdly, while most experts agree that the screwcap is the closure of choice for fresh white wines and early drinking reds, there's some debate about whether they are suitable for red wines destined for long ageing or oaked whites.

## The evidence
As well as all the anecdotal reports and opinions, good comparative data now exist on the performance of different closures. Important data came from a long-term closure study initiated by the AWRI in 1999. Fourteen different closures were analyzed: one ROTE ("roll-on tamper evident"; a posh name for a screwcap, or "Stelvin"), two "technical corks" (part cork, part synthetic), two different grades of standard cork, and nine different plastic corks. The wine used was a 1999 Clare Valley Semillon that had been fermented and stored in stainless-steel. Two batches, each of 300 bottles, were sealed with each type of closure, with the exception of the screwcap (which had a single bottling run of 800). The wines were then stored in a temperature-controlled facility where storage was randomized, with each bottle given a separate number. Tests were performed at three monthly intervals, with the variables studied – including extraction force required, ease of reinsertion into the neck of the bottle, incidence of leakage, concentration of free and total sulphur dioxide ($SO_2$), browning measures, and wine sensory analysis – using a panel of experienced tasters working under strict guidelines.

"Screwcaps still have a 'cheap' image in the minds of many consumers. People associate screwcaps with bargain-basement plonk. Some markets, particularly those in traditional European wine-producing countries, are highly resistant to alternative closures such as screwcaps, whereas others, such as Australia and New Zealand, are more receptive."

After only a couple of years, the results showed that wines that retained the highest concentration of free $SO_2$ showed the lowest degree of browning and tasted the freshest. It seems that free $SO_2$ concentration, which is relatively easy to measure, can act as a good predictor of future browning and a useful proxy for oxidation. Thus, it is a convenient way of measuring the effectiveness of a stopper. How did the different closures perform? The curves plotting free $SO_2$ concentration against time showed a pronounced dip with all the closures over the first year, which then began to flatten. The best performer was the ROTE closure, closely followed by the technical corks. The standard corks performed pretty well, as did six of the synthetics. Three synthetics performed badly.

The sensory analysis revealed some surprising results. The ROTE closure produced a rubber-like flavour/aroma in the wine after eighteen months. Considering that there is a long track record of bottling Riesling using screwcaps, and many library reference samples are available, it's an odd result. The AWRI scientists suggest that this taint is an unwelcome modification due to chemically reduced sulphur as a result of lack of oxygen. This potential reductive taint necessitates care on the part of the winemaker if screwcaps are to be used (*see* page 121). By thirty-six months, the data indicated that almost all the synthetics were showing an unacceptable amount of oxidation, with the screwcaps providing the best seal by some distance.

A similar study was published in 2004, when Hogue Cellars (Washington State, USA) announced the results from a four-year study on the effects of five different closures on its wines. Two wines, a Merlot and a Chardonnay, were sealed with a natural cork, two different synthetics, a screwcap with an Etain liner, and a screwcap with a Saranex liner. Over this period the only closure to show cork taint was the natural cork. The synthetics both showed oxidation characteristics. Both screwcaps and natural corks retained $SO_2$ better than the synthetics. At both twenty-four and thirty months, the screwcaps were preferred over the synthetics. Overall, the screwcaps were the preferred closure, but while this was true for both wines, the preference was stronger for the Chardonnay than for the Merlot.

## Screwcaps for red wines?

Screwcaps, therefore, give a better seal than other closures, and they are taint-free. The verdict seems to be that for fresh, fruity wines they are the closure of choice.

"Gibson suggests that, with Australian Riesling, changes have been documented in screwcapped wines that are not oxidative, and the wines are not locked in time."

The so-far unanswered question is whether they are the best closures for *all* wine types, including red wines destined for long-term ageing. People like the way that ageworthy reds such as classed-growth clarets age when sealed with a good quality, taint-free cork. Would screwcaps be a better closure for these sorts of wines, also?

The answer to this question hinges on whether a small amount of oxygen transmission through the closure is actually needed for successful bottle evolution of red wines. Little definitive data exist at the present time. Part of the difficulty in providing a conclusive answer is that the exact chemical changes that take place during successful ageing are still not completely understood. One thing we can safely say is that, if there is any significant influx of oxygen through a closure, the wine will rapidly oxidize and be spoiled. Therefore, the extent of any transmission under scrutiny here is very small.

Is there an oxidative component to desirable red-wine ageing? The AWRI's Peter Godden thinks that there is. "There is always oxygen present," he says. "It cannot be excluded completely, and certainly some phenolic reactions leading to the formation of stable pigments are oxidative." He suggests that the evidence is less clear-cut for white wines, although some people think oxygen is needed here, too, for successful evolution. "However, none of this should be taken to mean that it is desirable for oxygen to permeate through a closure," adds Godden. "Wines at bottling may well have absorbed enough oxygen for these reactions to proceed post-bottling."

Richard Gibson agrees. "I am inclined to think that bottle maturation is essentially anaerobic," he told me. "One of the issues here is that the gear to accurately measure the oxygen transmission of high-barrier closures is not available. What I do know is that oxygen transmission by closures over time simply causes oxidation. Synthetic closures have a small but finite oxygen transmission of 0.01cc per day per closure. Over time, wine sealed with them loses $SO_2$, then goes brown, as wine components react with oxygen. Oxygen-measuring data I have seen on screwcaps and good corks shows less than 0.001cc/day per closure. I am told that new Mocon equipment can measure down to 0.0001cc/day per closure. The testing is lengthy and expensive, however." Gibson suggests that, with Australian Riesling, changes have been documented in screwcapped wines that are not oxidative, and that the wines are not locked in time. "With reds, the question is vexed," he says. "I think that the key is to ensure maturation before the wine goes into bottle." He suggests that getting the anthocyanin polymerization along track before bottling is one of these important steps.

Godden adds, "There are certainly some 'age-worthy' red wines that have been under screwcap for three years or so, which are looking fine. We obviously won't know what they will look like after ten years until we get there, but personally I will be surprised if major problems develop, if they are not evident after three years." Godden expressed regret that no sizeable quantities of red wines from extensive screwcap trials that were initiated in Australia in the 1970s have survived. "It appears that all these wines were either dumped, or otherwise disposed of by the companies that established these trials when the market for white wines under screwcap turned so bad." Many of the whites were commercially bottled and thus found their way out, so this is probably why there are frequent anecdotal reports of twenty-year-old screwcapped Aussie Rieslings still tasting good.

# Screwcaps as an alternative to cork

Screwcaps were born in 1959, when French company La Bouchage Mécanique introduced the Stelcap-vin. The Stelcap closure had already proved successful for a range of spirits and liqueurs, and manufacturing rights were acquired by Australian Consolidated Industries (ACI) in 1970. It was renamed Stelvin for the Australian market, and trials at the ACI laboratories took place. The results were reported in 1976 in *The Australian Grapegrower and Winemaker.* Four closures (three screwcaps with different wadding materials, and a cork for comparison) were tested on six wines (three white, three red). The conclusions were that screwcaps were ideal for sealing wine bottles, but only if they had the right wadding and satisfactory seals were obtained between bottle and cap. Interestingly, the best-performing Stelvin closure at the time had agglomerated cork as part of the wadding (but this wasn't in contact with the wine). The trial continued to 1979. There was an industry push to move to screwcaps, but this lost momentum, partially through fears about consumer acceptance, and also because awareness of the shortcomings of cork were not as widespread at the time.

As dissatisfaction with cork increased, sporadic attempts to introduce screwcaps to the marketplace occurred. Yet a more united push was needed. As recently as the 2000 vintage, Clare winemakers, frustrated by the poor performance of cork, made a stand on the issue. Clare is famous for its Rieslings, and these are made in a style that shows almost any cork-related fault. The Clare winemakers had to overcome a major logistical obstacle before they could offer wines in screwcap: at the time, no Australian supplier could provide bottles and caps of the required style and quality. As a result, they had to drum together enough like-minded producers to generate an order for 250,000 bottles from Pechiney

in France. With a collaborative effort, they managed it, and the combined shift was large enough to make headlines for what, at the time, seemed a very brave move. Jeffrey Grossett, one of the winemakers involved, estimates that during the 2004 vintage, 200 million wine bottles were sealed with screwcaps in Australia.

The Clare initiative prompted New Zealand winemakers to form the New Zealand Screwcap Initiative in 2001. By 2004, estimates were that seventy per cent of New Zealand's wines are now screwcapped, up from one per cent three years earlier. Whether or not screwcaps establish such a presence in the more traditional European wine-producing countries remains to be seen.

Screwcaps consist of two components. First, is the cap itself, which comes attached to the sleeve. This is made of an aluminium alloy. Second, the business end of the screwcap – the liner, made of an expanded polyethylene wadding. This is typically covered with a tin foil layer that acts as a barrier to gas exchange, overlain by a PVDC film that provides an inert surface and will be in contact with the wine. Contrary to popular opinion, the screw cap isn't screwed on at all. Instead, the cap is held down tight over the end of the bottle (it is important for a tight seal that the lip is free of defects), and a set of rollers then moulds the sleeve of the cap to fit over the ridges on the outside of the top portion of the neck. This holds the whole closure firmly in place. The cap is joined to the sleeve by a series of small metal bridges, which break when the cap is twisted.

Although they are often considered as a single closure type, not all screwcaps are alike. The most significant difference is in the nature of the liner. In some caps this lacks the tin foil layer; the closure therefore has higher oxygen transfer properties and is less suited to long ageing of wines.

## Comparing screwcaps and corks

Normally the wine-bottle closure debate is a rather specialist (and some might add, dull) topic, yet in September 2003, it hit the big time. Corks and screwcaps were in the news after UK national newspapers, including the *Daily Mail* and the *Mirror*, picked up a press release issued by *Wine International* magazine about a comparative tasting of fine wines sealed with screwcaps and traditional corks. The results of this tasting were published in an article by Publishing Editor Robert Joseph in the October 2003 issue of the magazine.

The groundbreaking tasting – the first of its kind – was organized by *Wine International* and took place at Vinexpo, an international wine and spirits exhibition held in Bordeaux, in June 2003. Joseph and colleagues managed to get together forty-nine fine wines sealed by screwcap, and where possible these were paired alongside identical wines with natural corks. While many of the wines were from recent vintages, some dated back as far as 1980. In the forty cases where screwcapped and cork-sealed bottles were available for comparison, each member of the panel of some fifty tasters – which included Peter Gago, Michel Rolland, and Michel Laroche – was asked to give his or her preference. The results were striking: for the forty comparisons, tasters preferred the

"What these results show is that wines sealed with screwcaps in many cases taste different to those sealed with corks. Proponents of screwcaps argue that they taste better, fresher and age more slowly. But this may dissuade Old World producers who make wines destined for long bottle-ageing from turning to screwcaps, because they will argue that their customers like the way their wines taste (and develop in the bottle) when they are sealed by corks."

cork-sealed bottle only once, and opted for the screwcapped bottle a staggering twenty-one times.

An interesting issue, not discussed in Joseph's article, is raised by these results. What they show is that wines sealed with screwcaps in many cases taste different to those sealed with corks. Proponents of screwcaps argue that they taste better, fresher, and age more slowly. But this may dissuade Old World producers who make wines destined for long bottle-ageing from turning to screwcaps because they will argue that their customers like the way their wines taste (and develop in the bottle) when they are sealed by corks. This is likely to be an issue that will continue to be debated for some time to come.

### Making the switch

I asked Joseph whether he'd switch to screwcaps if he were a wine producer. "Switching across the board is either brave, foolhardy or suicidal – depending on a producer's relationship with his customers, and those customers' (retailers and sommeliers) relationship with the end-user," he replied. "While applauding those who've made the leap, I'd put a proportion of all my wines in screwcap and let the market grow into them. My experience at the Bordeaux tasting makes me every bit as keen to use screwcaps for age-able reds as on fresh, aromatic whites."

In his article, Joseph also criticized the use of environmental arguments by cork producers keen to persuade consumers against alternatives. He points out that far from being under threat, cork forests in Portugal are actually increasing by four per cent a year, and the Iberian lynx, whose demise has been blamed on the switch to alternative closures, has been in decline for a century. "I'm delighted that the debate is now out in the open," Joseph told me. "Hopefully there will be a lot more similar tastings – both behind winery doors and in public – and a lot more level-headed analysis of closures in general and the environmental issues (which should not be overlooked)." He added that, "In future, the cork manufacturers may find that their multimillion-pound campaigns fall on less fertile soil." Yet he still thinks there is some resistance in the trade to screwcaps for fine wine. "Sommeliers and older British importers and merchants are often certainly still either sceptical or downright negative, and this naturally communicates itself to producers," he explained.

How long does he think it will be until we see fine wines from the Old World sealed with screwcaps? "Well," he said, "Laroche, Paul Blanck, and Kuehn are already putting what I think of as fine wine under screwcap and crowncap (in the case of Kuehn) and I'd place a bet that Dourthe will use Stelvins for some higher-level Bordeaux. I'm not saying that screwcaps are necessarily the answer. The new Zork from Australia (*see* below) might work just as well, and there will certainly be other interesting innovations. However, I do believe that cork's days as the most widely used closure for wine are numbered."

## Conclusions: no "perfect" closure

What can we conclude? There is, as yet, no perfect closure. Instead, winemakers have to choose the closure that best suits their objectives. The data would seem to suggest that synthetic corks are the least effective closure: wines sealed with them tend to have a short shelf life and need to be drunk fairly soon after release. But there is still a place for them, especially the better-performing ones: with wines destined to be drunk within eighteen months of vintage, they represent an ideal solution for small wineries who are fed up with cork taint but don't

"'I'm not saying that screwcaps are necessarily the answer,' says Robert Joseph. 'The new Zork from Australia might work just as well, and there will certainly be other interesting innovations. However, I do believe that cork's days as the most widely used closure for wine are numbered.'"

want to incur the cost of switching their bottling line, since synthetics can be used with existing bottles and machinery. Now that there exist techniques that could vastly reduce – and even eliminate – taint problems with technical corks, the future for the new-generation Altec (called "Diam") and the ROSA-treated Twin Top seems quite bright, especially in countries where there is still consumer resistance to screwcaps.

Screwcaps themselves are on a bit of a roll: they are ideal for sealing most wine types and are gaining in consumer acceptance. It looks as if they will dominate certain markets, particularly in pragmatic, non-tradition-bound markets such as New Zealand and Australia. One question still remains: are screwcaps the best closure for red wines intended for long-term ageing? The data aren't there yet, but it looks like they may be suitable for all wine types. However, it would seem premature for winemakers to switch all their ageworthy reds to screwcaps before enough data has accumulated to suggest that this actually is the case. If I were a winemaker, I'd certainly be doing trials with screwcaps.

This leaves us with the good old cork. Taint rates of five per cent are clearly unacceptable. Can the cork manufacturers reduce this, and by how much? And how much of a reduction would be acceptable? These are key questions.

New closure types are also being developed to complement current choices. These include the glass Vino-lok closure now used by some German and Austrian producers (*see* www.vino-lok.de), and the Zork, a novel twist-off closure from Australia. There is also a promising closure system called Pro-cork, which uses a special membrane stuck to each end of the cork, preventing the cork from making contact with the wine and acting as a permeability barrier. It will be interesting to see how these are accepted by consumers and winemakers.

Finally, a "perspective" thought. If it weren't for corks, wine as we know it wouldn't have developed. It was the introduction of relatively inexpensive glass bottles coupled with a way of sealing them – the cork – that permitted the development of bottle-aged styles of wines in the seventeenth century. Cork therefore has a special place in the history of modern wine. And for all their faults, corks are proving to be rather difficult to replace.

**BELOW** The Vino-lok closure, *left*: the glass stopper revealed by removing the metal cap, *right*.

# Section Three
# **Our interaction with wine**

# 20 Flavour and its perception: taste and smell in wine tasting

There's an unspoken assumption in the world of wine. It's one that needs challenging, or at the very least, careful investigation. Let me try to explain. Take a critic and a bottle of wine. The wine possesses certain characteristics. If you take an array of scientific measuring devices, you can make a description of the wine in terms of its physical parameters, which will be correct within the margins of error of the devices used. You could prepare a document with this description, secure in the knowledge that if someone else were to measure these physical properties, or you were to come back later and reassess the wine, you would end up with a pretty similar description. Now it's time to let the critic assess the wine.

A critic assesses a wine in a very different way from a set of scientific measuring devices. Indeed, what a critic does in rating a wine is tell us about his or her interaction with it. Critics tell us about themselves as well as the wine, and it is hard to separate the two. They bring to wine not only their individual cultural and contextual differences, but also their perceptions of the wine itself, which depend on complex physiology and neurobiology. As with scientific instruments, we need to know the error margins in their performance: how consistent is their perception of the same liquid tasted at different times, in different contexts, on different days? The best critics should be consistent, but has anyone actually measured this? More importantly, we assume that our perceptions of the same wine are broadly similar – that we use the same physiological and neurobiological "tools" for assessing wine. But what if the differences between critics' opinions are not simply a matter of competence or preference, but reflect a more fundamental biological difference? This would change the way we look at wine tasting.

Similarly, we are familiar with the idea of continuous variation in the population for a variety of biological traits. Take height, for example. A random group of 100 people will range from tall to short, with most people somewhere in the middle. We're comfortable with the idea that variation in taste and smell is similar, meaning that sensitivity will vary across a group, with most people in the middle and progressively smaller numbers as we move towards the opposite ends of the distribution. But what if variation in taste is actually a discrete, discontinuous distribution, a bit like eye colour? So, rather than a spectrum of small differences in sensitivity, we are looking at separate groups, where the individuals in each group have similar sensitivity but the groups differ markedly from each other? We must bear such issues in mind as we consider the biological basis of wine tasting.

## The perception of wine

Most attempts to understand our interaction with wine focus on the sense of taste and smell, and on the detection of flavour molecules by the receptors in the mouth and nasal cavity. But this limited level of understanding just won't do if we want a proper explanation of how we actually perceive wine. Take a sip of wine. Your experience of this wine is a unified conscious event – a representation in the brain. There's a lot that happens to the signals coming from the tongue and nose before they are assembled into this mental construct. Taking things one step further, the way we share our experience of wine is through words. The transition from conscious flavour experience to verbal description is another complex one, but we're going to have to grapple with it if we are to gain a useful insight into the human response to wine tasting. Indeed, it seems that the verbal descriptors we use are instrumental in shaping our conscious representations. The subject of flavour and its perception is the focus of the next two chapters. We begin by looking at the senses of taste and smell, and how they interact. From this we move to how the brain makes sense of flavour, and then finish with a discussion of the way that we construct a representation of "wine" in our brains, and the role that language plays in this. It's a complicated story that is still in the process of being unravelled, but it is also a thoroughly interesting one.

## A matter of taste

Linda Bartoshuk, Yale University professor and respected authority on the science of taste, is giving a lecture. Midway through, she interrupts her presentation and begins to hand round strips of blotting paper that have been soaked in a solution of propylthiouracil (a thyroid medication, known more simply as PROP). The audience is surprised: science lectures aren't usually this interactive. Each person is told to place the paper on his or her tongue, and the result is surprising. One-quarter taste nothing at all. Of the others, most find the paper to taste quite bitter, and a sizeable minority experience an intense bitterness that is extremely unpleasant. What Bartoshuk is illustrating is the now well-documented individual variation in the ability to taste bitter compounds. Her research, building on an accidental discovery in the 1930s, has shown that people can be separated into three different groups according to their ability to taste PROP. Twenty-five per cent of the population are PROP non-tasters, fifty per cent are medium tasters, and the remaining twenty-five per cent are supertasters. The latter group are exquisitely sensitive to PROP and certain other bitter compounds. This hard-wired difference is thought to be genetic. Anatomically, Bartoshuk has shown that supertasters have an extremely high density of taste papillae – the structures that house the taste-buds – on their tongues, with non-tasters having relatively few.

This means that individuals in each group live in different "taste worlds" to the others. Although the main difference relates to bitter-tasting ability, the taste differences also extend to other flavour sensations. According to Bartoshuk, "Supertasters perceive all tastes as more intense than do medium tasters and non-tasters." As you'd imagine, these research findings could have significant implications for the way we approach wine. Bartoshuk certainly thinks so. "It is important for winemakers to test their wines on all three groups," she says. "It would be interesting to see if we could find systematic differences in preferences for specific wine types across the three populations."

## Sensory input: taste, smell, and touch

To interpret how these results relate to wine tasting, we need a grasp of the basic science involved. What we commonly think of as "taste" or "flavour" is actually a complex mix of three different sensory inputs: taste, smell, and touch. Strictly speaking, the sense of taste involves just the inputs from specialized taste-buds on the tongue. We can perceive five different tastes: sweet, salty, bitter, sour, and a fifth taste known as "umami". This is a Japanese word that loosely translates as "meaty" or "savoury", and refers to the taste of amino acids (the chemical building blocks of proteins) such as glutamate. The receptors for these different tastes are spread more or less evenly across the tongue. This may come as a surprise to those familiar with the tongue map of school biology texts, which shows sweet, salty, bitter, and sour flavours to be localized to different regions; another of Bartoshuk's contributions to the taste field has been to expose this map as one of the scientific world's most enduring myths. It's based on a German study from the early twentieth century, which showed very small differences in sensitivity to the different tastes around the perimeter of the tongue. An influential mistranslation of this study in the 1940s assumed that where sensitivity to the different tastes was at a minimum, it was absent altogether. The result? A diagram showing that bitter, salty, sweet, and sour are detected in different regions. Despite being wrong, this is still widely being taught to students of wine.

Yet taste provides us with relatively little information, compared with the sense of smell – known as "olfaction" in the trade. Whereas there are just five basic tastes, we can discriminate among many thousands of volatile compounds ("odorants"). Indeed, much of the character and interest in wine stems from the complex odours detected by the olfactory system; our taste-buds alone provide limited detail. How does olfaction work? Our olfactory epithelium, located in the top of our nasal cavity, contains olfactory receptor cells, each of which expresses just one type of olfactory receptor. Each of these receptors – and there are hundreds of them in humans – is tuned to recognize the particular molecular structure of different odorants. It's not yet clear how we can discriminate among thousands of different odours with only a few hundred different receptors, but it appears likely that there is some sort of combinatorial processing going on.

So where does the sense of touch kick in? The brain uses touch to localize flavours perceptually. When you put a piece of steak in your mouth, the input from both the taste-buds and the olfactory epithelium is combined in the brain in such a way that you think this information is coming from where you can feel the steak to be in your mouth. Likewise, take a swig of wine and the taste sensation appears to come from the whole mouth – not just where the taste-buds are found.

## Are you a supertaster? Test yourself

The way scientists assess taster status is by using a piece of blotting paper soaked in 6-propylthiouracil (PROP). But PROP is a prescription-only drug, so it's unlikely you'll be able to get hold of any. Unfortunately, scientists with access to PROP won't be able to supply PROP papers to interested parties because they'd need ethical clearance from their institution's review board. The good news is that there is a simple method you can use at home. It's a little messier, and not as dramatic, but it sort of works.

WHAT YOU'LL NEED
· Blue food colouring
· A piece of paper with a hole punched in it, about 7mm (about 0.5 inch) in diameter, or use a reinforcer for a ring-binder
· A hand lens or magnifying glass

METHOD
Swab some blue food colouring onto the tip of your tongue. Your tongue will take up the dye, but the fungiform papillae, which are small round structures, will stay pink. Pop the piece of paper on the front portion of your tongue and count how many pink dots there are inside the circle with the aid of a magnifying glass. I've tried it, and it works: the result correlates with my PROP taster status.

RESULTS
If you have...
Fewer than fifteen papillae: non-taster
Fifteen to thirty-five papillae: taster
More than thirty-five: supertaster

**RIGHT** Take a sniff: much of the sensory information we receive from wine comes via our olfactory receptors, in the back of our nose.

## Olfaction: the smell of success

Bartoshuk emphasizes that it is important to distinguish between "retronasal" and "orthonasal" olfaction. Orthonasal olfaction refers to what we typically call smell. When we sniff an odour, it moves through the nostrils into the nasal cavity, where it is detected by the olfactory receptors. In contrast, retronasal olfaction occurs when we chew and swallow food, or slurp a wine. Odours are forced behind the palate and into the nasal cavity by a back-door route. "We think that the two forms of input are even analyzed in different parts of the brain," says Bartoshuk. "We have evidence that taste plays an important role in telling the brain that the odour is coming from the mouth and should be treated as a flavour." She has found that in patients with taste damage, flavours are often diminished. Work in her lab involving the anaesthesia of taste shows that the intensity of taste also plays a role in the intensity of retronasal olfaction. The implications? "If this is so, then supertasters with their more intense taste sensations may also experience more intense retronasal olfaction." Taste and smell therefore overlap.

Since olfaction is a key element of wine tasting, do individuals differ in their ability to smell? We've seen good evidence that people can be separated into different groups in their ability to taste; do we also we live in different "smell worlds"? This question is harder to answer, because of the increased complexity of olfaction, but the answer seems to be a qualified yes, although to a much lesser extent than is true for taste.

This is where we need to appreciate the significant role of the brain in processing the information detected by our senses. So far, we have just been looking at the way the tongue and olfactory epithelium detect the chemical environment they are exposed to. For us to use this information, the brain has to interpret it and pull out the useful bits from the midst of all the noise, a function known as "higher-order" processing. It's a complex field of psychology, and one where experiments that provide firm answers are rare. For now, it's sufficient to note that the brain does quite a lot to the information that it receives from the tongue and nose. The role of learning is key here, and we take particular notice of what we have learned to be relevant information, and ignore what we think is unimportant. (This is discussed in greater detail in the following chapter.)

## Processing aromas

An example of the latter is habituation. Repeated or constant exposure to an odour reduces people's ability to detect it. Dr. Charles Wysocki, an expert in olfaction from the Monell Chemical Senses Center in Philadelphia, Pennsylvania, thinks that this could relate to the performance of professional wine tasters. "If individuals are constantly exposed over a lengthy session," he says, "they become less sensitive to odorants that repeat themselves, such as oak." This overlaps with a phenomenon known as sensory-specific satiety, discussed in the next chapter – it's the brain's way of telling us that we have had enough of something, and causes us to find a particular flavour or smell less appealing in quite a specific manner.

It is clear that people differ in their sensitivity to different odours. Wysocki comments, "If a large enough sample of people is tested – say, twenty – the range in sensitivity to a single odorant can be 10,000-fold on a single day." Others put this figure a little lower. Dr. David Laing, from Australia's University of Western Sydney, suggests that in a sample of 100 people, "You could expect a variation of about 100 times between the most and least sensitive persons." This is still a significant difference, and enough to explain the reported differences in perception of the cork-taint compound trichloroanisole. But Laing adds that, as with all things biological, "The natural distribution of sensitivities means that many of us differ in sensitivity by only a few times – for example, fewer than ten." Another olfaction researcher, Professor Tim Jacob from Cardiff University in Wales, supports this idea. "It is possible," he says, "that we do each have different smell universes, but it is remarkable that we agree about smells to the degree we do."

A more extreme variation is where individuals are completely unable to detect certain odours, a condition known as specific anosmia. An example of this which is familiar to doctors is the ability – or lack thereof – to smell ketones, found in the breath of patients with poorly controlled diabetes. This ability is an all-or-none phenomenon, with about a quarter of doctors failing to detect this smell. Anosmias such as this – and it is not clear how many there are, or whether any relate to odours commonly found in wine – are usually genetic in origin. Fascinatingly, though, Wysocki points out that environmental exposures to certain odours can influence gene expression, turning on receptors in the olfactory epithelium. "Some people who cannot smell androstenone (a pig pheromone found in pork meat) can be induced to perceive its odour by repeated, short exposures to the odorant over a few weeks." The implication for wine-tasting ability here would be that we can learn to detect new smells of which we have been previously unaware. Again, it is not clear how widespread this is.

Our noses are temperamental performers. According to Jacob, women have a heightened sense of smell at ovulation. Appetite also stimulates smell, making us more perceptive when we're hungry. "There are centrifugal neuronal pathways leading from the brain to the olfactory bulb which modulate odour perception," says Jacob. "These act as a gate, allowing more or less information through." He also suspects that humidity affects the perception of smell, and has noticed as yet unquantified seasonal and weather-associated differences. Intriguingly, some odours can also counteract others, so that small quantities can cancel the smell experience of another, unrelated odour. Age also modulates the senses of taste and smell, although in different ways. There is a clear loss of smell with age, and while there is a much smaller loss in taste ability over a lifetime, it affects men and women differently. Males show a steady decline in the ability to taste bitter substances, whereas women show a sharp decline in this ability at the menopause.

## The skill of the wine taster

So the picture emerging is a complex one. We see that there are significant individual differences in tasting ability, with three distinct populations each living in different "taste worlds". We also see that there are complex and less clear-cut individual differences in the sense of smell, with the two senses of taste and smell overlapping to a certain degree. But how do these rather surprising results relate to wine? Would supertasters make the best wine tasters? "No," says Bartoshuk. "There is too much learning involved. Much of the skill of a wine expert comes from learning the odour complexes produced in wine. We know that learning plays a very important role in the naming of odours." Jacob agrees that learning is crucial. "The inexperienced person does not have a smell vocabulary," he says. "This hugely restricts their ability to describe and define

## Are women better wine tasters than men?

It's frequently asserted that women are better wine tasters than men. What is the science behind this claim? These gender differences seem to be related mainly to olfaction. A review by French scientists G. Brand and J.L. Millot raises some interesting issues that could relate to wine perception.

Women show variations in their sensitivity to smells during their menstrual cycle, with olfactory performance reaching a peak during ovulation and then decreasing during menstruation. But the fact that women on the pill (whose hormone levels don't cycle in the same way as those of menstruating women) still showed this variation indicates that this is not hormone-dependent, but dependent on a more central rhythm.

Does pregnancy affect olfactory ability? One study evaluated the reactions of pregnant women and a control group to twelve odours. How sensitive were the subjects to each odour, could they discriminate between odours, and how pleasant was each odour? The results showed no consistent differences in olfactory sensitivity or odour evaluation between the two groups. Two of the odours tested were considered to be of social significance (*i.e.* biologically relevent), and these were the only ones rated as more intense during pregnancy.

There are other explanations for sex differences in wine tasting. Women have been shown to do better than men in verbal tasks, and the brains of men and women are organized differently for language. This better performance of females in olfaction could reflect this cognitive advantage. One suggestion is that odour processing shares cortical resources used in processing language.

A fascinating study published in 2004 used Functional Magnetic Resonance Imaging (fMRI: a scanning technique that looks at activation of brain areas, based on the increased blood flow to local vasculature that accompanies neural activity; *see also* page 175) to measure the response to both imagined and real odours. Men had greater brain activation for both real and imagined odours, but the relative ratios of these responses differed: the responses to both the real and imaginary odours were about twice as high in women as in men. This suggests that some smells might have greater meaning, and consequently greater effect, on women than men. These results are consistent with a hypothesis that women may respond more efficiently to some olfactory stimuli than men, and that this is related in part to gender differences in cognitive style – in other words, because they think slightly differently.

odours." Even for wine experts, a common problem is the impoverished language we have for describing tastes and smells. In Jacob's opinion, "A large part of the wine taster's skill comes from being able to develop some sort of classification system, and then to associate words/categories with smells."

## PROP studies

One researcher has directly addressed this issue of individual differences in wine tasting. Gary Pickering, a professor of oenology at Brock University in Ontario, Canada, is studying whether PROP tasting status has any effect on wine perception and appreciation. The initial findings are illuminating. "We've just shown for the first time that PROP supertasters and tasters perceive the acidity, bitterness, and astringency of red wines more intensely than non-tasters," he explains. "Also, these differences appear to be moderated by the red-wine style being evaluated."

So far, Pickering's research has just looked at three different red-wine types. But he's planning to extend this research to include other wine styles, including white wines. Pickering suspects that the different taster groups will show different consumption patterns for wine, and have different preferences. Intriguingly, he also plans to assess the proportion of non-tasters, tasters, and supertasters among writers and winemakers. Along these lines, Bartoshuk recalls that a journalist once asked her how to distinguish the different groups so she could test food critics. But the results were unpublishable, because the critics considered their classification to be pejorative and wouldn't let their names be used. "The non-tasters thought they were being described as insensitive," explains Bartoshuk, "while the tasters thought they were being described as picky."

So we come to the key question. If the supertasters live in a world of enhanced flavour sensations, are they better wine tasters? And by that measure, are non-tasters disadvantaged? Perhaps a significant observation here is that women are more likely than men to be supertasters. In the USA, where this has been studied, about thirty-five per cent of females are supertasters, but just fifteen per cent of men. Does this mean that women are at an advantage when it comes to wine tasting? Not according to Pickering. In fact, he suggests that the opposite might even be true. "I would speculate that supertasters probably enjoy wine less than the rest of us," he explains. "They experience astringency, acidity, bitterness, and heat (from alcohol) more intensely, and this combination may make wine – or some wine styles – relatively unappealing."

## To err is human?

Finally, a humbling thought for those of us who evaluate wine professionally. Judged by our mammalian peers, we humans have a pretty poor sense of smell. Our olfactory epithelium covers just one-fifth of the range of that in cats, while dogs can distinguish between the smell of clothing worn by non-identical twins. In fact, for most other mammals the smell world is just as vivid and important to them as the visual world – something that anyone who has taken a dog for a walk will be all too aware of. And as for discriminating among a number of aromas in a complex mixture such as wine – well, we're just not very good at it. According to David Laing, "Humans can only identify up to a maximum of four odours in a mixture, regardless of whether the odours are a single molecule (*e.g.* ethanol) or more complex (*e.g.* smoke)." Worth bearing in mind next time you are tempted to write a flowery tasting note?

# 21 Wine and the brain: making sense of flavour

When people think about taste and smell, their focus is invariably on the tongue and nose, which carry the taste and olfactory receptors that interact with the outside world. This is, after all, where aromas and flavours are translated into electrical signals. But, relatively speaking, that's the easy bit – if we really want to understand these senses and how they work, we need to look at the brain and how it processes this information. That's a whole lot harder, and spans the fields of neurobiology, psychology, and even philosophy.

How is it that electrical currents from nerve cells are translated into a unified conscious experience in the brain? Science is a long way from being able to address this head-hurtingly complex question directly. But, a relatively new technique, Functional Magnetic Resonance Imaging (fMRI), has transformed brain research in recent years by allowing us to visualize the brain in action.

During a regular MRI scan, a subject is placed inside a large cylindrical magnet and exposed to a massive magnetic field. A sophisticated detection device then creates three-dimensional images of tissues and organs from the signals produced. fMRI is a twist on this, where the technique is used specifically to measure changes of blood flow in the brain. When a group of brain cells become more active, they need more blood, and this generates a signal in the scan. Although there was initial controversy about whether a direct correlation exists between the blood flow detected in an fMRI scan and actual brain activity, the consensus in the field is that this is the case. The power of fMRI is that it can show how we use our brains when, for example, we think of chocolate, or move our middle finger; the limitation is that to detect these signals reliably, subjects are required to lie inside a large metal cylinder with their heads completely still.

In this chapter we are going to look at how brain scientists have used fMRI and other techniques to unravel how taste and smell are processed in the brain. I'll also touch on research work which examines the way a representation of a wine that has just been tasted is constructed in our minds. Because of the practical and experimental difficulty of these sorts of studies, it's an area where there's still a lot of uncertainty. However, even the limited data obtained so far are highly relevant for wine tasting, and is important if we want to provide a robust theoretical basis for the human interaction with wine.

## Do trained tasters process wine differently?

In 2002, the Santa Lucia Foundation in Rome organized an international congress for neuroscientists. Benigna Mallebrein, who was involved in coordinating a wine and olive-oil tasting at the congress (intended to coincide with the session where papers on taste and smell were presented), had the bright idea of using fMRI to look at what happens to the brains of wine tasters when they experience wine. In particular, how do experienced tasters' brains respond to wine compared to those of novices? Mallebrein's idea was taken up by researchers from the Functional Neuroimaging Laboratory of the Santa Lucia Foundation, Rome, headed by Dr. Alessandro Castriota Scanderberg, who put together a simple yet elegant study.

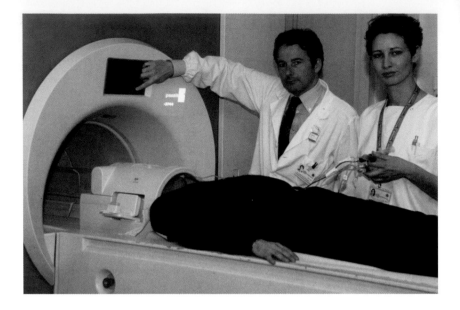

The researchers took seven professional sommeliers and seven other people matched for age and sex but without specific wine-tasting abilities, and monitored their brain responses while they tasted wine. Tasting wine while you are having your brain scanned is no trivial feat. "The experience was pretty uncomfortable," recalls Andrea Sturniolo, one of the sommeliers involved. "I was under a tunnel with four plastic tubes in my mouth, totally immobile." The researchers fed subjects a series of four liquids: three different wines and a glucose solution as a control. Subjects tried to identify the wines and form a critical judgement on them. They were also asked to judge when the perception of the wine was strongest: while it was in the mouth ("taste"), or immediately after swallowing ("after-taste"). "The experiment lasted a good fifty minutes," says Sturniolo, "which seemed endless. Certainly, they were not ideal conditions to carry out such a delicate experiment, but as they were identical for all participants, I think the results are reliable."

So what did the scans show? Some brain regions – notably the primary and secondary taste areas in the insula and orbitofrontal cortex – were activated in both sets of subjects during the "taste" phase. But during this period, another area was activated only in the sommeliers. This was the front of a region called the amygdala-hippocampal area. In the "after-taste" phase, the untrained subjects also showed activation of this amygdala-hippocampal area, but only on the right side, whereas in the sommeliers it was activated on both sides. In addition, the sommeliers exclusively showed further activation in the left dorsolateral prefrontal cortex (*see* page 179).

## How the brain constructs "flavour"

Now, unless you are a neuroscientist, this won't mean much to you. If we are going to make sense of these results, we need to examine how the brain processes taste and smell, and uncover the roles of these activated brain regions. The senses of taste and smell work together to perform two important tasks: identify nutritious foods and drinks, and protect us from eating things that are bad for us. The brain achieves this by linking food that we need with a reward stimulus – it smells or tastes "good" – and making bad or unneeded foods aversive. To do this, flavour perception needs to be connected with the processing of memory

"Hunger and appetite are powerful physical drives. They are also finely tuned. It is striking that most of us are able to eat what we need and not a lot more or less: even a slight imbalance, over decades, would result in gross obesity or starvation."

(we remember which foods are good and those which have made us ill) and emotions (we have a strong desire for food when we are hungry that then motivates us to seek out a decent meal). Because seeking food is a potentially costly and bothersome process, we need a strong incentive to do it. Hunger and appetite are thus powerful physical drives. They are also finely tuned. It is striking that most of us are able to eat what we need and not a lot more or less: even a slight imbalance, over decades, would result in gross obesity or starvation.

## Processing flavour

Taste begins on the tongue, where we have some 5,000 specialized structures called taste-buds, embedded in lumps called papillae. Each taste-bud contains fifty to 100 sensory cells responding to one of five different primary tastes (*see* page 170): sweet, salty, sour, bitter or "umami". These sensory cells convert this chemical information into electrical signals, which pass through to the primary taste cortex in the brain. This is located in a region called the insula, which, as you might expect, is one of the areas that was activated in the aforementioned fMRI study during wine tasting. Taste provides us with relatively little information compared with the sense of smell, more commonly referred to in scientific texts as "olfaction". Whereas there are just five basic tastes, we can discriminate among many thousands of volatile compounds ("odorants"). Our olfactory epithelium, located in the top of the nasal cavity, contains receptor cells, each of which expresses just one type of olfactory receptor. This information is also turned into electrical signals by the receptor cells, which are then conveyed to the olfactory cortex via a structure known as the olfactory bulb.

## Creating the sensation of flavour

At this stage, when the information exists at the level of the primary taste and smell areas of the brain, it is likely that all that is coded is the identity and intensity of the stimulus. Alone, this information is of relatively little value. But

**RIGHT** Representing flavour in the brain. This diagram shows a rather approximate and idealized network of relationships between the various inputs and brain processes that contribute to the unified representation of flavour in the brain. The key point is that flavour is a consequence of some complex processing steps, and there is no simple, linear pathway from the primary sensations of taste and smell to our conscious experience of these inputs. The grey circle indicates the various higher-order processing steps taking place. The position of some of the arrows is open to debate: connections shown here are for the purposes of illustrating concepts, and do not all represent solid data on these interrelationships.

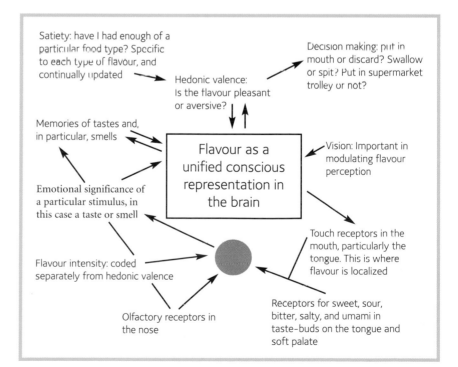

Satiety: have I had enough of a particular food type? Specific to each type of flavour, and continually updated

Hedonic valence: Is the flavour pleasant or aversive?

Decision making: put in mouth or discard? Swallow or spit? Put in supermarket trolley or not?

Memories of tastes and, in particular, smells

Flavour as a unified conscious representation in the brain

Vision: Important in modulating flavour perception

Emotional significance of a particular stimulus, in this case a taste or smell

Flavour intensity: coded separately from hedonic valence

Touch receptors in the mouth, particularly the tongue. This is where flavour is localized

Olfactory receptors in the nose

Receptors for sweet, sour, bitter, salty, and umami in taste-buds on the tongue and soft palate what the brain does next is very clever. It extracts the useful information from this mass of data, and begins to make sense of it – a process known as higher-order processing. Here we turn to the work of Edmund Rolls, a professor of experimental psychology at Oxford University, who has studied a region of the brain called the orbitofrontal cortex.

The work of Rolls and others has shown that taste and smell are brought together to form the sensation of flavour in the orbitofrontal cortex. Information from other senses, such as touch and vision, is also combined at this level to create a complex, unified sensation that is then localized to the mouth; after all this is where any response to food or drink, such as swallowing it or spitting it out, must take place. Rolls has also demonstrated that the orbitofrontal cortex is where the reward value (the "niceness", known as "hedonic valence") of taste and smell is represented. In other words, this is where the brain decides whether what we have in our mouths is delicious, dull or disgusting. This conclusion is echoed by a 2003 fMRI paper by Anderson and colleagues. This study showed that the brain uses two dimensions to analyze smells, intensity, and hedonic valence. The amygdala responds to intensity, while the orbitofrontal cortex decides whether the smell is good or bad.

Some nerve cells in this brain region respond to combinations of senses, such as taste and sight, or taste and touch, or smell and sight. This convergence of inputs is acquired by learning, but it is a slow process, typically requiring many pairings of the different sensations before it is fixed. This could explain why we often need several experiences with a new food or wine to be able to appreciate them fully. It is also at this level that stimulus-reinforcement association learning takes place. In this situation, for example, you encounter a new food (stimulus) which tastes good, but then it makes you violently sick (association). Next time you pop some of this in your mouth, you immediately spit it out in disgust. It saves you the bother of being sick again, and is therefore a protective mechanism.

### Sensory-specific satiety

One aspect of Rolls's research on the orbitofrontal cortex that has direct relevance to wine tasting is his work on sensory-specific satiety. This is the observation that when enough of a particular food is eaten, its reward value decreases. However, this decrease in pleasantness is greater than for other foods. Putting it more simply, if

## The Pepsi challenge and what it tells us about wine tasting

Read Montague, a neuroscientist at Baylor College of Medicine in Texas, devised a fascinating experiment that has implications for wine tasting. It stemmed from a series of TV commercials in the 1970s and 1980s where individuals took the "Pepsi challenge". In this test, Pepsi was pitted against Coke in a blind tasting, with subjects not knowing which was which. They invariably preferred the taste of Pepsi, but this wasn't reflected in their buying decisions.

Montague wanted to know why, so he re-enacted the Pepsi challenge with volunteers. The difference was that this time their brain activity was being scanned by an MRI machine. On average, Pepsi produced a stronger response in the ventral putamen, a region thought to process reward. In people who preferred Pepsi, the putamen was five times as active when they drank Pepsi than it was in Coke-preferring subjects drinking Coke.

In a clever twist, Montague repeated the experiments, yet this time telling the subjects what they were drinking as they drank it. Remarkably, most of them suddenly preferred Coke. Their brain activity also changed, with activity occurring in the medial prefrontal cortex, a region that shapes high-level cognitive powers. In effect, the subjects were allowing what they knew about Coke – its brand image – to shape their preferences. Remarkable.

The implications for wine tasting are clear. When we don't taste blind, our preferences are liable to be shaped by pre-existing information we have about the wine. Try as hard as we might to be objective, this isn't possible. What we know about wine will shape how we perceive the wine, and will even influence how much we enjoy a particular bottle. This brings another fascinating level of complexity to wine tasting.

"This all makes perfect sense at a practical level. When you haven't eaten for a long time, even simple foods can taste great; their hedonic valence has been altered by your state of hunger. I love raspberries, but they would lose their appeal if I had already eaten five punnets of them."

you like both bananas and chocolate, and then eat lots of banana, you can't stomach the thought of another banana but you will still fancy a chocolate. This clever brain trick makes us want the sorts of foods that we need at a given time, and helps us to balance our nutritional intake. Rolls has shown that the orbitofrontal cortex response to the odour of a food eaten to satiety decreases, but the response to another odour that has not been eaten doesn't change. The subjects' perception of the intensity of the smell of the consumed food doesn't change, but their perception of its hedonic valence does. In another study, he showed that swallowing is not necessary for sensory-specific satiety to occur. Rolls is cautious about speculating, but agreed that this could have some effect when a taster is repeatedly encountering the same sort of taste or smell. At a large trade tasting it is quite common to taste as many as 100 wines in a session. If these results of sensory-specific satiety are extrapolated to this sort of setting, then it's likely that the brain will be processing the last wine you taste differently to that of the first, assuming that there are some components to the taste or smell in common – for example, tannins, fruit, or oak.

This all makes perfect sense at a practical level. When you haven't eaten for a long time, even simple foods can taste great; their hedonic valence has been altered by your state of hunger. I love raspberries, but they would lose their appeal if I had already eaten five punnets of them. I'd still recognize them as raspberries, though. My brain would simply be changing how attractive I found various flavours according to other information it was receiving.

## Why trained tasters are different

Not surprisingly, given its importance in the processing of flavour, the orbitofrontal cortex is one of the regions activated in the brains of both trained and untrained wine tasters in the Italian fMRI study (*see* page 176). What about the other areas – the ones that were highlighted specifically in the sommeliers?

Firstly, we have the amygdala-hippocampal area. This zone plays a key role in processing motivation (the amygdala) and memory (the hippocampus). According to Dr. Scanderberg, "Finding an early and consistent activation of the amygdala-hippocampus complex in the sommelier group suggests a greater motivation for the recognition process." This may indicate that the sommeliers were expecting a reward and thus pleasure from the tasting process. The other key area is the left dorsolateral prefrontal cortex, a zone involved in the planning and use of cognitive (thinking) strategies. The sommeliers' unique activation here is consistent with the idea that only experienced tasters follow specific analytical strategies when wine is in their mouths. These strategies might be of a linguistic kind, associating words with specific flavours. We'll return to this later.

In parallel with fMRI studies on musicians, which show that music activates different areas of trained musicians' brains compared with those of casual listeners, it seems that sommeliers experience something different to the average person when they taste wine. "There is clear evidence that the neural connections of the brain change with training and experience," says Dr. Scanderberg. "There are two apparently contradictory ways that the brain adjusts its structural network in parallel with increasing expertise of the subject." The first, and most common, is to assign a specific function to a smaller cluster of cells higher up in the brain's hierarchy. For example, in the recovery of stroke patients, it is common to see a particular task activate a smaller but higher region in the brain at the end of rehabilitation than it did at the start. The second strategy is to recruit more brain areas to help with a complex task. Experienced tasters seem to follow this second strategy, pulling in new brain areas to help with the analysis of sensory stimuli. The implications for wine tasting are clear. I'm assuming here that, as a reader of this book, you may well be someone who has drunk a fair bit of wine over a number of years. Do you remember a wine that first really appealed to you? If you were to go back in time now and taste that wine again, but with your current wine-drinking history, you'd actually perceive something quite different the second time around. Your brain has been changed by drinking all that wine – and we aren't talking about alcohol-induced neural degeneration. By paying attention as you've been drinking, just like the sommeliers in this study, your response to wine differs from that of untrained subjects. This also underlines the importance of the learning component in wine appreciation. People versed in one culture of wine may need to re-learn about wine when exploring another. Even if you have years of expertise in Australian reds, for example, you may have to start from scratch when trying to appreciate German Riesling.

While this study is of great interest, some unanswered questions remain. Firstly, the sommeliers seem to be using more of their brain areas in the process of wine tasting, but are they actually enjoying the wine more? Do wine experts get more pure "pleasure" from their wine, or is the extra appreciation solely at an intellectual level? Secondly, some tastes are innate, whereas others are acquired, and it is often these acquired tastes that are more enduring, even if, initially, they might have been quite off-putting. Does the brain process these innate versus acquired tastes differently?

According to Mallebrein, further studies like this are planned. For example, the scientists at the Santa Lucia Foundation intend to carry out the same study in a group of female sommeliers and age-matched controls, since the initial study was done with males. For now, we are left with the tantalizing thought that each time we taste wine and think about it, our brain is undergoing subtle changes, which will then alter our perception of the next glass of wine. So it seems that, even if we are tasting the same wine together, our brains might be constructing subtly different conscious experiences for each of us.

## Words and wine: the psychology of tasting

Frédéric Brochet, a cognitive psychologist, has done some important work that is highly relevant here. He has studied the practice of wine tasting as carried out by professionals. His claim is that the practice and teaching of tasting rests on a fragile theoretical basis, and his work seeks to redress this imbalance. "Tasting is representing," says Brochet, "and when the brain carries out a 'knowledge' or 'understanding' task, it manipulates representations." In this context, a "representation" is a conscious experience constructed by the mind on the basis of a physical experience – in this cases the taste, smell, sight, and mouth-feel of a wine. Brochet uses three methodologies in his work: textual analysis (which looks at the sorts of words tasters use to verbalize their representations), behavioural analysis (inferring cognitive mechanisms from looking at how subjects act), and cerebral function analysis (looking at how the brain responds to wine directly through the use of fMRI).

### Textual analysis: studying the words tasters use

Textual analysis involves the statistical study of the words used in a text. Brochet used five data sets, consisting of tasting notes from *Guide Hachette*, Robert Parker, Jacques Dupont, Brochet himself, and notes on eight wines from forty-four professionals collected at Vinexpo. Employing textual-analysis software called ALCESTE, he studied the way different tasters used words to describe their tasting experiences. He summarizes his six key results as follows. (1) The authors' descriptive representations are based on the types of wines and not on the different parts of the tasting. (2) Representations are "prototypical": that is, specific vocabularies are used to describe types of wines, and each vocabulary represents a type of wine. Putting this another way, when tasters experience a particular wine, the words they use to describe it are those that they link to this sort of wine. (3) The range of words used (lexical fields) is different for each author. (4) Tasters possess a specific vocabulary for preferred and non-preferred wines. No taster seems to be able to put aside his or her preferences when their representations are described. Brochet adds that this dependence of representations on preferences is well-known in the fragrance world. (5) Colour is a major factor in organizing the classes of descriptive terms used, and has a major influence on the sorts of descriptors used. (6) Cultural information is present in the sensorial descriptions. Brochet states that "Certain descriptive terms referring to cognitive representation probably come from memory or information heard or read by the subject, but neither the tongue nor the nose could be the object of the coding. All takes place as if the information proposed on the label or by a potential salesperson generates sensorial information and the described characteristics."

### Behavioural analysis: perceptive expectation

In the next set of experiments, Brochet invited fifty-four subjects to take part in a series of experiments in which they had to describe a real red wine and a real white wine. A few days later, the same group had to describe the same white wine, although now it had been coloured red with a neutral-tasting food colourant. Interestingly, in both experiments, they described the "red" wine using identical terms (this was shown statistically) even though one of them was actually a white wine. Brochet's conclusion was that the perception of taste and smell conformed to colour – vision has more of an input in the wine-tasting process than most people would think. Brochet notes a practical application of this observation, which has

## Lost for words: the difficulty of describing taste and smell

One of the frustrations faced by tasters, novice and experienced alike, is that it is extremely difficult to describe our experience of wine. To quote Hugh Johnson, "Words follow lumberingly after the clear, precise, yet indefinable impressions of the tongue." Our senses are dominated by vision. This is why it is possible to describe what we see, such as a landscape, to another person so that they will have a reasonably clear idea of the scene before us. But have you ever tried to explain to someone what a peach tastes like, or your impression of steak and chips? It's almost impossible.

On one level, we can try to identify the different flavours present in a wine, such as "raspberries", "spice", "vanilla", and so on. This sort of description has an aura of precision to it, but one that may be illusory. As Brochet's work suggests, the cues for these descriptors are factors such as colour and type of wine, and the author's own cultural background and preferences. Studies have shown that even experienced tasters are unable to detect more than four odours in a mixture. In effect, tasters are usually "making up"

tasting notes, on the basis of factors other than strictly what is in the glass. Besides, much of the interest in a wine lies in factors such as texture, balance, and structure, which are even harder to describe in precise terms than specific flavours or aromas.

This sounds a little negative. If this is the truth, then why do we bother writing tasting notes? The short answer is because it's the best we can manage, so it will have to do. The whole process might be more useful, though, if the wine trade recognized the imprecision of this process. What we are doing with our tasting notes is using a "code" language that gives information about a number of aspects of the wine. It would also be helpful if the more creative among the wine-writing fraternity stopped writing tasting notes with dozens of stacked (and often exotic) descriptors, as if this proved they operated on a higher gustatory and olfactory plane than the rest of us. Brochet's results suggest that we should take ourselves a little less seriously when we are attempting the difficult job of describing wine in words.

been known for a long time in the food and fragrance industries: almost no one sells colourless products any more.

In a second, equally mischievous experiment, Brochet served the same average-quality wine to people at a week's interval. The twist was that on the first occasion it was packaged and served to people as a *vin de table*, and on the second as a *grand cru*. We'd probably all like to think we'd not have been taken in by this ruse, but Brochet's tasters fell for it, hook, line, and sinker. He analyzed the terms used in the tasting notes, and it makes telling reading. For the "*grand cru*" wine versus the *vin de table*, "a lot" replaces "a little"; "complex" replaces "simple"; and "balanced" replaces "unbalanced" – all because of the sight of the label. Brochet explains the results via a phenomenon called "perceptive expectation": subjects perceive what they have pre-perceived, and find it difficult to back away from that. For humans, visual information is more important than chemosensory information, so we tend to trust vision more. Brochet uses this to explain Emile Peynaud's observation that "Blind tasting of great wines is often disappointing".

### Variation in representations

A further study in this series examined how the qualitative ratings of a series of wines differed among a group of wine tasters. A group of eight tasters was asked to rank eighteen wines, which they tasted blind, in order of preference. The results differed widely. With a similar methodology to that used by the Italian researchers, Brochet then used fMRI to assess the brain response of four subjects to a series of wines. One of the most interesting results obtained was that the same stimulus produced different brain responses in different people. In terms of brain area activated, one was more verbal, another more visual. Also, when a subject tastes a wine several times, the images of each tasting are different. Brochet concludes that this demonstrates the "expression of the variable character of the representation". The representation is a "global form, integrating, on equal terms, chemosensorial, visual, imaginary, and verbal imagination".

## Conclusions

While there's a lot still to be learned about how the brain constructs our experience of wine, it is already clear that this is a complex area that we often try to simplify. It is our attempts to simplify the concepts underlying wine tasting and iron out the very real inter- and intra-individual variations that lead to problems in the interpretations of results from tastings. There is a lot more to the wine experience than just smell and taste; the basic information from these chemical senses is supplemented in a very real way by other input: for example, from vision, touch, and memory. In addition to this, the higher-order integration of all this input is a flexible and complicated processing stage that then forms our unified perception (or "representation") of the tasting experience.

The results of Brochet and others show that factors such as tasting blind make a crucial difference to the nature of this representation, and that representations of the same wine differ markedly among tasters. In addition, the past experiences of tasting will change the nature of our current experiences. This information should help our understanding of the scientific underpinnings of the wine-tasting process, and help in the design of tastings. For example, panel tastings where consensus is sought look doomed to failure. It is likely that further studies using similar techniques to those described here will give us a greater understanding of the rather complex business of tasting and describing wine.

# 22 Wine-flavour chemistry

Wine is a complicated chemical soup, the nature of which scientists are only just beginning to understand. It is estimated that wine contains more than 1,000 volatile flavour compounds, of which more than 400 are produced by yeasts. Despite decades of research, scientists are only now beginning to get a fuller understanding of the true nature of the chemical composition of wine. Part of the difficulty is that the picture is a dynamic one. The volatility of various flavour compounds can be altered by other components of the wine. Added to this, human perception of various flavour chemicals is altered by their context – the suite of other chemicals present in the wine. Thus chemical "A" might be below detection level in one wine and above it in another, even though its concentration is the same in both.

One further complicating factor is that many of the most important chemicals that shape a wine's specific character are present at very low concentrations. Look at our old adversary 2,4,6-trichloroanisole (TCA), the chief culprit in cork taint, as an example. This is detectable at fantastically low concentrations of less than five parts per trillion (a concentration which is usually simplified into terms of drops in an Olympic-sized swimming pool, or seconds in many centuries; it is not many of either). The most prevalent constituents of wine are often relatively unimportant in terms of the sensory qualities of the wine. And the actual compounds we currently know the most about do not necessarily reflect their importance in determining wine flavour, but rather our ability to sample them with the techniques available. This is changing, and as I write, new progress is being made, driven largely by advances in sampling technology.

What is the goal of wine-flavour chemistry? Do we need to be able to put a chemical name to all the nuances of a fine wine in order to appreciate it? No, clearly not. But if we understand the precise mechanisms by which certain components of the grape must are transformed into beneficial flavour molecules – for example, by the metabolic action of yeast, or barrel-ageing, or bottle maturation – then winemakers can adapt their techniques to maximize positive flavour development. In a similar vein, viticulturalists can adapt their techniques to encourage the formation of precursors of positive flavour molecules and avoid the development of grape constituents that impact negatively on wine characteristics.

However there is also a dark side to this branch of wine science. A greater understanding of the impact of particular flavour compounds that occur naturally in wine will aid those who fancy a bit of "creative" winemaking. It would be very hard to spot the addition of flavour compounds to wine, particularly if these were added in tiny amounts (it doesn't take much of most volatile wine compounds to have a significant effect) or as aroma precursors. As well as being dishonest, undisclosed manipulation of this sort could have the potential to mar the "natural" image of wine in the eyes of consumers (*see* chapter 11).

"In volume terms, after water, ethyl alcohol is the most important component of wine, and is produced by the fermentation of sugars by yeasts. Alone, it doesn't taste of much, but the concentration of alcohol in the final wine has a marked effect on the wine's sensory qualities."

# Wine-flavour compounds

Wine chemistry has already been discussed to some extent in other chapters of this book, particularly with respect to reduction (chapter 16), *Brettanomyces* (chapter 18), yeasts (chapter 17), and barrels (chapter 13). For the purposes of this chapter, it will be useful to take an overview of the key classes of wine flavour compounds, highlighting a few that are of particular interest. These compounds can be divided neatly into five groups: acids, alcohols, sugars, polyphenols, and volatile compounds, although there is some overlap.

## Acids

Grapes contain a range of acids, and acidity is a vital component of wine composition. Tartaric, malic, and citric acid are present in grapes (the latter only in small quantities); upon fermentation, these are joined by lactic and succinic acids. If malolactic fermentation takes place, much of the tart malic acid is converted into the softer lactic acid. A range of other acids (over thirty) also occurs at lower concentrations. The relationship between the acid composition of wine and its actual acidic taste is complex; some acids are naturally more acidic by virtue of their chemical structures. The perception of acidity is also strongly influenced by other flavour components of the wine, notably sweetness, which counters the perception of acidity quite markedly. Acidity in wine is important for reasons other than flavour: it affects wine stability (directly, by inhibiting the growth of microbes, and indirectly, by increasing the efficacy of sulphur dioxide administrations), and is important in red wines in influencing colour (put simply, the more acidic the wine, the redder the anthocyanin pigments are).

## Alcohols

In volume terms, after water, ethyl alcohol is the most important component of wine, and is produced by the fermentation of sugars by yeasts. Alone, it doesn't taste of much, but the concentration of alcohol in the final wine has a marked effect on the wine's sensory qualities. This is evidenced by the "sweet spot" tastings carried out by the likes of California-based wine-technology company Vinovation. If a wine with a high natural alcohol level is subjected to alcohol reduction via reverse osmosis, a series of samples of the same wine can be prepared differing only in alcohol levels – say, at half degree intervals from twelve to eighteen per cent alcohol (*see* pages 110–111). Panels of tasters show marked preferences for some of these wines over others, and different descriptors are commonly used to describe the sensory properties of the different samples. Excessive alcohol can lead to bitterness and astringency in a wine. It may also taste "hot".

## Sugars

Grapes are rich in sugar. Indeed, grapes are the sweetest of all berries, and contain increasing levels of fructose and glucose as they mature. During fermentation, nearly all of this sugar is turned into alcohol for the majority of wines. However, winemakers sometimes deliberately retain some residual sugar in their wines, even if they are marketed as dry, to improve body and offset high acidity levels.

## Polyphenols

These are probably the most important flavour chemicals in red wines, but are of much less importance in whites. Polyphenols are a large group of compounds that use phenol as the basic building block (*see* table, opposite). An important property of phenolic compounds is that they associate spontaneously with a wide

| Polyphenolic compounds | |
|---|---|
| Non-flavonoid polyphenols | There are two types of these smaller non-flavonoid polyphenolic compounds: the benzoic acids (such as gallic acid) and cinnamic acids. They are often present in grapes in a conjugated form (*e.g.* as esters or glycosides). |
| Flavan-3-ols | These are important in wine, and include catechin and epicatechin. They are particularly important in their polymeric forms, where they are called procyanidins (often referred to as condensed tannins). |
| Flavonoids | Umbrella term used to describe a large group of polyphenols, including anthocyanins, flavonols, and flavones. |
| Anthocyanins | These are the red/blue/black pigments in grapes, which are almost always found in the skins. Five different anthocyanin compounds are found in red wines, the dominant one being malvidin. They are not stable in young wines, but react with tannins to form complex pigments which gradually become larger as wine ages, to the point where they become insoluble and precipitate. Oxygen has an important role in facilitating the process of phenolic polymerization. The colour of pigments depends on the acidity of the grape must and the concentration of sulphur dioxide: they tend to be redder at lower pH (more acid) and more purple at higher pH. |

range of compounds such as proteins and other phenolics, by means of a range of non-covalent forces (which don't share electrons: for example, hydrogen bonding and hydrophobic effects). Phenolic compounds are widely thought to have health-enhancing effects, but their propensity to bind with proteins such as salivary proline-rich proteins (PRPs) will conspire against them reaching sites in the body where they might be active.

### Volatile compounds

This is where things get really complex, but it is also where much of the action is. Volatile compounds give wine its smell, known more respectfully as the "bouquet" or "aroma". They come directly from the grapes themselves, but more commonly are secondary aromas arising from fermentation processes, or even tertiary aromas developing during maturation and ageing. Most occur in extremely low concentrations, which, before the advent of highly sensitive analytical techniques, made their study a difficult business. Rather than list the 400 or so which are thought to be important in wine, the table opposite gives a description of the main classes, with some specific examples.

## Tannins

The term "tannin" is chemically rather imprecise, but it is one used by almost all wine tasters. It is used to describe a group of complex plant chemicals found principally in bark, leaves, and immature fruit which form complexes with proteins and other plant polymers such as polysaccharides. It is thought that the role of tannins is plant defence; they have an astringent, aversive taste that is off-putting to herbivores. Tannins in wine come from grape skins, stems, and seeds, and their extraction is heavily dependent on particular winemaking processes. Some tannins

"Can we, through dissection, really enhance a wine's ability to lift our soul? Is the beauty and viscerality delivered by a wine – or a cuisine, or a piece of music – really improved by manipulating the pieces? I don't think so."

also come from new barrels where these are used to age wine. Tannin management is a crucial step in red winemaking. Tannins are thought to taste astringent because they bind with salivary PRPs and precipitate them. They may also react directly with tissues in the mouth.

There are two classes of tannins: condensed and hydrolyzable. The former are the main grape-derived tannins. They are formed by the polymerization of polyphenolic monomers such as catechin and epicatechin into chains, which are referred to by using the unit DP (for degree of polymerization). Tannins are reactive and will form complexes with other aromatic (*i.e.* benzene-ring-containing) compounds. The main variables in tannins are the length of the polymer and the nature of the individual subunits that compose it. In wine, the bonds between tannin polymers are repeatedly breaking and reforming. Research is currently under way that is attempting to work out the relationship between tannin structure and mouth-feel qualities; it is still unclear how different tannins affect perception of wine. Emerging research is suggesting that the traditional account of red-wine ageing (that over time tannins get bigger, become insoluble, and fall out of solution) is wrong. It could well be that tannins are breaking up in the acidic environment of the wine and are getting smaller. Some wines age wonderfully with very little or no bottle deposit. Dr. Paul Smith, a research chemist with the Australian Wine Research Institute (AWRI), says we are "still very much at the stage of trying to understand and characterize wine tannins".

## Concluding perspective

But before we get carried away by all this knowledge of the flavour components of wine, here's a useful perspective from Vinovation's Clark Smith. "In the twentieth century," he says, "scientific reductionism, a technique which divides a problem into manageable pieces, has attempted to crack the code of wine quality. The UC-Davis approach, popularized as the Aroma Wheel school of sensory science, has attempted to manipulate wine flavour through viticultural and oenological experiments, seeking to enhance the 'good' aromas and minimize the 'bad'. But, can we, through dissection, really enhance a wine's ability to lift our soul? Is the beauty and viscerality delivered by a wine – or a cuisine, or a piece of music – really improved by manipulating the pieces? I don't think so. I contend that reductionist winemaking yields fruity, varietally correct, alcoholic soda-pop which doesn't ring anybody's bell at much over ten bucks."

While Smith's comments seem a little unfair to UC Davis, he's got a point. Wine quality can't be made sense of by a reductionist approach; it is an emergent

## Colour in red wines

Researchers are now beginning to understand the nature of colour in red wines, and the story that is emerging is challenging traditional understanding in this area. Colour in red wines falls into three categories. First come the anthocyanins, the primary pool of colour from the grape. Young wine is packed with anthocyanins, which are very reactive; they interact with both sulphur dioxide and oxygen, which bleaches them.

In addition to anthocyanins, there are two major fermentation-derived colour groups. The first of these is the pigmented polymers. These are formed by the chemical linkage between tannins and anthocyanins. This is a covalent linkage, and is very important in forming stable colour in wines.

The third group is called the anthocyanin-derived pigments, which arise from reactions between anthocyanins and other phenolics and aldehydes. This is a massive, complicated class of non-bleachable pigments; new members are being added all the time. These are still quite reactive, and they can form further combinations with tannins to form pigmented polymers.

| The main classes of volatile compounds | |
|---|---|
| Esters | Important to wine flavour. They are formed by the reaction of organic acids with alcohols, during both fermentation and ageing. Ethyl acetate (or ethyl ethanoate) is the most common ester in wine, formed by the combination of acetic acid and ethanol. Most esters have a distinctly fruity aroma; some also have oily, herbaceous, buttery, and nutty nuances. |
| Aldehydes | Present in grape must, but of relatively minor importance in wine flavour. The exception is acetaldehyde (ethanal: oxidized ethanol), a component of some sherries. Vanillin (4-hydroxy-methoxy-benzaldehyde) can be an important aroma molecule in wine aged or fermented in oak. |
| Ketones | Ketones include diacetyl (butane-2,3-dione), which gives a buttery odour at higher levels that can be negative. Acetoin (3-hydroxybutan-2-one) has a slightly milky odour. $\beta$-damascenone and $\alpha,\beta$-ionones are known as the complex ketones, or isoprenoids. The former has a rose-like aroma and is most commonly found in Chardonnay; the latter occur in Riesling and smell of violets. Benzoic aldehydes are taint compounds with a bitter almond flavour. Sometimes produced as a result of the incorrect application of epoxy resin vat linings. |
| Higher alcohols | Also known as fusel oils. At least forty have been described in wine. Most important are the amyl alcohols. With pungent odours, they are negative at higher levels, but kept in check they can be positive. For example, hexanol has a grassy flavour. |
| Lactones | Lactones (furanones) have been identified both in grapes and oak barrels. The oak lactones (*cis*- and *trans*-$\beta$-methyl-$\gamma$-octalactone) are important in barrel-aged wines, imparting sweet and spicy coconut aromas with woody characteristics. Sotolon (3-hydroxy-4,5-dimethyl-5(H)-furan-2-one) is associated with botrytized wines and has sweet, spicy, nutty aromas. |
| Volatile acid | The most significant volatile acid in wine is acetic acid, produced during fermentation, but more significantly a result of *Acetobacter* activity. It tastes sour and smells of vinegar. |
| Volatile phenols | Important in wine aroma. 4-ethylphenol and 4-ethylguaiacol, found predominantly in red wines, are formed by the yeast *Brettanomyces*, and have distinctive gamey, spicy, animally aromas. 4-vinylphenol and 4-vinylguaiacol are rare in red wines and more common in whites, and have largely negative aromatic properties. These are formed by the enzymatic decarboxylation of cinnamic acids, a process inhibited by some grape phenols in red wines. |
| Terpenes | A large family of compounds, widespread in plants. Grapes contain varying amounts, which contribute to wine odour. Over forty have been identified, but only six are thought to add to wine aroma. Highest in Muscat wines: the distinctive floral character is due to the likes of linalool and geraniol. Grapes like Gewürztraminer and Pinot Gris also have a terpene component. |
| Methoxypyrazines | Nitrogen-containing heterocyclic compounds formed by the metabolism of amino acids. 2-methoxy-3-isobutyl-pyrazine is a distinctive element of the aroma of varieties such as Cabernet Sauvignon and Sauvignon Blanc. At high concentrations it can be overly herbaceous and is generally seen as a problem in red wines, but an asset in certain styles of white when it contributes fresh, grassy aromas. Methoxypyrazines have extremely low detection thresholds. |
| Sulphur compounds | Important in wine aroma. Mercaptans (thiols) are negative at higher amounts, but in controlled quantities they are important in the aroma of Sauvignon Blanc and some other white varieties. Some sulphur compounds have positive effects on wine aroma at extremely low levels. |

Wine is usually defined as "fermented grape juice as an alcoholic drink", but there is also a supplementary definition of a "fermented drink resembling this made from other fruits, etc., as specified (elderberry wine; ginger wine)". Unless specified otherwise, therefore, the assumption is that wine is the product of fermented grape juice.

Yet, with fantastically rare exceptions, winemakers add things to wine. At the simplest level, this addition may be limited to a little sulphur dioxide. Most commonly, more things are added, including yeast starter cultures, fining agents, tannins, acidity, oxygen, sugars, and flavour compounds via oak barrels or barrel substitutes. Who's to say which additives are acceptable, and which aren't? Is it more acceptable to add more of a component that is already present in the wine, than to add one which isn't? Bear in mind also that there are viticultural and winemaking techniques that will ensure that more (or less) of a particular chemical component ends up in the final wine. Is manipulation acceptable when, as in this case, it is indirect, but not if it involves the direct addition or subtraction of a chemical from the must or wine? And are direct manipulations that are traditional, such as chaptalization (the adding of sugar to must), more acceptable than ones that are novel (such as the removal of alcohol from a wine by reverse osmosis)? And what about the selective use of yeast strains known to enhance the presence of certain flavour molecules in the finished wine? These are difficult questions to answer with any degree of certainty.

property of the manifold components of wine (*see* page 205). By breaking wine down into its constituents, we can fail to see the wood for the trees. It is the property of the whole that matters. As well as specific flavours and aromas, we need to consider the texture, structure, and overall depth of the wine. What makes one wine great and another ordinary is a subject in need of plenty more research, addressed elsewhere in this book (chapters 2, 3, 8, 11, 16, and 18).

## Supplementing wine

Wine is a complex mixture of chemicals, and many hundreds of these play a role in determining its flavour and aroma properties. Now that we know more about the important flavour molecules, a time is approaching where it could be possible to synthesize a manufactured wine from first principles, by combining chemicals in the right proportions. But even if we knew enough to make such an artificial wine, it is likely to be much more straightforward and a whole lot cheaper to let the grapes and fermentative microbes do all the work, with just a few necessary additions such as sulphur dioxide. Totally manufactured wines may never be a big hit, but a more realistic prospect is wines that are flavour "supplemented". These could already be with us, albeit illegally. Advances in wine-flavour chemistry have pinpointed chemicals that are important in flavour and aroma; some present at very low levels. Judicious additions to certain wines would be very hard to detect where these additions involved molecules already present in the wine. Rather than drive this sort of activity underground, where it is hard to be detected, shouldn't it just be allowed? It seems a bit hypocritical to allow some additions but not others, merely on the grounds of tradition. Surely a more defensible regulatory strategy would be to permit more, but require full disclosure; perhaps a separate category could be devised for those wines where flavour compounds have been added.

Wine has considerable added value because of factors such as tradition, authenticity, local characteristics, cultural richness, and healthfulness. The danger is that if it is turned into just another manufactured beverage by the unregulated addition of just about anything, then some of this added value will be lost. It's a tough decision, but one that will have to be faced by the wine industry over the coming decades.

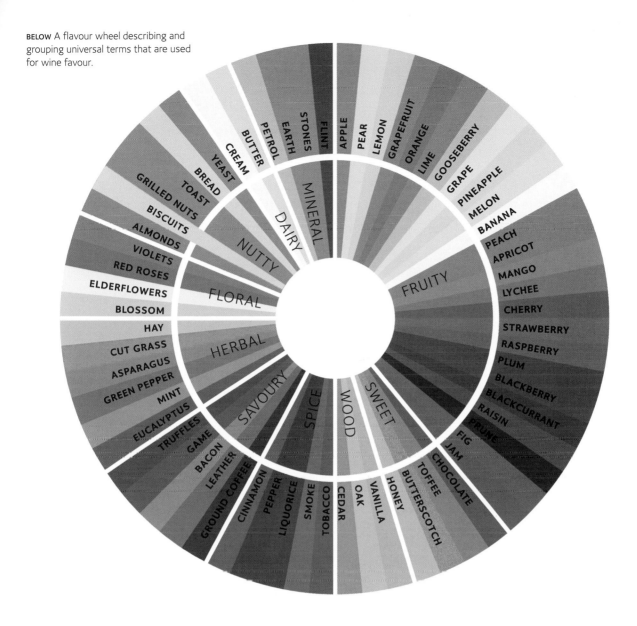

The flavour wheel includes the following groupings and terms:

**MINERAL:** FLINT, STONES, EARTH, PETROL

**DAIRY:** BUTTER, CREAM

**NUTTY:** YEAST, BREAD, TOAST, GRILLED NUTS, BISCUITS, ALMONDS

**FLORAL:** VIOLETS, RED ROSES, ELDERFLOWERS, BLOSSOM

**HERBAL:** HAY, CUT GRASS, ASPARAGUS, GREEN PEPPER, MINT, EUCALYPTUS

**SAVOURY:** TRUFFLES, GAME, BACON, LEATHER, GROUND COFFEE

**SPICE:** CINNAMON, PEPPER, LIQUORICE, SMOKE, TOBACCO

**WOOD:** CEDAR, OAK, VANILLA

**SWEET:** HONEY, BUTTERSCOTCH, TOFFEE, CHOCOLATE, JAM

**FRUITY:** APPLE, PEAR, LEMON, GRAPEFRUIT, ORANGE, LIME, GOOSEBERRY, GRAPE, PINEAPPLE, MELON, BANANA, PEACH, APRICOT, MANGO, LYCHEE, CHERRY, STRAWBERRY, RASPBERRY, PLUM, BLACKBERRY, BLACKCURRANT, RAISIN, PRUNE, FIG

# Wine mimicry

Let's be theoretical for a moment. If it were possible to analyze a great wine, such as Chave's Hermitage from a great vintage, and replicate this wine accurately by chemical means, would this be an evil thing to do? It would certainly be wrong if the resultant liquid were passed off to consumers as Hermitage. But what if it were sold without such labelling deceit, at a low price? It would offer someone of limited means a great sensory experience for relatively little money.

Whether or not this is desirable depends on your view of wine. Is wine more than just what is in the bottle? Or is the experience of wine confined wholly to the mental representation that results from our response to sniffing and slurping the liquid we have in our glasses? Neurobiology answers this question to

a degree (*see* page 175). Our knowledge of and beliefs about the wine we are drinking help shape the sensory representation we have. Thus, for me, if I were drinking a fake wine almost identical to Chave's Hermitage in chemical properties, it would be a lesser experience than knowing that I was drinking the real deal, with the cultural context that this confers. On another level, someone who neither knew nor cared about Chave or Hermitage would have a near-equal experience of both the real wine and the manufactured liquid.

The tentative conclusion might be that, for certain markets, a manufactured wine-like beverage would be perfectly acceptable, although manufacturing fine wine is unlikely to prove a success, unless you are prepared to be fraudulent at the same time.

# 23 Wine and health

Any British wine-lovers unfortunate enough to suffer a heart attack should make sure they are living in the catchment area of the Great Western Hospital in Swindon. Why? Because then they'd be likely to come under the care of William McCrea, a consultant cardiologist who prescribes his patients a couple of glasses of red wine a day. And it's not any old plonk, either. Unlike hospital food, the wine served to patients is pretty respectable: Montes Alpha Cabernet Sauvignon, to be precise, from Chile. This unusual measure was prompted by a research study showing that drinking red wine protects heart-attack survivors against a second heart attack, and by other studies indicating that Chilean Cabernet Sauvignon is particularly rich in the molecules that some people think are responsible for this protective effect.

The health claims made for wine are truly amazing. If you believed everything you heard about wine's benefits, you'd wonder why people bother with other drugs. A quick trawl through the scientific literature comes up with reports suggesting that wine (and red wine in particular) protects to a certain degree against heart disease, strokes, various cancers, AIDS, dementia, diabetes, benign prostatic hypertrophy, and osteoporosis. There have even been a couple of recent reports showing that teetotal women trying for babies take longer to conceive and that drinking two glasses of red wine counteracts the damage to the cardiovascular system caused by smoking one cigarette.

But can this all be true? The goal of this chapter is to take a critical look at some of the evidence, focusing on some of the mechanisms that have recently been proposed for the potential health benefits for wine-drinkers. I'll also try to explain why the results so far have been frustratingly imprecise and, in some cases, contradictory.

## Moderate drinking seems to be good for you

It's well-established that in Western populations, moderate drinkers live longer than non-drinkers, who in turn live longer than heavy drinkers. It is a consistent finding in what are known as "epidemiological" studies – those that look at the incidence and distribution of diseases and their causal factors.

This phenomenon is known as the "J-shaped curve", which is the shape of the line you get if plot mortality (the risk of dying) against alcohol consumption on a graph. Studies have shown that moderate drinking increases life expectancy, mainly through its protective effects on the cardiovascular system – your heart and blood vessels. This benefit is also enjoyed by heavy drinkers, but their risk of death starts to increase as they are more likely to suffer from the various conditions related to heavy drinking, such as liver cirrhosis, stroke, certain cancers, and increased risk of accidental or violent death. It is a pretty robust finding that has been replicated in countless studies, to the degree that it is no longer controversial. It's also quite a significant effect – one large study looking at research spanning back twenty-five years on the subject indicates that moderate drinkers cut their risk of heart attack by as much as a quarter.

While the overall message is clear, though – that moderate drinking is healthier than heavy drinking or being a teetotaller – there has been quite a bit of debate about the details, and also the significance of this finding. Should doctors be advising abstinent patients to take up moderate drinking? Is it just red wine that has this beneficial effect, or is it shared by all alcoholic drinks? And what are the mechanisms that could explain alcohol's (or wine's) health-promoting properties?

## A question of mechanisms

Let's deal with the last issue first: the mechanisms by which moderate drinking might protect against certain diseases. This has proved particularly difficult to unravel, and there is little consensus. There is currently a range of plausible theories, each supported by varying degrees of evidence. It should be pointed out that these potential mechanisms are not exclusive; some or all of them could be contributing to the protective effect documented.

### 1. Antioxidant effects

One of the most strongly advocated claims for red wine's health benefits stems from the antioxidant compounds that it contains. These could prevent the oxidation of molecules in the circulation such as LDL (low-density lipoprotein, the "bad" cholesterol, which, in its oxidized state, is a major contributor to atherosclerosis). In the laboratory, phenolic compounds from red wine, such as resveratrol, have been shown to have potent antioxidant effects, protecting against the oxidation of LDL. Many *in vitro* studies (experiments outside the body) have indicated that lipoprotein oxidation increases its uptake by cells, and can cause macrophages to fill up with cholesterol, just as occurs with foam cell formation in the atherosclerotic process, so preventing this oxidation would seem to be a very good thing.

The problem with this attractive theory is that large clinical trials of dietary antioxidants have failed to demonstrate any health benefits. It's a large step from showing the activity of a compound in the laboratory to demonstrating that it is taken up by the gut, finds its way to target tissues in the body, and has the required activity in human subjects. In addition to this, some of the largest epidemiological studies have suggested that moderate consumption of all alcoholic drinks, and not just red wine, confers health benefits. But the antioxidant story is one of enduring appeal. People can understand it easily because it is conceptually simple, and the idea that these healthy-sounding phenolic compounds in red wine are good for us has a degree of resonance with our own preconceptions. It's much harder for people to accept the second mechanism, that alcohol itself is having a protective effect, even though the evidence for it is probably stronger.

### 2. Direct effects of alcohol

A more plausible mechanism concerns the effects of alcohol itself on the lipids in the bloodstream. Several studies have shown that alcohol consumption has the favourable effect of increasing the concentration of HDL (high-density lipoprotein, the "good" cholesterol), which is anti-inflammatory and decreases the risk of atherosclerosis (*see* "How atherosclerosis works" on page 192). The degree of increase is similar to that achieved with other interventions, such as exercise programmes. This finding would explain why some large studies have shown that not only red wine but also other alcoholic drinks protect against cardiovascular

"While the overall message is clear, though – that moderate drinking is healthier than heavy drinking or being a teetotaller – there has been quite a bit of debate about the details, and also the significance of this finding."

Atherosclerosis, a major killer in Western societies, is a progressive disease of the blood vessels that often begins early in life. It involves the formation of plaques – a build-up of cholesterol, waste products, and other substances – in the inner lining of blood vessels and arteries. Over time, these plaques can grow large enough to reduce blood flow, but they are at their most dangerous when they rupture, causing clots to form.

When these clots block coronary arteries, they cause heart attacks, and when they affect brain vessels, they cause strokes. Atherosclerosis is thought to begin with damage to the endothelium (inner cell layer) of blood vessels. Controllable risk factors for atherosclerosis include high levels of LDL cholesterol, elevated blood pressure, smoking, obesity, physical inactivity, and diabetes.

disease when consumed in moderation. While the evidence for this mechanism is quite good, critics suggest that the benefit is fairly small, and can be negated by other factors such as being overweight or smoking. It's also a hard idea for people to accept. Alcohol is the bad bit, isn't it? The other components of wine sound much healthier.

### 3. Platelet function

The third mechanism concerns the effects of wine on reducing the "stickiness" of platelets, specialized cells in the blood that are responsible for clot formation. This is known as an anti-thrombotic effect. This may be important in preventing events such as heart attacks (caused by clots in the blood vessels supplying the heart) and strokes (clots in vessels supplying the brain), but it might not have an important role in the long-term development of atherosclerosis. The anti-thrombotic benefit of moderate drinking is similar to the beneficial effect of taking aspirin.

### 4. Protecting the endothelium

Intriguingly, a fourth mechanism has recently been suggested by the work of London-based scientist Roger Corder, professor of experimental therapeutics at the William Harvey Research Institute. His research group has shown that polyphenols from red wine inhibit the formation of a compound called endothelin 1 (ET1) in cultured cells. The effect is a potent one, requiring only relatively small amounts of these compounds. ET1 is an important molecule because it causes the constriction of blood vessels, encouraging the development of atherosclerosis (*see* above). This fits in with other research showing that red wine modifies the function of the endothelium, a layer of plate-like cells lining the inner surfaces of blood vessels. The importance of this observation lies in the fact that the first stage of atherosclerosis in vessels is damage to the endothelium. If red wine can prevent these early events, then it is likely that it can inhibit the development of heart disease. So far, these studies have been conducted on cultured bovine (that's cow to you and me) cells from the endothelium of the aorta, a major artery. While this ET1 effect looks to be a very promising explanation for red wine's beneficial properties on cardiovascular disease, it needs to be shown that this is what is happening in the human body. Roger Corder is keen to do some studies on human volunteers, but needs increased funding.

Corder's current work is focused on studying wine from different origins to see whether all red wine is likely to be protective, or whether some wines confer more benefit than others. To this end he visited Sardinia, where there is an unusually high proportion of centenarians. Sardinians have twice to three times the chance of living to 100. Could it be that red wines from higher altitudes,

"Several studies have shown that alcohol consumption has the favourable effect of increasing the concentration of HDL (high-density lipoprotein, the "good" cholesterol), which is anti-inflammatory and decreases the risk of atherosclerosis. The degree of increase is similar to that achieved with other interventions, such as exercise programmes."

where there is a greater exposure of grapes to ultraviolet light, which stimulates polyphenol production, could have a greater protective effect? Corder found that the Sardinian wines collected on his trip had unusually high levels of polyphenols, as did some Argentinian wines tested. Mendoza in Argentina has some of the highest vineyards in the world, consistent with the notion that polyphenol production is a protective response to ultraviolet light. Red wines from both Sardinia and Argentina were both potent inhibitors of ET1 production in Corder's *in vitro* experiments.

## A complex picture

It's likely that the mechanisms underlying the health-giving effects of moderate alcohol consumption, and specifically red wine, will be complex, involving more than one of the above systems. This will take quite some unravelling by researchers, although they seem to be on the right track. Part of the difficulty is that it's very difficult – and expensive – to do the sorts of trials that need to be done on human populations to settle this issue once and for all.

Cardiovascular-disease expert François Booyse is director of molecular cardiology at the School of Medicine at the University of Alabama in Birmingham, Alabama, USA. In 2003, he landed a grant of US$7.6 million over five years to form a research group that would study the cellular, molecular, and genetic mechanisms by which wine components work to reduce mortality. Booyse is keen to emphasize the complexity of this area, and stresses that the four potential mechanisms which I have outlined above represent only part of the real story. "We should not be so naïve to think that wine components exert their overall protective benefits through only a few select, altered, vascular functions," he says.

"There are many excellent and detailed mechanistic studies that describe the effects of wine components (alcohol and polyphenols) on a diverse number of other vascular, haemostatic, and myocardial functions that may each and all have an important contribution to the overall cardiovascular disease protection attributed to wine consumption. The select functions you have listed can be affected by both alcohol and by a number of individual, principal wine polyphenols. It is highly unlikely that only one function plays a particularly major role in overall protection. It is much more plausible that it is the combined effects of alcohol plus multiple polyphenols on a diverse number of vascular, haemostatic, and myocardial functions that can then act in combination, or perhaps synergistically, to afford the overall cardioprotection attributed to moderate wine consumption."

## Resveratrol and Sir2

Perhaps even more speculatively, a further potential mechanism by which moderate drinking might protect against certain diseases is suggested by a recent study which examined the effect of red-wine extracts on yeast cells. Resveratrol, a polyphenolic compound in red wine, has been found to boost the levels of an enzyme called Sir2, which is thought to stabilize DNA. The net effect is that the lifetime of the yeast is extended by up to seventy per cent. Other studies apparently show the same effect in fruit flies. The important background to this story is that severe calorific restriction (typically a third fewer calories than normal) is known to extend life span in mammals, and Sir2 elevation mimics this process.

An even more recent study has uncovered the mechanism by which Sir2 has its life-prolonging effects. Of course, it's a long way from yeast or flies to humans, but if you wanted to extend your life span by a third, most people would choose to drink wine as opposed to cutting their diet to near-starvation levels! This subject is discussed in depth in chapter 25.

### Cardiovascular protection: the analysis

What does Booyse think of the four mechanisms suggested above?

*(1) Antioxidant effects.* "Resveratrol and other polyphenols reduce LDL oxidation/aggregation and can be protective," says Booyse. "However, whether wine polyphenols actually exert their potential protective benefits in the blood primarily via their antioxidant potential/properties remains controversial. A more interesting suggestion has been that these antioxidant effects may be more important in the gut, during digestion, prior to lipoprotein/fatty acid absorption."

*(2) Direct effects of alcohol.* "The beneficial effect of alcohol itself on blood lipid fractions is well documented," he says. "Both alcohol and polyphenols affect blood lipid profiles/fractions, particularly the increase in HDL cholesterol (primarily the HDL2 and HDL3 sub-classes). An increase in HDL cholesterol can contribute to one of the many protective benefits."

*(3) Platelet function.* Again, Booyse thinks that postive effects on platelet function are well-documented. "Alcohol and various wine polyphenols will reduce platelet function and aggregation. This is important in vascular haemostasis, will contribute to the further overall reduced risk for thrombosis, and provide protection."

**BELOW** A diagram illustrating the effects of alcohol on the endothelium of blood vessels. Tne detail is not so relevant here; the important point is the complexity of the interaction.

*Picture courtesy of Francois Booyse*

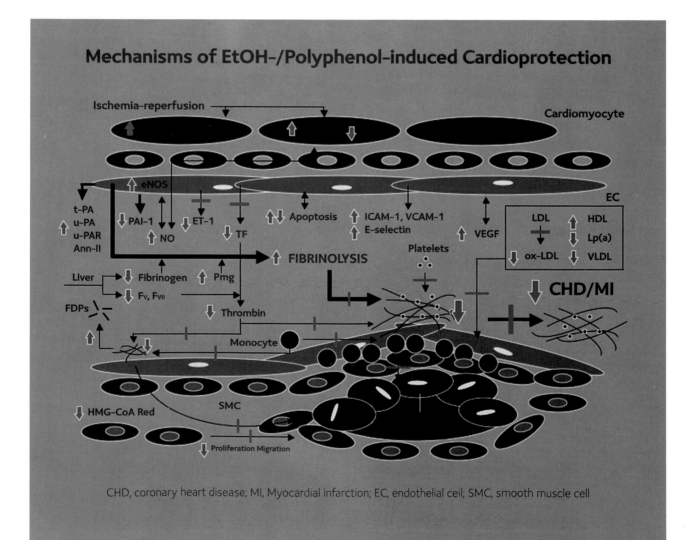

## Mechanisms of EtOH-/Polyphenol-induced Cardioprotection

CHD, coronary heart disease; MI, Myocardial infarction; EC, endothelial ceil; SMC, smooth muscle cell

## Polyphenolic compounds in red wine

Red wine contains many chemicals belonging to a group known as polyphenols, which are derived from grapes. They are responsible for the differences between red and white wines, especially the colour and flavour. And, according to many studies, polyphenols protect against cardiovascular disease and have other health-enhancing properties. Typically, a glass of red wine will contain 200mg of phenolic compounds, whereas a white will have about 40mg. These include the flavonoids, phenolic acids,

and their derivatives anthocyanins (the red pigments in grapes), and tannins.

Wine contains more of these compounds than grape juice or its extracts. This is thought to be because the alcohol in the fermentation vat assists in the extraction of these compounds from the skins. Research is currently under way to see how red wines differ in their polyphenol content, so soon it may be possible to identify a subset of particularly heart-friendly reds.

*(4) Protecting the endothelium.* "Both alcohol and individual polyphenols affect a number of different endothelial cell functions that can all have equally important protective benefits," Booyse reports. "Nitric oxide produced by the endothelial cell enzyme, eNOS, is a key regulator of vascular homeostasis, including vascular tone and blood pressure, equally or more important than changes induced by ET1. Wine component-induced increased nitric oxide has been widely implicated as a major contributor to vasorelaxation and protection. Other affected functions include altered clotting factors, fibrinolytic components, apoptosis (programmed cell-death) pathways, and expression of adhesion molecules."

## "Confounding"

But before we get too carried away, it should be pointed out that there exist nay-sayers who suspect the health benefits of moderate drinking are actually an artifact of what is known as "confounding" (*see* page 9). Two recent reports, one from Sweden and the other from Denmark, have studied the characteristics of the different drinking groups in various studies. They've found that moderate wine-drinkers tend to be richer, better educated, and have a more favourable psychological profile – all factors which tend to be associated with better health. Although most serious studies try to control for confounding (for instance, by trying to balance the different consumption groups in terms of socio-economic status) it's possible that some of the associations between wine-drinking and various diseases are a little muddied by this factor.

What sort of experiments would we need to carry out in order to obtain a definitive answer? Well, off the top of my head, I suspect we'd need a large group of volunteers in order to have sufficient statistical power. These people would need to be prepared to control their diets very closely for decades, because the diseases we are talking about take a long time to develop, and we don't have good surrogate measurements that would tell us reliably about how such diseases are increasing in likelihood over shorter periods. We'd need these people to eat an identical diet, and live lives very closely related in terms of stresses, exercise, and general well-being. Then we'd have to randomize these people in terms of alcohol and wine exposure, which would need to be monitored accurately; current studies rely on self-reported drinking behaviour, which is a problem for two reasons.

Firstly, as already discussed, there might be something different about people who freely choose to drink or not, and the level of drinking they undertake. Choice of beverage might also be linked to some other factor that influences health. Secondly, people routinely under-report how much they drink,

"It still remains, though, that wine could just be a marker of other, so far unidentified factors that are beneficial to health – guilty by association, but in itself not health-promoting."

whether deliberately or not. If we had a large enough group of people who differed only in how much they drank, the pattern of this drinking (a further complication; most studies ignore this potentially important factor and just look at net consumption), and their choice of alcohol delivery medium, whether beer, wine or whisky, then we might be able to come up with more definitive answers.

It still remains, though, that wine could just be a marker of other, so far unidentified factors that are beneficial to health – guilty by association, but in itself not health-promoting. The J-shaped survival curve has indeed been suggested to be an artifact caused by the fact that non-drinkers are actually a less healthy population than moderate drinkers. Dubbed the "sick-quitter" syndrome, the idea is that people who aren't well stop drinking, joining the ranks of the genuine teetotallers. On balance, however, the epidemiological evidence for the health benefits of moderate drinking are strong enough, so it looks like booze is indeed having some benefit: a reassuring and surprising message for drinkers worldwide.

## Prescribing wine?

So should doctors be prescribing wine? On the one hand, there's strong evidence that a couple of glasses of red wine a day could dramatically cut the risk of heart disease, particularly in susceptible groups, such as middle-aged men. On the other hand, alcohol has a dark side, and most doctors are reluctant to start encouraging non-drinkers to start imbibing because of the risk that their patients will end up with a drink problem. Now, I'm not medically qualified, but if I were to become my GP for a day, this is the advice I think I'd give myself. Don't smoke, eat a balanced diet, watch your weight, and exercise regularly. And then, seeing as I'm trying my best to do all these, I'd prescribe myself a couple of generous glasses of red wine a day – preferably something decent!

## The dark side of booze

While the message that moderate drinking has a beneficial effect on health seems to have been well-received by most people, there's no getting around the fact that heavy alcohol consumption damages health. Public health messages about alcohol are complicated by the fact that there is no "one-size-fits-all" ideal level of consumption; it varies depending on age, body mass, sex, and medical history. Furthermore, how much is in a "standard drink"? In the USA, it is fourteen grams of alcohol (roughly the equivalent of a five-ounce glass of wine), in the UK just eight grams and in Japan 19.75 grams.

Some authors claim that alcohol public-health messages have been given a "soft ride" because the media and other influential sectors of society like a drink themselves. What are the negative effects of drinking? Probably the most well-publicized is cirrhosis of the liver. This is the result of destruction of liver cells by toxic breakdown products of alcohol, and it is a disease that eventually causes liver failure. The liver is normally very good at regenerating itself, so you have to drink heavily over a sustained period to suffer from this. Consistent heavy drinking also elevates blood pressure (causing hypertension) and results in alcoholic cardiomyopathy (where damage to the heart muscle is sustained). Heavy drinking

also increases the risk of a range of cancers. Alcohol's neurobiological effects cause increased numbers of accidental deaths and injuries. Alcoholism has devastating effects on the lives of those caught in its grip, and their families.

But how much alcohol can you drink before you start experiencing negative health effects? Is half a bottle of wine a day going to cause problems? Most governments issue a set of guidelines on this subject. The UK government guidelines define a "drink" or "unit" as eight grams (1cl) of pure alcohol and define moderation as three to four drinks a day for men and two to three drinks a day for women. To work out how many "drinks" there are in a bottle of wine, multiply the alcoholic strength by 0.75. For example, if you drink half a bottle of thirteen percent wine you have consumed 13 x 0.75 ÷ 2 = 4.875 standard drinks.

Some, however, feel that these limits are deliberately set low, because people typically underestimate how much they really drink. Since most studies on alcohol and health involve self-reports of drinking behaviour, this tendency to under-report consumption is also likely to skew results of such studies. Besides, many of us judge "moderation" to be very similar to our own consumption levels.

# 24 Wine allergies

The last time I had a bad reaction to wine, I put it down to the fact that I'd just consumed a heroic quantity of it. But for some people, even just one glass can cause extremely unpleasant reactions such as headaches, flushing, itching, and nausea. To investigate this, I decided to play doctor (in the professional sense, of course,) and took some case histories.

## Case studies

Jill has adverse reactions to French red wine. "The first time it happened, I'd had less than half a bottle," she recalls. "I felt like I'd drunk five bottles, and I felt bad for the whole day." On this occasion Jill made no connection between the wine and the splitting headache and nausea she experienced. But when she tried the second bottle of the case she'd bought, she had the same reaction. She gave the remaining ten bottles away, and the lucky recipient didn't experience any adverse reaction. Jill also had the same response with a couple of other French reds she has tried since, and the same thing has happened on a few occasions with Belgian beer. She hasn't seen a doctor, but instead controls the problem by avoiding French reds altogether.

"I think I've got a wine allergy," says Susie. "On one occasion, I can have just one glass of wine and I'll get a most horrendous headache the next day. On another occasion I can have a bottle and a half with no reaction." She told me that this is a fairly random occurrence that happens perhaps once a month, but she's sure it's not related to pre-menstrual syndrome and she doesn't get it with other alcoholic drinks. Susie hasn't been able to pinpoint a grape variety or a certain type of wine, but it seems to happen more with white wines than reds. She also hasn't been to see a doctor, but the symptoms of intense headache and sinus blockage are very real.

Alison went out one Friday night and got very drunk. "The next morning my face started to swell," she recalls. This continued all Saturday and Sunday morning. "I looked like the elephant man," she says, "so in the end I went to hospital." She was given Piriton, an antihistamine, and over the next days the swelling went down. For the following six months, every time she drank wine she got angry red weals on her arms, legs, and sometimes her stomach. Alison doesn't drink red wine, so this was a white-wine reaction; she didn't react to any other forms of alcohol. Remarkably, after six months, this all cleared up and she's now happily drinking wine again.

## Allergy or intolerance?

These three cases give a snapshot of the range of different "allergic" reactions caused by wine, and demonstrate just how difficult it can be to work out common patterns. It's also hard to assess how frequent these sorts of responses are, because people experiencing them rarely report them to their doctors; they just learn to live with their "allergy". And there haven't been any proper scientific studies looking at the occurrence of these types of complaints. Yet anecdotal reports of unpleasant reactions to wine seem to be quite common.

Most, if not all, bad reactions to wine aren't "allergies". A true allergic reaction involves an immune response to an allergen, most usually a protein. These can be quite serious, but fortunately are rather rare. More common is food intolerance, where someone has an adverse reaction to a food without any immune-system involvement. An example would be lactose intolerance, which is found in around ten per cent of the population. Lactose is a protein present in milk, and affected individuals have a deficiency of lactase, the enzyme needed to digest it. Some foods also contain compounds that are pharmacologically active, such as histamine, tyramine or serotonin, and these may have effects on the body that resemble allergic reactions, but which don't involve the immune system.

## How to diagnose a food allergy

The most reliable method for confirming a diagnosis of food allergy is the double-blind, placebo-controlled food challenge. Patients are tested with the allergen, together with a range of other foods, without them knowing what they are being exposed to. Studies like this reveal that around two per cent of the population have genuine food allergies. This compares with around twenty per cent of people who have consistently reported self-diagnosed food allergies when large-scale surveys have been carried out.

Dr. Pamela Ewan, from Addenbrooke's Hospital in Cambridge, is one of the UK's leading experts on food allergies. She confirms that adverse reactions to wine are not thought to be true allergic reactions. "The sensitivity to wine is thought to be due to the direct effect of various – poorly defined – chemical components of the wine," Ewan reports. A recent scientific paper published by an Italian research group has reported allergen-induced anaphylactic shock reactions in people who have drunk wine. They have identified two proteins they believe to be responsible for this allergic response: an endochitinase, and a lipid-transfer protein. Consequently, the possibility remains that there are some people who do have genuine allergic responses to wine. Clearly more work is needed in this area.

## The role of sulphites and histamines

Which components of wine might be causing these adverse reactions? Wine is a complex mix of chemicals, which makes this a difficult question to answer, but the two leading culprits are sulphites and histamines. Sulphites are present in all wines,

RIGHT By law labels on wines from the USA must contain the declaration "contains sulphites" – this has led many consumers to assume that any reaction to the wine must be because of the presence of the sulphites.

## ALDH deficiency: feeling flushed

Acetaldehyde is a compound formed by the breakdown of alcohol in the liver by the enzyme alcohol dehydrogenase. It's a toxic compound that is one of the leading causes of hangovers, but most of the time it is broken down by aldehyde dehydrogenase (ALDH) into the less harmful acetic acid. However, some eighty-five per cent of Japanese and Chinese populations have a deficiency in ALDH, which results in an unpleasant flushing response when affected individuals consume alcohol. As well as flushing of the face and neck, other symptoms include headaches, low blood pressure, and nausea. This deficiency in ALDH is relatively rare in non-Asian populations. Of course, if you are affected in this way, then all alcoholic drinks will have this effect – not just wine.

but at varying levels. They are added during winemaking to maintain hygiene, and added to bottled wine as a preservative, as well as being a natural product of fermentation. Sulphites are frequently implicated in adverse reactions to wine, and it is commonly thought that they are a trigger that sets off asthma. As a result, in the USA, wines must be labelled as "contains sulfites" (the "f" spelling is American) unless they have extremely low levels, in which case the concentration must be disclosed. This leads many people to conclude, often falsely, that if they have a bad reaction to wine, it must be because of the sulphites present in the wine.

A study examining individuals with a history of wine-induced asthma involved testing them with wines of differing sulphite levels, but results were inconclusive. The conclusion was that wine-induced asthma is a complex phenomenon that may involve several mechanisms. If you suspect that your wine intolerance is due to sulphites, then check to see whether you have a similar reaction to prepared salads and dried fruit (such as apricots), both of which typically contain higher levels of sulphites than wine. If you react to these too, then you might want to find low-sulphur wines. Interestingly, Europe's largest wine shop, Lavinia in Paris, has a section for low- or no-sulphur wines.

Histamine, one of the pharmacologically active chemicals released by mast cells in the true allergic response, is widely considered to be the main cause of adverse reactions to wine. Red wine contains 0.6 to four grams per litre of histamine, white far less. It's thought that patients intolerant to wine cannot degrade histamine properly due to a deficiency of diamine oxidase, the enzyme that fulfils this role. However, a recent study showed no correlation between histamine content and wine intolerance. The picture is unclear. If you have a hunch that histamine in wine may be causing a problem for you – for example, if you only have problems with red wines and not whites – then it may be worth seeing if taking an antihistamine before drinking makes any difference.

## Treating allergies

Because the exact cause of adverse reactions is so hard to diagnose medically, and due to the lack of positive treatment other than just simple avoidance, food allergies and intolerances are fertile ground for untested – and often untestable – complementary therapies. There is little or no scientific evidence that techniques such as cytotoxic testing, applied kinesiology, electrodermal screening, Nambudripad's allergy elimination technique (NAET), or sublingual testing are useful in diagnosing or treating food allergies and intolerances. For those who suffer from adverse reactions to wine, it's a frustratingly cloudy picture that emerges. While some people might be able do the detective work needed to find out precisely which types of wine cause them problems, and then avoid them, there's very little that can be done for those who seem to have more-or-less random bad reactions.

# 25  Extending life span by drinking wine

The Holy Grail. According to medieval legend, it was the cup with which Christ celebrated the Last Supper, which was used shortly therafter by Joseph of Arimathea to catch the Lord's blood as he hung from the cross. Thus the story goes; it is imbued with supernatural powers – one sip from this cup, and you'll live forever.

Extending life span has become the Holy Grail of modern medicine. While most of us accept we're never going to live forever, many people would like to postpone the inevitable for as long as possible. In Western societies life expectancy has risen steadily, yet the question remains: what is the upper limit on life span? In contrast to the average age of the population, this limit doesn't seem to have shifted much; more people are living longer, but the very oldest people aren't any older. Now, however, research is beginning to shed new light on a biological mechanism that could hold the key to longer life. And, in a fascinating twist on the Holy Grail legend, one of the components of red wine could provide the age-busting drug that has been sought for so long. In addition to this, the same mechanism might represent part of the explanation for the well-documented health benefits of moderate alcohol consumption (*see* previous chapter).

## Limits to longevity

One of the founding observations about ageing was made in 1961 by the scientist Leonard Hayflick. He noticed that cultured human cells had a finite life span, and would only continue to divide a certain number of times: around fifty. The only way researchers were able to confer on cells the ability to divide indefinitely was by introducing into them genes called oncogenes, thus effectively turning them into cancer cells. This restricted potential for division became known as the Hayflick limit, but its basis remained obscure until the late 1970s, when researcher Liz Blackburn discovered that the mechanism behind the Hayflick limit involved caps, known as telomeres, at the end of chromosomes. Each time a cell divides, the telomeres shorten, conferring a finite life span on them known as "replicative senescence". As you might expect, cancer cells don't undergo this replicative senescence, as their telomeres don't shorten on division. Instead, they are kept long by the activity of an enzyme called telomerase. It was hoped that the discovery of such a fundamental, life-limiting mechanism might lead to rejuvenation therapies, as well as to a cure for some cancers. As yet, there's no indication that this will be the case. Currently, the common view among gerontologists is that growing old is a syndrome of separate diseases, and if progress is to be made in overcoming the limits of life span, it will be through the painstaking effort of conquering diseases and age-related deficits, one by one.

But the emerging story that is the focus of this chapter is different. It suggests that the process of ageing is under direct control of a particular signalling switch. This is potentially exciting to scientists, because, if the switch mechanism is simple enough to be unravelled in the lab, then this could represent a target for therapeutic intervention.

# Caloric restriction

As yet, the only intervention that has been proven to reliably extend life span is caloric restriction (CR). In a surprisingly wide range of organisms, ranging from yeast to mammals, reducing calorie intake to levels only just sufficient to maintain life has the surprising effect of increasing life span. In yeasts, the effect is dramatic, with a life extension of almost double. The same is true in another model organism that has been widely studied: the nematode worm *Caenorhabditis elegans*. In rats and mice, caloric restriction is also protective against cancer. Scientists have been struggling for an explanation of this robust effect for many decades.

But caloric restriction isn't really an option for humans. Not if you like your food, that is. You might live a longer life, but it wouldn't be much fun. The drawbacks of eating just half to two-thirds of the normal recommended intake (the sort of reduction needed in animals for the life-prolonging benefit to be seen) include feeling very hungry and having a reduced reproductive drive. Caloric restriction is not exactly the rock-and-roll lifestyle. However, a quick web search revealed that there is a caloric-restriction society, aimed at encouraging people who are prepared to half-starve themselves in the name of well-being and longevity. If you are interested in joining this merry band of rather thin people, the URL is www.calorierestriction.org.

In addition to this, until recently no one has demonstrated that this effect really works in humans in the same way it does in lab rats. Who'd go through the deprivation of caloric restriction for an uncertain benefit? Then, in April 2004, a paper was published suggesting that caloric restriction can have benefits in humans also. A research group led by Luigi Fontana at Washington University (St Louis, Missouri, USA) examined eighteen people who had voluntarily been

## Resveratrol: a wonder drug from red wine?

A lot of the attention in the wine and health discussion has focused on one molecule, resveratrol (*see* page 193). Its proper chemical name is 3,5,4-trihydroxystilbene, and it belongs to a class of plant-defence molecules called phytoalexins. These are synthesized by plants to protect themselves from fungal disease, and levels are elevated in response to attack. Resveratrol has been shown to possess antioxidant and anti-tumour properties. For example, it can inhibit the oxidation of low-density lipoprotein (LDL), which is what happens during the first stage of atherosclerosis (*see* page 192).

A study by Jennifer Burns, Alan Crozier, and colleagues from Glasgow University investigated sources of resveratrol in the diet. They found that both fresh red grapes and red wine had relatively high levels of resveratrol. In the wines they tested, concentrations varied from 98 μg to over 1800 μg per 100ml. However, they conclude that before we advocate resveratrol as a therapy, we need to know more about how (and whether) it is absorbed from the diet, and what happens to it once it is inside the body.

The amount of resveratrol present in wine varies substantially. Because it is found mainly in grape skins, a key factor governing its prevalence is the amount of time the grape skins are in contact with the must; consequently, white wines have very little, and more extracted reds have the most. Most attention has

focused on resveratrol's potent antioxidant properties and its capacity to reduce platelet aggregation (platelets are the clot-forming blood cells). But most of the research demonstrating this activity has been done *in vitro* (in artificial experiments outside the body), not *in vivo* (in real-life situations within the body).

Yet another role for resveratrol has been suggested by recent work from a group led by Dr. Gail Mahady of the University of Illinois. Mahady suggests that resveratrol in red wine might be acting as an antibiotic, killing microbes that some think have a role in the development of atherosclerotic plaques in blood vessel walls.

Mahady took the bacterium that has recently been identified as a possible causative factor of atherosclerosis, *Chlamydia pneumoniae*, and studied the effect of wine extracts (Californian Pinot Noir) and pure resveratrol on cultures of this bug. They found that both resveratrol and the red-wine extracts demonstrated antimicrobial action against the two test strains of bacteria, when used at relatively low concentrations. Mahady suggests that this concentration equates to "about one glass of Pinot Noir". *Chlamydia* is not the only bacterium that wine acts on. "We have good evidence that red wine and resveratrol inhibit the growth of *Helicobacter pylori* [the bacterium associated with stomach ulcers]," Mahady says. She is hoping to do further studies on the subject.

practising CR for an average of six years each, and compared them with normal, healthy people who had been on typical diets. The results were striking. On a battery of tests aimed at uncovering general health status and propensity to cardiovascular disease, the CR people did much better. Could this be saying something about the sort of people who would willingly embrace CR? This selected population might have been healthier to start with. Not so, it seems, because the medical records of these CR practitioners showed that before they began this alternative diet, their scores were roughly similar to those of the control group. This is the first demonstration that CR in humans decreases the incidence of certain diseases, although it is brave to extrapolate this result to suggest that CR will make people live longer.

Scientists now postulate that there are two metabolic strategies common to many different organisms: live fast/die young and live slow/die later. The reasoning behind this is that, if food is plentiful, then you want to get on with life, have kids, and once they are reared get out of the way so you are not competing for resources with them. Yet if food is scarce, you want to put off reproducing and hang in there, hoping that things will change: hence the extended life span and lower reproductive drives of calorie-restricted animals. A complex set of signalling molecules has been implicated in this control of metabolism, and this is where the significant new research comes in.

## The Sirtuin story

Leonard Guarente is a biology professor at the prestigious Massachusetts Institute of Technology (MIT). He researches the biology of ageing, and has recently focused on a group of molecules called sirtuins. These are molecules known as histone deacetylases, responsible for modifying the protein (histone) around which DNA is coiled in chromosomes. In the confines of the cell nucleus, histone modifications have an important role in controlling which genes are expressed, and when.

Initially, it was thought that the mechanism behind CR was passive, through reducing metabolism and thus lowering oxidative damage to cells and tissues. This was challenged when, in 2002, Guarente's lab showed that in yeast, CR was a highly regulated response involving a sensing step that kicked off a programme to extend life span. Sir2, one of the sirtuins, is responsible for promoting survival in response to scarce resources, and it is ideally equipped for this task, because its deacetylase activity is dependent on a molecule heavily involved in metabolic activity, NAD. What is remarkable is that this metabolism-sensing switch seems to have been conserved from organisms such as yeast all the way through to mammals (in the latter, Sir2 is known as Sirt1). If this is all sounding a bit too biochemical, here's where red wine comes in. In 2003, a group led by David Sinclair at Harvard Medical School screened a variety of compounds for their effects on Sir2, and hence the life span of yeast. Resveratrol was shown to activate Sir2, and increase yeast life span by some seventy per cent. This finding created much media interest, with the inevitable flow of "drink red wine and live longer" stories. But more was to come.

Back at MIT, Guarente and colleagues published a groundbreaking study in June 2004, in which they unravelled the mechanism by which Sirt1 has its effects. Through a detailed series of experiments in cultured mammalian cells, they demonstrated that Sirt1 activates mobilization of fat from adipocytes, a critical element of caloric restriction. When food is scarce, Sirt1 binds to and represses genes controlled by a molecule called PPARγ, which regulates fat. This causes a reduction in adipose tissue, which then results in an increased life span, perhaps through influencing other hormonal systems connected with fat mass. This story is supported by the fact that mice lacking SIRT1 don't show this fasting-induced mobilization of fat. Guarente and colleagues then turned to resveratrol, which had been shown to activate Sir2. They showed that 50 and 100 $\mu$M concentrations of resveratrol caused a significant reduction in fat in cultured adipocytes. The involvement of Sirt1 in this process was confirmed by showing that this effect didn't occur in cells lacking Sirt1. Turning to real mice rather than cultured cells, they then showed that Sirt1 is indeed recruited to PPAR$\gamma$ DNA-binding sites on fasting.

It's a slightly complicated, but compelling story, giving a possible mechanism for the regulation of life span by diet. In addition, it is appealing to suppose that red wine, which contains resveratrol, has a pharmacological effect, activating Sirt1. In turn, Sirt1 mobilizes fat from adipocytes causing a reduction in adipose tissue, a key step in caloric restriction. As a result, red-wine consumption confers the benefits of caloric restriction without the discomfort of a drastically reduced food intake.

## Spoiling the party?

The red wine/resveratrol/sirtuin hypothesis is a very seductive one. Losing weight, cutting cancer risk, and living longer – just by drinking a respectable quantity of red wine? Count me in. However, despite the fascinating science involved, there is one major hurdle: the bioavailability of dietary resveratrol. People assume that when they ingest something, be it food, pills or drink, it is automatically taken into the body. Not so. Drugs entering via our mouths have to survive a complex, sometimes hostile, gut environment, negotiate its epithelial barrier, and then find their way through to sites of action. Before we get too excited about wine-borne resveratrol and its possible health-enhancing effects, we need to know if there's enough present in red wines for a pharmacological effect to occur. If this is the case, we need to know what happens to this resveratrol in the gut. Is it taken up in the intestine? Does it get into the bloodstream? And how long does it last?

Red wine varies in its resveratrol content. At the higher end of concentrations, is there enough to have an effect on sirtuins? Professor Roger Corder (*see* page192), well-known for his studies on wine and health, thinks not. Refering to Guarente's recent paper, he says, "I don't consider the effects of resveratrol that are described to have any significance in relation to wine consumption, as it was necessary to use concentrations of 50 $\mu$M and 100 $\mu$M to see a response." How much wine would we need to drink? "Wine typically contains 2mg/litre of resveratrol, with a circulating plasma volume of 2.5 to three litres in an average man," he explains. "Many of the studies on SIR2 use concentrations of 10 $\mu$M (2.28mg/litre)." Corder calculates that we'd need to consume 2.5 litres of wine and all the resveratrol would have to be absorbed. It doesn't look positive, but the issue isn't closed yet.

More problematic is the bioavailability story. Data in humans are currently rather limited, although it is beginning to emerge. And it threatens to rain on the resveratrol parade when it does. At the Medical University of South Carolina, Professor Thomas Walle has looked at this, and he's emphatic that resveratrol isn't going to get to where it's needed in the body. "Based on our studies, as well as those of others," he says, "the bioavailability of resveratrol – that is, the amount of intact resveratrol reaching the blood circulation – is virtually zero in humans."

These initial results are not encouraging, but neither are they fatal to the wine/resveratrol/sirtuin story. It's likely that there will be further twists and turns in this fascinating tale, but as yet this particular Holy Grail is a tantalizing goal for intrepid researchers – a legend that may yet prove to be true.

"Before we get too excited about wine-borne resveratrol and its possible health enhancing effects, we need to know that there's enough present in red wines for a pharmacological effect to occur. If this is indeed the case, we need to know what happens to this resveratrol in the gut. Is it taken up in the intestine? Does it get into the bloodstream? And how long does it last?"

# Concluding remarks

It is my hope that anyone who has read at least a few chapters of this book will come away with some answers, but even more questions. There is a pressing need for more good quality research on many of the issues covered in these pages. The wine world is still burdened by too much received wisdom, folklore, and practice, based on tradition and anecdotal observation. While many traditional practices have a sound scientific basis, it is likely that others don't, and it would be helpful to know the difference. At the same time, an important part of wine's appeal, at least at some levels of the market, is tradition – its historical context and cultural roots. Application of new technology needs to be sensitive to this. To finish with, I'd like to touch on two subjects that have formed common threads running through many of the subjects in this book, the common practice of blaming tools, and the limits of reductionist science.

## Don't blame the tools

Much of this book has been focusing on the science behind the various tools, techniques, and manipulations that are available to both the winemaker and viticulturalist. But, ultimately, what is more important than the specific techniques used is the will or intent of the producer. Good producers who make interesting wines will be able to utilize scientific and technological tools, should they choose to, in order to help them achieve their goals for particular wines. Indeed, the choice of which technologies to adopt and which to leave alone is an important one, and is aided by an understanding of the likely benefits and any drawbacks of these technologies.

Meanwhile, producers who are simply aiming to make wine as cheaply as possible will no doubt find technologies that will help them in their goals, too. But just because technology puts tools into the hands of producers whom we might view as misguided – for example, those wanting to flavour-enhance cheap wines to make them taste expensive, or who want to make soupy, over-extracted, concentrated, point-chasing wines, or even those who want to cheat blatantly – this doesn't mean that the technologies themselves are bad. They are neutral. Of course, some technologies might be provoking a near-irresistible temptation for winemakers to cheat, in which case perhaps they should be regulated. But as with most tools, there are legitimate as well as dubious uses.

Let's use an analogy to illustrate this concept. Henri Cartier-Bresson took some of the twentieth century's most compelling photographs with a 35mm Leica rangefinder, which was a new style of camera back in the 1930s. This camera was a tool, albeit one which, with its compact dimensions, facilitated his sort of photojournalism. The tool was important to Cartier-Bresson, but much more significant was his genius as a photographer. He could have taken bad pictures with the Leica; that he didn't is down to his skill and intent more than just the characteristics of the camera he used. Perhaps, some might argue, in wine we focus a little too much on the tools and not enough on the intent and ability of the wine-grower.

## How useful are reductionist approaches?

Reductionism, the splitting down of a system into its component parts, and then studying these bits in isolation, has been a tremendously useful way of doing science. Most science is done this way, but researchers are now beginning to realize that what the philosophers of science have been saying for a while – that there are limits to reductionism – is actually true. Reductionist science has allowed biologists to unravel the human genome. But making sense of this genetic code is another matter altogether, a process that will require more than reductionist approaches. And while neurobiologists have uncovered in minute detail the working of the nerve cells in the brain, how much does this tell us about consciousness? In a similar vein, how useful are reductionist approaches in yielding understanding about wine? Advances in wine-flavour chemistry mean that we now have a large body of knowledge about many of the specific chemical components that are important in wine flavour. However, doubts are being expressed in certain quarters about the usefulness of this knowledge, and whether this is a fruitful avenue of research for improving wine quality.

Why is this? It is because wine quality is what is known as an "emergent" property. It is a characteristic of the whole system – all the various components of the wine working together to yield a sensory experience that is not evident from studying these components in isolation. Let's imagine you have spent years honing your analytical skills, and are expert in identifying specific aroma and taste sensations in wine. You could write a list of all the compounds you can spot in a particular wine, and demonstrate that they are actually there by analytical chemistry techniques. But does this really tell me much about this wine, and the experience I will have with it?

Bear in mind that the sensory experience of wine depends on both the nature of the wine and the physiological and mental response of the taster to this wine. The understanding of wine yielded by chemical analysis is just one part of a complex picture, and our brains don't work in a similar way to analytical chemistry devices such as a gas chromatograph or mass spectrometer. When we taste wine we are doing much, much more than chemical analysis. This is quite a complicated concept, but it is an important one. Trained sensory analysis of wine is useful in that it facilitates a way of measuring, in a scientific and statistically analysable way, some of the properties of wine. But, in reality, it is rather crude, and there is noise in the system, introduced by inter-individual variance in perception, taster skill, and the difficulty of expressing flavour sensations in words. Sensory analysis is certainly a vital tool for wine research, but it is a blunt, limited tool when it comes to giving us useful information about what really matters in a wine.

In the mid-1990s Vinovation's Clark Smith expressed some of these ideas in a witty, thoughtful and highly controversial article in *Vineyard and Winery Management*, entitled "Does UC Davis have a theory of deliciousness?" He took the Department of Viticulture and Enology at the University of California at Davis to task for failing to recognize a paradigm shift that has taken place in the world of wine surrounding definitions of wine quality. In essence, he suggested that Davis was stuck in a reductionist rut. He advocated a fusion of the Davis analytical approach, often responsible for clean but dull wines, with an "older, visceral, holistic method of assessment", to produce an integrated view of what makes wine "delicious". Smith uses an analogy. "I find myself facing similar dilemmas in the health industry. I'm in pretty good health; I just want advice on how to live to be a hundred. My doctor, schooled in western medicine, checks my blood pressure, cholesterol, bilirubin and so forth, and tells me to come back when I'm sick. He thinks wellness is the absence of disease.

So I try an acupuncturist. I find out he's got a theory of wellness. He looks me over, gives me a tune-up with the needles and some herbs, makes some useful suggestions. I feel good. I ask him for some advice on prostate cancer and it turns out he doesn't know what disease is. Just as Western medicine has no conception of wellness, UC Davis offers no theory of deliciousness." He concedes: "What it does offer is just as vital." Smith concludes, "The Davis approach, like Western medicine, is analytic, and their counterpoints are holistic. What we need is a synthesis that integrates both approaches." It seems a little unfair to blame UC Davis researchers for doing science the way all scientists are trained to work, but Smith's point is well taken.

## The holistic approach

One of the problems has been that scientists' notions of "improving wine quality" have often been at odds with those of people who actually make and drink the stuff. Consider the following scenario. One by one, scientists identify a series of wine faults – *Brettanomyces*, reduction, poor sulphur-dioxide usage, "green" flavours and aromas, and so on. They set about instructing winemakers how to correct these faults. They also identify flavour molecules that have a positive effect, and instruct winemakers how to maximize these by, for example, vineyard interventions, maceration techniques or the use of specific yeast strains. The result is often a perfect, fault free wine, but one which doesn't excite the senses; which fails to thrill. The weakness of the reductionist, analytical approach is that, in Smith's words, "It does not, by itself, contain the tools for a sophisticated appreciation of wines as a whole". There are concepts that relate to the properties of wine as a whole, which are important for wine quality, or "deliciousness", but which cannot be understood by a reductionist approach. If wine science is to progress in aiding our understanding of wine quality, then it will have to break free of the shackles of a purely reductionist, analytical approach, and seek to integrate this with a holistic view of the wine experience.

Researchers will probably read these comments with a degree of frustration. I imagine they will feel the same way as athletes or footballers do when they hear coaching tips from spectators. It's all very well talking about "holistic" approaches, but what does this mean in practice? Scientists are doing reductionist science because that's the way they've been trained to work, it seems to be the most sensible way to proceed, and it is yielding useful results that are relevant to the wine industry. In effect, they are still in a data-gathering phase, but there may come a point when further data collection is no longer insightful, and becomes confusing, redundant or overwhelming. Then it will be necessary to sit back and try to make sense of the big picture. It is also possible that a broad-perspective, holistic view could help inform the reductionist, data-gathering aspect of wine science right here, right now. So, in closing, I leave you with one thought: although science is a powerful, useful tool, as I argued in the introduction to this book, could strict reductionist thinking be limiting the utility of wine science?

# Glossary

Entries in SMALL CAPITALS are cross references.

**Abscisic acid (ABA)** An important plant hormone (also known as plant growth regulator), involved particularly in signalling during episodes of stress, such as cold or drought. *See* chapter 9.

**Acetaldehyde** The most common ALDEHYDE in wine, formed when oxygen reacts with ETHANOL. Present in small amounts in all wines. Not nice: smells bad, and one of the reasons that oxidized wines aren't very pleasant. It's also the initial breakdown product of alcohol in the body, and responsible in large part for the unpleasantness of hangovers. Acetaldehyde is important because it is involved in the copolymerization of phenolic compounds. Combines readily with SULPHUR DIOXIDE.

**Acetic acid** A volatile acid that is the main signature compound of vinegar. Formed by the action of ACETOBACTER bacteria on alcohol in the presence of oxygen. All wines have a bit of it because it is a natural product of fermentation. But you don't want too much.

**Acetobacter** Bacteria that spoil wine by turning it into vinegar in the presence of oxygen.

**Acids** Important flavour constituents of wine. Provide tart, sour flavours which balance the other components. Wine contains a range of acids, most notably tartaric and malic acid (present in grapes), and lactic acid and succinic acid (produced during fermentation). Acidity is important in wine: as well as the flavour, it affects the colour, and also the effectiveness of SULPHUR DIOXIDE additions. It is commonly measured as total acidity, which is the sum of fixed and volatile acids. Acidity is also measured as pH, although this doesn't correlate exactly with total acidity. The relationship between the acid composition of wine and its actual acidic taste is a complex one: some acids are naturally more acidic than others for chemical reasons. The perception of acidity is also strongly influenced by other flavour components of the wine, notably sweetness, which counters the perception of acidity quite markedly.

**Alcohol** Common name for ETHANOL.

**Aldehydes** Also known, along with KETONES, as carbonylated compounds. Rapidly combine with SULPHUR DIOXIDE in wine. These are formed whenever wine is exposed to oxygen. The most important aldehyde in wine is ACETALDEHYDE. Other aldehydes present in wine can be important in terms of flavour development: some higher aldehydes contribute to wine aroma, and vanillin is a complex aromatic aldehyde that can be present in wine because of fermentation or ageing in oak barrels.

**Amino acids** The building blocks of proteins, present in wine at appreciable levels, and responsible for the taste of UMAMI. There are just twenty of them, responsible for the many thousands of different proteins produced by living creatures.

**Ampelography** The science of vine identification.

**Anthocyanins** PHENOLIC COMPOUNDS responsible for the colour of red and black grapes. In wine, they interact with other components to form pigmented polymers and are responsible for wine colour. *See* chapter 22.

**Antioxidant** Chemical compound that prevents oxidation by reacting with oxidation: it takes the hit to protect other compounds. *See* chapters 7, 23 and 25.

**Apiculate yeast** Group of yeasts involved in wild or indigenous yeast fermentations. *See* chapter 14.

**Ascorbic acid** Also known as vitamin C, and sometimes used in wine as an antioxidant. Acts synergistically with sulphur dioxide, but controversially the two together have been implicated in some incidences of RANDOM OXIDATION.

**Astringency** Perceived in the mouth by the sense of touch, astringency in wine is contributed by TANNINS – a drying, mouth-puckering sensation.

**Autolysis** In wine, the self destruction of yeast cells, releasing flavour components into the wine.

**Bâtonnage** Stirring the lees, the yeast-cell deposit at the bottom of a fermentation vessel.

**Baumé** A measure of dissolved compounds in grape juice, used as an approximate measure of sugar levels. Common in Europe.

**Bentonite** A clay used to fine (remove suspended solids from) wine.

**Biodynamic** Controversial form of organic viticulture with a cosmic slant. *See* chapter 8.

**Bitterness** Taste sensation, not all that common in wine, and commonly confused with ASTRINGENCY and sourness.

**Botrytis** Genus of fungus, but also a common term to describe infection of grapes by *Botrytis cinerea*. If it affects already-ripe grapes it can be beneficial, and is responsible for many of the world's great sweet wines. But it also has a malevolent influence, causing grey rot.

**Brettanomyces** Yeast genus that is, at sufficient concentrations, a spoilage organism in wine. Controversial. *See* chapter 18.

**Cane** A one-year old stem of a grape vine, used as the basis of cane (*a.k.a.* ROD AND SPUR) pruning. *See* chapter 10.

**Carbon dioxide** The well-known gas, vital to plant growth as the carbon source of photosynthesis, and also contributing to global warming (*see* chapter 4). Used in winemaking to protect grapes, must, and wine from oxygen. Naturally produced in fermentation, and while in most wines this dissipates, in some styles appreciable levels remain where it helps to preserve freshness.

**Catechin** A Flavan-3-ol (the other significant one in wine is epi-catechin), a group of PHENOLIC COMPOUNDS that are the building blocks of TANNINS. In their polymeric forms, where they are called procyanidins (often referred to as condensed tannins). *See* chapter 22.

**Chaptalization** The addition of sugar to must to boost alcoholic strength.

**Chloranisoles** Group of chlorine-containing compounds largely responsible for musty taint caused by rogue corks. Most well known is 2,4,6-TRICHLOROANISOLE (TCA).

**Clonal selection** Taking cuttings from a superior vine in the vineyard for further propagation. While vineyards are often planted by using genetically identical material (a single clone of a variety), after some years some vines are seen to perform better than others, over and above site-specific influences. This might be because of spontaneous mutations, but is commonly because of disease pressure. It's worth noting that the most vigorous, actively growing vines in a vineyard are usually not the ones producing the best quality fruit, and shouldn't automatically be chosen to take cuttings from.

**Clone** In viticulture, a group of vines all derived from the same parent plant by vegetative propagation (cuttings), and thus genetically identical.

**Colloids** Very tiny particles, smaller than a micrometer in diameter, usually made up of large organic molecules, that are important for the body of a wine. These can be removed by filtration, which can have the effect of stripping flavour from a wine if done clumsily.

**Congeners** Imprecise term for impurities in a spirit, thought to be responsible in part for hangovers.

**Copigmentation** Trendy but controversial term used to describe the fixing of colour in red wines by the presence of non-coloured phenolic compounds. For example, one of the reasons Shiraz is sometimes fermented with a dash of Viognier is because copigment phenolics from the white grapes facilitate production of a darker wine.

**Copper** Element often present in the vineyard because of the use of Bordeaux mixture (which contains copper sulphate) to combat fungal disease. Can also be used to remove volatile sulphur compounds from wine to prevent reductive taints (*see* chapter 16).

**Cordon** Name for the woody arm or branch of a vine, growing horizontally from the main trunk and which bears spurs (when spur pruning is adopted).

**Cover crop** Plants grown between the vine rows during the dormant season. They are then ploughed into the soil before the vine growth kicks in. *See* chapter 7.

**Cross-flow filtration** Also known as tangential filtration, this is the technique behind reverse osmosis. *See* chapter 14.

**Cryoextraction** The controversial use of freezing fresh grapes before crushing to extract only the sweetest, richest juice. Used by producers of sweet wines to soup them up a bit, but some consider this to be cheating.

**Cytokinins** A group of PLANT HORMONES. Particularly involved in regulating cell division, thus affecting growth stages.

**Dekkera** The spore-forming form of the yeast BRETTANOMYCES.

**Diacetyl** Common name for butane-2,3-dione, this is a ketone produced during fermentation or by the action of lactic-acid bacteria. Smells buttery and slightly sweet.

**Downy mildew** Significant fungal disease of vines caused by *Plasmopara viticola*. Introduced to Europe from the USA in the 1880s, this caused significant damage, until it was managed by spraying Bordeaux mixture. Still a major problem.

**Enzymes** Proteins that catalyse chemical reactions (make them go faster, or reduce the temperatures needed for them to occur). Commercial preparations exist that can be used in winemaking for various reasons, some more justified than others.

**Esters** Important to wine flavour. They are formed by the reaction of organic acids with alcohols, and are formed during both fermentation and ageing. ETHYL ACETATE (also known as ethyl ethanoate) is the most common ester in wine, formed by the combination of acetic acid and ethanol. Most esters have a distinctly fruity aroma, with some also possessing oily, herbaceous, buttery and nutty nuances.

**Ethanal** Another term for ACETALDEHYDE.

**Ethanol** Common name for ETHYL ALCOHOL, even more commonly referred to as just ALCOHOL.

**Ethyl acetate** A common ESTER in wine formed by the combination of ACETIC ACID and ethanol. Also known as ethyl ethanoate.

**Ethyl alcohol** In volume terms, ethyl alcohol is the most important component of wine, and is produced by fermentation of sugars by yeasts. On its own, it doesn't taste of much (just a slight sweetness at wine-like concentrations), but the concentration of alcohol in the final wine has a marked effect on the wine's sensory qualities.

**4-ethylguaiacol** *See* VOLATILE PHENOLS.

**4-ethylphenol** *See* VOLATILE PHENOLS.

**Extraction** In winemaking, the removal of PHENOLIC COMPOUNDS from the grape skin during the winemaking process.

**Fan leaf virus** One of the most common vine diseases. Caused by a range of viruses. A big problem, and a good reason for planting with specially treated virus-free rootstock. Although planting in areas where the nematode vectors for this disease exist is a virtual death sentence for vines.

**Fixed acids** A term used to describe the non-volatile acids, tartaric and malic. Some acids are intermediate between volatile and fixed, though.

**Flavonoids** A large group of plant PHENOLIC COMPOUNDS, including pigments such as ANTHOCYANINS.

**Fructose** One of the main sugars in grapes, along with glucose.

**GC–MS** Stands for gas chromatography-mass spectrometry. A sensitive analytical technique for separating and identifying volatile compounds or gases.

**Gibberellins** A group of PLANT HORMONES important for influencing the growth and development of vines. Sometimes applied artificially. Important in shoot elongation and release from dormancy.

**GIS** Stands for geographical information systems, in viticulture used to gather data about physical characteristics of a vineyard for PRECISION VITICULTURE.

**Glucose** Produced by photosynthesis, this is the most important sugar of the grape.

**Glycerol** Produced during fermentation, this is a polyol that can make a wine taste slightly sweeter, but which, contrary to popular opinion, doesn't affect viscosity.

**Higher alcohols** Also known as fusel oils, these are products of fermentation. Can contribute some aromatic character to wines.

**Histamine** Chemical involved in allergic reactions in humans. Present in some wines, but not thought to be responsible for adverse reactions, sometimes termed wine "allergies". *See* chapter 24.

**Homoclimes** Trendy New World viticultural term for areas with similar climates.

**Hybrid vines** Vines that are produced by crossing two different species. Also known as interspecific crosses. Typically, disease-resistant American species are crossed with *Vitis vinifera* vines to produce resistant vines, without the foxy flavours characteristic of the American species. These are also commonly called American hybrids or French hybrids.

**Hydrogen sulphide** Smells of rotten eggs, and a potential spoilage element formed during fermentation. It is caused by a nitrogen deficiency in the must. *See* chapter 16.

**Integrated pest management** Known simply as IPM, this is an agricultural system that aims to reduce inputs of herbicides, fungicides and pesticides through intelligent use. *See* chapter 7.

**Internode** The bit of a stem between two nodes (where the buds occur).

**Ketones** Usually produced during fermentation. β-damascenone and α- and β-ionone are called complex ketones and are thought to exist in grapes. β-damascenone smells rose-like. α- and β-ionone occur most notably in Riesling grapes.

**Laccase** An enzyme that results from botrytis infection of grapes that is highly problematic in encouraging oxidation of musts.

**Lactic acid** A softer tasting acid produced by the bacterial metabolism of the harsher malic acid during malolactic fermentation.

**Lactones** Compounds that can be present in grapes, but which more commonly come from oak (the oak lactones, *see* chapter 13). Sotolon is a lactone characteristic of botrytized wines.

**Leafroll virus** A problematic viral disease that can only be eradicated through using virus-free planting material.

**Maceration** Important in red wine, this is the process of soaking the grape skins to remove PHENOLIC COMPOUNDS. There are lots of ways of doing this, including modern innovations such as an extended maceration period at cool temperatures before alcoholic fermentation is allowed to start.

**Maderization** The process of a wine becoming oxidized – to become maderized, usually by heat.

**Malic acid** Along with tartaric acid, this is one of the two main organic acids in grapes. Transformed to the softer lactic acid by the action of lactic-acid bacteria during MALOLACTIC FERMENTATION.

**Malolactic fermentation** The conversion of malic acid to lactic acid effected by lactic-acid bacteria. *See* chapter 17.

**Mercaptans** Sulphur compounds sometimes found in wine. *See* chapter 16.

**Methoxypyrazines** Nitrogen-containing heterocyclic compounds produced in grapes by the metabolism of amino acids. 2-methoxy-3-isobutylpyrazine is the compound responsible for the bell pepper, grassy character common in Sauvignon Blanc and Cabernet Sauvignon wines. Concentrations of methoxypyrazine decrease with ripening; sunlight on grapes also reduces the concentration.

**Micro-oxygenation** Technique of slow oxygen addition to fermenting or maturing wine. *See* chapter 12.

**Monoterpenes** Chemical group contributing to the aroma and flavour of varieties such as Muscat and also Riesling.

**Mouthfeel** Fashionable tasting term which is used to describe textural characters, most specifically structure, of a wine.

**Nodes** The parts of the grapevine stem that contains the bud structures, separated by internodes.

**Oechsle** Measure of sugar concentration in grapes, primarily used in Germany and Austria.

**Oenological tannins** Commercially produced tannins, usually of non-grape origin, used to add to wines. More commonly used than you'd think.

**Oïdium** Fungal disease commonly known as POWDERY MILDEW.

**Oxidation** Substances are oxidized when they incorporate oxygen and lose electrons or hydrogen. Oxidation is always accompanied by the opposite reaction, reduction, such that when one compound is oxidized, another is reduced. In wine, oxidation occurs on exposure to air and is almost always deleterious.

**Pectins** Carbohydrates that glue plant cell walls together.

**pH** Technically, the negative logarithm of the hydrogen ion concentration in a solution. A scale used to measure how acid or alkaline a solution is (more acid = lower pH). Very important in winemaking.

**Phenolic compounds** Also known as POLYPHENOLS, this is a large group of reactive polymers with the phenol group as the basic building block. Very important in wine. *See* chapter 22.

**Physiological ripeness** Also known as phenolic ripeness. Trendy term used to distinguish the stage of maturity of the vine and grapes, as opposed to just the sugar levels. In warm climates, picking by sugar levels alone can result in unripe, herbaceous characters in the wine.

**Phytoalexins** Important antimicrobial compounds produced by plants in response to attack.

**Pigmented polymers** Also known as pigmented tannins. Complex group of chemicals now implicated in red-wine colour production. Formed by the combination of ANTHOCYANINS with CATECHINS during fermentation. *See* chapter 22.

**Plant hormones** A group of signalling molecules that influence plant growth and development, and also stress responses. Also known in the trade as plant-growth regulators. This group includes auxins, cytokinins, gibberellins, abscisic acid and ethylene. Some researchers also include the brassinosteroids and jasmonic acid in this club.

**Polymers** Molecules that form as the result of POLYMERIZATION of smaller sub-units.

**Polymerization** Making larger molecules by joining together smaller sub-units.

**Polyphenols** These are probably the most important flavour chemicals in red wines, but are of much less importance in whites. Polyphenols are a large group of compounds that use phenol as the basic building block. An important property of phenolic compounds is that they associate spontaneously with a wide range of compounds, such as proteins and other phenolics, by means of a range of non-covalent forces (for example, hydrogen bonding and hydrophobic effects). *See* chapter 22.

**Polyphenol oxidase (PPO)** An enzyme that causes browning by reacting with PHENOLIC COMPOUNDS and oxidizing them. Grapes that have been infected with fungi have high levels of PPO and this can cause oxidation of the wine, both directly and by combining with free SULPHUR DIOXIDE.

**Polysaccharides** Carbohydrate POLYMERS with sugars (monosaccharides) as the main subunits.

**Powdery mildew** Also known as OÏDIUM. Nasty fungal disease that devastated European vineyards when it was introduced from the USA in the late 1840s. Was eventually countered by dusting vines with sulphur, a treatment still used today by some. The fungus responsible is *Uncinula necator*.

**Precision viticulture** Selectively applying vineyard inputs according to relevant data. *See* chapter 3.

**Proteins** Polymeric molecules made from combinations of the twenty naturally occurring AMINO ACIDS. Encoded by genes.

**PVPP** Shorthand for poly(*N*-vinylpyrrolidinone), sometimes used to remove bitter phenolic compounds from white wine.

**Quercitin** A common FLAVONOID in grapes.

**Quercus** The genus comprises the various species of oak. *See* chapter 13.

**Random oxidation** Also known as sporadic post-bottling oxidation, describes the premature browning that occurs in some white wines some months after bottling. It is a problem common enough that some industry figures have referred to this as the "new cork taint". The main explanation for this phenomenon is variable oxygen transfer through the cork. Wines are protected against oxidation through the addition of sulphur dioxide ($SO_2$) at bottling. If the free $SO_2$ falls to very low levels, then the wine is unprotected, and browning can occur. Corks have been shown to vary dramatically in their oxygen-transfer properties, and random oxidation is thought to be caused by the subset of corks that let in significantly more oxygen than others. However, some scientists suspect that random oxidation may be caused by as-yet poorly understood chemical reactions independent of the closure. It has been suggested that common winemaking addition of the antioxidant ascorbic acid to keep white wines fresh may have the paradoxical effect of rendering the added $SO_2$ less effective, and making some wines susceptible to oxidation. Another proposed cause of random oxidation is poor procedure or intermittent failure on the bottling line, allowing some wines to have much higher levels of dissolved oxygen from the outset. Random oxidation is mainly a problem with white wines: while oxygen ingress through the closure will certainly damage red wines, they are more resistant to oxidation because of their high phenolic content. Oxidation is also more likely to be spotted in white wines because of the dramatic colour change that accompanies it.

**Redox potential**  Stands for reduction-oxidation potential. Can be measured. *See* chapter 16.

**Reduction**  Shorthand term used to refer to sulphur compound flavours in wine. Technically, it is the opposite of OXIDATION. *See* chapter 16.

**Resveratrol**  PHENOLIC COMPOUND that is also a PHYTOALEXIN, present in grapes and red wines. May have some health-enhancing properties (*see* chapter 25).

**Reverse osmosis**  Controversial filtration technique used to concentrate wines, and also for alcohol removal. *See* chapter 14.

**Rod and spur**  Alternative name for cane pruning. *See* chapter 10.

**Saccharomyces cerevisiae**  The yeast species responsible for alcoholic fermentation, known colloquially as brewer's or baker's yeast. Comes in many different strains. *See* chapter 14.

**Saignée**  Also known as vat bleeding, a winemaking technique for taking juice of skins to increase the solids to juice ratio in red wine making, thus souping up the phenolic content of the resulting wine.

**SO₂**  Chemical formula for SULPHUR DIOXIDE.

**Sorbitol**  An alcohol present in low levels in wine with a hint of sweetness to it, occasionally used by fraudsters as an illegal addition.

**Sotolon**  A lactone present in botrytized wines.

**Spinning cone**  Technically a gas-liquid counter-current device. A way of stripping alcohol from wines without removing important volatiles, used commonly to concentrate fruit juices without taking out interesting bits. Widely used, but because of the expense of the equipment this is just a service industry. *See* chapter 14.

**Spur**  A stubby grape-vine shoot pruned back to just a few nodes.

**Spur pruning**  A way of pruning vines that leaves just short spurs on a permanent cordon. *See* chapter 10.

**Succinic acid**  An acid present at low concentrations in grapes and wine.

**Sulphides**  Reduced sulphur compounds that occur during winemaking.

Usually negative, but can be complexing at the right levels. *See* chapter 16.

**Sulphur dioxide**  $SO_2$. Hugely important molecule added in winemaking to protect wine from oxygen and microbes. *See* chapter 15.

**Tangential filtration**  *See* CROSS-FLOW FILTRATION.

**Tannins**  Tannins are found principally in the bark, leaves and immature fruit of a wide range of plants. They form complexes with PROTEINS and other plant POLYMERS such as POLYSACCHARIDES. It is thought that the role of tannins in nature is one of plant defence. Chemically, tannins are large polymeric molecules made up of linked subunits. The monomers here are PHENOLIC COMPOUNDS that are joined together in a bewildering array of combinations, and can be further modified chemically in a myriad of different permutations. There are two major classes of tannins: condensed and hydrolyzable. Hydrolyzable tannins aren't as important in wine. The condensed tannins, also known as proanthocyanidins, are the main grape-derived tannins. They are formed by the polymerization of the polyphenolic flavan-3-ol monomers CATECHIN and epicatechin.

**Tartaric acid**  The most important grape-derived acid in wine. Often precipitates out as harmless tartrate crystals.

**TCA**  Abbreviation for 2,4,6-TRICHLOROANISOLE.

**Terpenes**  A large family of compounds that are widespread in plants. Grapes contain varying amounts, which survive vinification to contribute to wine odour. More than forty have been identified in grapes, but only half a dozen are thought to contribute to wine aroma. They are highest in Muscat wines: the distinctive floral, grapey character is down to the likes of linalool and geraniol. Other varieties such as Gewürztraminer and Pinot Gris also have a terpene component to their aromas.

**Total acidity**  An important measurement for winemakers, made by titration. Given in terms of grams per litre of tartaric or sulphuric acid. It includes measurement of both fixed and volatile acids.

**2,4,6-Trichloroanisole**  Potent, musty-smelling compound largely responsible for cork taint. *See* chapter 19.

**Umami**  The fifth basic taste, only recently recognized. It's the taste of "savouriness" and results from the detection of AMINO ACIDS. *See* chapter 20.

**Vitis vinifera**  The species name for the Eurasian grape vine, to which the varieties we know and love all belong.

**Volatile acidity**  The acidity contributed by the various volatile acids, the most significant of which is ACETIC ACID. A little is OK, but too much makes the wine smell of vinegar.

**Volatile phenols**  Important in wine aroma. 4-ethylphenol and 4-ethylguaiacol, found predominantly in red wines, are formed by the action of the spoilage yeast BRETTANOMYCES, and have distinctive gamey, spicy, animally aromas (*see* chapter 16). 4-vinylphenol and 4-vinylguaiacol are rare in red wines and more common in whites, and also have largely negative aromatic properties.

**Yeasts**  Unicellular fungi important for fermenting grape juice to wine. *See* chapter 14.

# Bibliography

Rather than a full list of references, this is a selected, much abbreviated bibliography of some key sources. These would be a good place to start for anyone who wants to explore the issues covered in this book in more depth. Where appropriate, this list is annotated.

## GENERAL REFERENCES

**Bisson L.F., Waterhouse A.L., Ebeler S.E., Walker A.M., Lapsley J.T.** "The present and future of the international wine industry", *Nature* 418:696–699, 2002

**Jackson R.S.** *Wine Science: Principles, Practice, Perception*, Academic Press, 2000

**Peynaud E.** *Knowing and Making Wine*, Wiley, New York, 1984

**Ribéreau-Gayon P., Dubourdieu D., Doneche B., Lonvaud A.** *Handbook of Enology. Volume 1: The Microbiology of Wine and Vinifications*, Wiley, Chichester, 2000

**Ribéreau-Gayon P., Glories Y., Maujean A., Dubourdieu D.** *Handbook of Enology. Volume 2: The Chemistry of Wine Stabilization and Treatments*. Wiley, Chichester, 2000

**Robinson J.** (ed) *The Oxford Companion to Wine*, 2nd Edn. Oxford University Press, 1999

**Winkler A.J., Cook J.A., Kliewer W.M., Lider L.A.** *General Viticulture*, University of California Press, Berkeley, 1974

## CHAPTER 1

**Aradhya M.K., Dangl G.S., Prins B.H.** *et al* "Genetic structure and differentiation in cultivated grape, *Vitis vinifera* L.", *Genetic Research* 81:179–192, 2003

**Boss P.K., Buckeridge E.J., Poole A., Thomas M.R.** "New insights into grapevine flowering", *Functional Plant Biology* 30:593–606, 2003

**Bowers J.E., Meredith C.P.** "The parentage of a classic wine grape, Cabernet Sauvignon", *Nature Genetics* 16:84–87, 1997

**Carmona M.J., Cubas P., Martínez-Zapater J.M.** "VFL, the grapevine FLORICAULA/LEAFY ortholog, is expressed in meristematic regions independently of their fate", *Plant Physiology* 130:68–77, 2002

**Franks T., Botta R., Thomas M.R.** "Chimerism in grapevines: implications for cultivar identity, ancestry and genetic improvement", *Theoretical and Applied Genetics* 104:192–199, 2002

**McGovern P.E.** *Ancient Wine: The Search for the Origins of Viniculture*, Princeton University Press, Princeton, NJ, 2003

**Vouillamoz J., Maigre D., Meredith C.P.** "Microsatellite analysis of ancient alpine grape cultivars: pedigree reconstruction of *Vitis vinifera* L. 'Cornalin du Valais'", *Theoretical and Applied Genetics* 107:448–454, 2003

## CHAPTER 2

**Wilson J.E.** *Terroir: The Role of Geology, Climate, and Culture in the Making of French Wines*, Mitchell Beazley, London, 1998

**Maltman A.** "Wine, beer and whisky: the role of geology", *Geology Today* 19:22–29, 2003

**Seguin G.** "'Terroirs' and pedology of wine growing", *Experientia* 42:861–873, 1986

## CHAPTER 3

**Bramley R.G.V., Hamilton R.P.** "Hitting the zone – making viticulture more precise". In Blair RJ, Williams PJ, Hoj PB (Eds) *Proceedings of the 12th Australian Wine Industry Technical Conference*, Winetitles, Adelaide, in press, 2004

## CHAPTER 4

**Jones G.V., White M.A., Cooper O.R.** "Climate change and global wine quality", *Climatic Change*, in press, 2004

## CHAPTER 5

**Hails R.S.** "Assessing the risks associated with new agricultural practices", *Nature* 418:685–688, 2002

**Iocco P., Franks T., Thomas M.R.** "Genetic transformation of major wine grape cultivars of *Vitis vinifera* L.", *Transgenic Research* 10:105–102, 2001

**Trewavas A.J.** "The population/biodiversity paradox. Agricultural efficiency to save wilderness", *Plant Physiology* 125:175–179, 2001

**Vivier M.A., Pretorius I.S.** "Genetically tailored grapevines for the wine industry", *Trends in Biotechnology* 20:472–478, 2002

## CHAPTER 6

**Campbell C.** *Phylloxera: how wine was saved for the world*, Harper Collins, London, 2004

**Granett J., Walker A., Kocsis L., Omer A.D.** "Biology and management of grape phylloxera", *Annual Review of Entomology* 46:387–412, 2001

**Omer A.D., Granett J., Walker A.M.** "Influence of plant growth stage on grape phylloxera (Homoptera: Phylloxeridae) populations", *Environmental Entomology* 31:120–126, 2002

**Ordish G.** *The Great Wine Blight*, Sidgwick & Jackson, London, 1987

## CHAPTER 8

**Mader P., Fliessbach A., Dubois D., Gunst L., Fried P., Niggli U.** "Soil fertility and biodiversity in organic farming", *Science* 296:1694–1697, 2002

**Waldin M.** *Biodynamic Wines*, Mitchell Beazley, London, 2004

## CHAPTER 9

**Gu S., Du G., Zoldoske D.** *et al* "Effects of irrigation amount on water relations, vegetative growth, yield and fruit composition of Sauvignon blanc grape vines under partial root-zone drying and conventional irrigation in the San Joaquin Valley of California, USA", *Journal of Horticultural Science and Biotechnology* 79:26–33, 2004

**Sobeih W.Y., Dodd I.C., Bacon M.A., Grierson D., Davies W.J.** "Long-distance signals regulating stomatal conductance and leaf growth in tomato (*Lycopersicon esculentum*) plants subjected to partial root-zone drying", *Journal of Experimental Botany* 55:2353–2363, 2004

**Souza C.R., Maroco J.P., Santos T.P.** *et al* "Partial root zone drying: regulation of stomatal aperture and carbon assimilation in field-grown grapevines (*Vitis vinifera* cv. Moscatel)", *Functional Plant Biology* 30:653–662, 2003

## CHAPTER 10

**Howell G.S.** "Sustainable grape productivity and the growth-yield relationship: a review", *American Journal of Enology and Viticulture* 52:165–174, 2001

## CHAPTER 14

**Gibson R.L.** "Crossflow membrane technology for the wine industry", *Australian Grape Grower and Winemaker* April 1986

## CHAPTER 15

**Robinson E.M.C., Godden P.E.** "Revisiting sulphur dioxide use", *Australian Wine Research Institute Technical Review* 145, 2003

## CHAPTER 17

**Esteve-Zarzoso B., Manzanares P., Ramón D., Querol A.** "The role of non-*Saccharomyces* yeasts in industrial winemaking", *International Microbiology* 1:143–148, 1998

Fleet G.H. "Yeast interactions and wine flavour", *International Journal of Food Microbiology* 86:11–22, 2003

Pretorius I.S., Bauer F.F. "Meeting the consumer challenge through genetically customized wine-yeast strains", *Trends in Biotechnology* 20:426–432, 2002

Romano P., Fiore C., Paraggio M., Caruso M., Capece A. "Function of yeast species and strains in wine flavour", *International Journal of Food Microbiology* 86:169–180, 2003

## CHAPTER 18

Chatonnet P., Dubourdieu D., Boidron J.N. "The influence of *Brettanomyces/Dekkera* sp. yeasts and lactic-acid bacteria on the ethylphenol content of red wines", *American Journal of Enology and Viticulture* 46:463–468, 1995

Comitini F., Ingeniis De J., Pepe L., Mannazzu I., Ciani M. "*Pichia anomala* and *Kluyveromyces wickerhamii* killer toxins as new tools against *Dekkera/Brettanomyces* spoilage yeasts", *FEMS Microbiology Letters*, 238:235–240, 2004

Coulter A., Robinson E., Cowey G.I. *et al* "*Dekkera/Brettanomyces* yeast – an overview of recent AWRI investigations and some recommendations for its control." In: *Grapegrowing at the Edge, Managing the Wine Business, Impacts on Wine Flavour*, ASVO Proceedings, Adelaide, p.41–50, 2003

Fugelsang K.C., Zoecklin B.W. "Population dynamics and effects of *Brettanomyces bruxellensis* strains on Pinot Noir (*Vitis vinifera* L.) wines", *American Journal of Enology and Viticulture* 54:294–300, 2003

## CHAPTER 19

Duncan B.C., Gibson R.L., Obradovic D. "2,4,6-trichloroanisole and cork production", *Wine Industry Journal* 12:180–184, 1997

## CHAPTER 20

Bartoshuk L.M. "Genetic and pathological taste variation: what can we learn from animal models and human disease?" *Ciba Foundation Symposium* 179:251–267, 1993

Duffy V.B., Peterson J.M., Bartoshuk L.M. "Associations between taste genetics, oral sensation and alcohol intake", *Physiology of Behaviour* 82:435–445, 2004

Kim U.K., Breslin P.A., Reed D., Drayna D. "Genetics of human taste perception", *Journal of Dental Research* 83:448–453, 2004

Lindeman B. "Receptors and transduction in taste", *Nature* 413:219–225, 2001

Pickering G.J., Simunkova K., DiBattista D. "Intensity of taste and astringency sensations elicited by red wines is associated with sensitivity to PROP (6-n-propylthiouracil), *Food Quality and Preference* 15:147–154, 2004

Schoenfeld M.A., Neuer G, Tempelmann C., Schussler K., Noesselt T., Hopf J.M., Heinze H.J. "Functional magnetic resonance tomography correlates of taste perception in the human primary taste cortex", *Neuroscience* 127:347–353, 2004

## CHAPTER 21

Anderson A.K., Christoff K., Stappen I. *et al* "Dissociated neural representations of intensity and valence in human olfaction", *Nature Neuroscience* 6:196–202, 2003

Brochet F., Dubourdieu D. "Wine descriptive language supports cognitive specificity of chemical senses", *Brain and Language* 77:187–196, 2001

Castrioto-Scanderberg A., Hagberg G.E., Cerasa A. *et al* "The appreciation of wine by sommeliers: a functional magnetic resonance study of sensory integration" *Neuroimage* 25: 570–578, 2005

De Araujo I.E.T., Rolls E.T., Kringelbach M.L., McGlone F., Phillips N. "Taste-olfactory convergence, and the representation of the pleasantness of flavour, in the human brain", *European Journal of Neuroscience* 18:2059–2068, 2003

Kringelbach M.L., De Araujo I.E.T., Rolls E.T. "Taste-related activity in the human dorsolateral prefrontal cortex", *Neuroimage* 21:781–788, 2004

Morrot G., Brochet F., Dubourdieu D. "The color of odors", *Brain and Language* 79:309–320, 2001

Verhagen J.V., Kadohisa M., Rolls E.T. "The primate insular/opercular taste cortex: neuronal representations of the viscosity, fat texture, grittiness, temperature, and taste of foods", *Journal of Neurophysiology* 92:1685–1699, 2004

## CHAPTER 22

Clarke R.J., Bakker J. *Wine Flavour Chemistry*, Blackwell, Oxford, 2004

## CHAPTER 23

Booyse F.M., Parks D.A. "Moderate wine and alcohol consumption: beneficial effects on cardiovascular disease", *Thrombosis and Haemostasis* 86:517–528, 2001

Corder R., Douthwaite J.A., Lees D.M., Khan N.Q., Viseu Dos Santos A.C., Wood E.G., Carrier M.J. "Endothelin-1 synthesis reduced by red wine", *Nature* 414:863–864, 2001

Novartis Foundation "Alcohol and cardiovascular disease", Novartis Foundation Symposium 216, Wiley, Chichester, 2000

Schriever C., Pendland S.L., Mahady G.B. "Red wine, resveratrol, *Chlamydia pneumoniae* and the French connection", *Atherosclerosis* 171:379–380, 2003

## CHAPTER 24

Cordova A.C., Jackson L.M., Berke-Sclessel D.W., Sumpio B.E. "The cardiovascular protective effect of red wine." *Journal of the American College of Surgeons* 200: 428–439, 2005

Stockley C. "Can histamine in wine cause adverse reactions for consumers?" *Australia and New Zealand Grapegrower and Winemaker, Annual Technical Issue*, 2004

## CHAPTER 25

Corder R., Crozier A., Kroon P.A. "Drinking your health? It's too early to say", *Nature* 426:119, 2003

Howitz K.T., Bitterman K.J., Cohen H.Y. *et al* "Small molecule activators of sirtuins extend *Saccharomyces cerevisiae* lifespan", *Nature* 425:191–196, 2003

Picard F., Kurtev M., Chung N. *et al* "Sirt1 promotes fat mobilization in white adipocytes by repressing PPAR-gamma", *Nature* 429:771–776. Erratum in: *Nature* 430:921, 2004

Wood J.G., Rogina B., Lavu S. *et al* "Sirtuin activators mimic caloric restriction and delay ageing in metazoans", *Nature* 430:686–689, 2004

# Index

Page numbers in *italic* refer to
illustration captions.

## A

ABA *see* abscisic acid
abscisic acid (ABA) 78-80, 82
acetic acid 110, 187
Achaval, Santiago 27
Achaval-Ferrer 27, 28
acidity 115-16, 184; *see also*
  minerality
Adamson, Warren 148
additive-free wines *see* natural
  wines
additives in wine 94-5, 183, 188;
  *see also* sulphur dioxide
Advanced Wine Assessment Course
  (AWAC) 150-1
ageing, human 200, 202
ageing, wine 117, 125, 162
ALCESTE 180
alcohol consumption *see* drinking
  wine
alcohol levels 22, 44, 95, 109, 110-
  11, 112, 114, 135, 184
alcohols 184
ALDH *see* aldehyde dehydrogenase
aldehyde dehydrogenase (ALDH)
  199
Allemand, Thierry 119
allergies to wine 197, 198-9
Altec 152-3, 154, 156, 165
Amisfield 28
Amorim 157, 158
Anderson, AK 178
animal experiments 9, 10
anthocyanins 24, 77, 81, 100, 186
antioxidants 94, 191, 194, 201
Antiyal 75
Aracil, Jean-Marie 156
archaeology, molecular 20
Argentina 27-8, 47, 91
Mendoza 28, 193
Arnst, Bart 83
aroma/aromas 123, 124, 125, 127,
  128, 172-3, 186, *189*
asthma 199
atherosclerosis 191, 192
Australia 20, 35, 54, 75, 80, 81, 83,
  97, 98, 112, 121, 143, 164, 165,
  172
New South Wales
Hunter region 43
Queensland 62
South Australia 58, 59
Barossa Valley 27, *33*, 42, *53*, *64*,
  *87*, *99*
Clare Valley *22*, *23*, 26, *87*, 160,
  *161*, 163
Coonawarra 36

Padthaway *39*
Victoria
Mildura 36
Western Australia
Margaret River 36, 141
Australian Wine Research Institute
  (AWRI) 44, 117, 118, 122, 127,
  132, 137, 138, 139, 140, 150, 152,
  153, 161, 162, 186
Austria 91 165
AWAC *see* Advanced Wine
  Assessment Course
AWRI *see* Australian Wine Research
  Institute

## B

Bacon, Mark 78, 79, 82
barrels 95, 101-8
Barros, Antonio de 157-8
Bartoshuk, Linda 169, 171, 173, 174
Baverstock, David 97
Beaucastel, Ch. de 123, 132, 142
Bennett, Malcolm 34
Bertagna, Dom. 119
biodiversity 61, 64, 66
Biodynamic viticulture 11, 50, 68-77
Biodyvin 74
Blackburn, Liz 200
Blanck, Dom. Paul 164
blended wines 29
*blocage* 79
Bonny Doon 30, 97, 139
Bonterra 72, 73
Booth, David 89, 90
Booyse, François 193, 194
Bordeaux mixture 66, 71
Dosch, Daniel 37, 39
bottle closures *see* closures,
  alternative; corks *and* screwcaps
Boulard, Francis 72
Boulton, Roger 98, 111, 116
bouquet *see* aroma/aromas
Bouschet, Henri 57
Bowen, Anita 27
brain processing of wine flavour
  175-82
Bramley, Rob 35, 36, 39
Brand, G 173
Breton, Catherine and Pierre 119
*Brettanomyces* 108, 110, 136-43
Broadley, Martin 34
Brochet, Frédéric 180, 181, 182
Burns, Jennifer 201

## C

Cabral, Miguel 158
Calatrasi 136
California 21, 30, 35, 37-8, 42, 56,
  57, 63, 77, 83, 97, 106, 112, 132,
  139

Central Valley 43, 98, 111
Mendocino 73
Napa Valley 43, 44
Sonoma Valley 43, 147
California, University of (Davis) 20,
  24, 49, 98, 111, 116, 186, 188,
  205, 206
caloric restriction (CR) 201-2
Campden and Chorleywood Food
  Research Organization (CCFRA)
  153, 159
Canada 47, 50, 174
*Candida stellata 133*
cane toads 62
canopy management 89-90
carbonic maceration 119
cardiovascular protection 190-6
Carey, Victoria 32
Carpenter-Bloggs, Lynne 75
Cartwright, Bob 141
Castriota-Scanderberg, Alessandro
  175, 179
CCFRA *see* Campden and
  Chorleywood Food Research
  Organization
Ceago 75
champagne 124
Champagne Raymond Boulard 72
Chapoutier, Michel 74, 75
chaptalization 112, 188
Chatonnet, Pascal 103, 123, 124,
  138, 139, 140, 141, 147
Chauvet, Jules 119
chemistry of wine flavours 183-9
Chile 38, 42, 43, 58, 72-4, 75, 91,
  98
Casablanca region 72
Colchagua region 72
Maipo region 72
chimerism 23-4
China 47, 49, 199
climate 40-3
Clos de la Coulée-de-Serrant 70,
  75
Clos Roche Blanche 75
closures, alternative 159-65
Cloudy Bay 124
Collins, Charles 141, 142
colour *see* grapes: colour; *veraison*
  *and* wine: colour
Commonwealth Scientific and
  Industrial Research Organization
  (CSIRO) 35, *47*, 49, 81
complexity, wine 123, 125
  and *Brettanomyces* 141
concentration
  finished wine 113
  must 112, 113
Cone-Tech 111
confounding 9, 195-6

cooperage 103, *104*
copper fungicides 71
Corbet-Milward, John 148
Corder, Roger 192, 203
cork bark *145*
cork taint 145-65, 172
corks
  natural 144-5, 152, 161, 163-4
  synthetic 159-60, 164-5
Cornelissen, Frank 96, 120
Corney & Barrow 68
Coturri 120
cover cropping 37, 64-5, *64*, 73, 83
CR *see* caloric restriction
Crasto, Quinta do *28*
Croser, Brian 121
Crozier, Alan 201
CSIRO *see* Commonwealth
  Scientific and Industrial Research
  Organization

## D

Daniel, Steve 149
DAP *see* diammonium phosphate
Davidian, Jean-Claude 31, 32
Deiss, Marcel 75
*Dekkera see* Brettanomyces
Delteil, Dominique 31, 122, 125,
  126, 127
Demeter 71, 73, 74
Denmark 195
descriptors, tasting 180-1
diammonium phosphate (DAP) 122,
  139
diseases of vines 70
  botrytis 50, 63, 66, 73, 116
  downy mildew 66
  leafroll virus 67
  phylloxera 37, 52-9
  Pierce's disease 50, 63
  powdery mildew (oïdium) 50, 52,
  63, 66, 73
Doll, Sir Richard 9
Dourthe 164
drainage 32-3, 80
Dressner, Joe 119, 120
drinking wine
  effects on health 190-6
Dry Creek winery 147
Dubourdieu, Denis 123
Ducournau, Patrick 97
Dupont, Jacques 180
Dyson, John 91

## E

ecological compensation areas
  63-4, 65, 66
*élevage* 97
endothelium protection 192-3, *194*,
  195

## Acknowledgments

This book relies heavily on the input from scientists, winemakers, viticulturalists, editors who have commissioned my work, wine merchants, PR bods and even other wine writers. The danger with a lengthy list like this, which aims at comprehensiveness, is that some people who deserve to be included will likely be omitted inadvertently. If you fall into this category, I apologize. Several chapters in this book started life as articles in the UK wine trade journal *Harpers Wine and Spirit Weekly*, and consumer magazine *Wine International*. I thank the editors of these publications, Tim Atkin and Christian Davis of *Harpers* and Catharine Lowe of *Wine International*, for having the vision to commission these articles, then allowing me to use expanded versions here. Special thanks are also due to the excellent scientists of the Australian Wine Research Institute (AWRI), particularly Peter Godden, who has been unusually generous with his time and advice. At Mitchell Beazley, Hilary Lumsden, Julie Sheppard, and Jamie Ambrose have been fantastic in seeing this project through.

### Thanks are due to (in alphabetical order)

Nick Alabaster, Jean-Marie Aracil, Tim Atkin, Kent Bach, Mark Bacon, Linda Bartoshuk, David Baverstock, Malcolm Bennett, David Booth, Francois Booyse, Daniel Bosch, Francis Boulard, Roger Boulton, Rob Bramley, Michael Brajkovich, Martin Broadley, Nathan Burley, Miguel Cabral, Danny Cameron, Victoria Carey, Bob Cartwright, Michel Chapoutier, Pascal Chatonnet, Charles Collins, Jaysen Collins, Roger Corder, Frank Cornelissen, João Costa, Tim Crane, Jean-Claude Davidian, Christian Davis, Dominique Delteil, Joe Dressner, Brian Fletcher, Brian Forde, Leigh Francis, Ken Fugelsang, Richard Gibson, Mark Gishen, Peter Godden, Randall Grahm, Jeffrey Grosset, Lenny Guarente, Sam Harrop, James Healy, Marteen Van Helden, Eric Hervé, Jack Hibberd, Tim Jacob, Andrew Jefford, Carlos de Jesus, Lee Johnson, Nicolas Joly, Gregory Jones, Phil Jones, Robert Joseph, Susan Keevil, Shozo Kobayashi, Dominique Lafon, David Laing, James Lawther, Anne-Claude Leflaive, Ernst Loosen, Brian Loveys, Catharine Lowe, Hilary Lumsden, Gail Mahady, Benigna Mallebrein, Alex Maltman, Michael McCarthy, Jacques Mell, Charles Melton, Anne Mendenhall, Carole Meredith, Andrew Mitchell, Chris Mitchell, Jane Mitchell, Michael Moosbrugger, Dorli Muhr, Dirk Niepoort, Rebecca Palmer, Wendy Parr, Robert Paul, Francois Peretti, Marc Perrin, Pierre Perrin, Gary Pickering, Rachel Plecas, Sakkie Pretorius, Mike Ratcliffe, John Reganold, Rui Reguinga, Raymond Reynolds, Jancis Robinson, Simon Robinson, Edmund Rolls, Anthony Rose, Dawid Saayman, Alessandro Castriota Scanderberg, Peter Schell, Jayson Schwarz, Nicolas Serpette, Julie Sheppard, Richard Smart, Jeff Sinnott, Barry Smith, Clark Smith, Steve Smith, Charles Spence, Phil Spillman, Dan Standish, Andrea Sturniolo, Laura Taylor, Sean Thackrey, Alexandre Thienpont, David Thomas, Mark Thomas, Reinhard Töpfer, Domenic Torzi, Joe Wadsack, Monty Waldin, Larry Walker, Corinna Wilson, Amy Wislocki, Charles Wysocki, and Christiano Van Zeller.

## Picture credits

**663.2**
**Goode**     **Goode, Jamie**

**The science of
wine**

DUE DATE

| | | | |
|---|---|---|---|
| | | | |
| | | | |
| | | | |
| | | | |
| | | | |
| | | | |
| | | | |
| | | | |
| | | | |
| | | | |
| | | | |